Pluralist Universalism

Pluralist Universalism

An Asian Americanist Critique
of U.S. and Chinese Multiculturalisms

WEN JIN

The Ohio State University Press | Columbus

Library of Congress Cataloging-in-Publication Data
Jin, Wen, 1977–
 Pluralist universalism : an Asian Americanist critique of U.S. and Chinese multiculturalisms
/ Wen Jin.
  p. cm.
 Includes bibliographical references and index.
 ISBN 978-0-8142-1187-8 (cloth : alk. paper)—ISBN 978-0-8142-9288-4 (cd)
 1. Multiculturalism in literature. 2. Cultural pluralism in literature. 3. Ethnic relations in
literature. 4. Cultural pluralism—China. 5. Cultural pluralism—United States. 6. Multicul-
turalism—China. 7. Multiculturalism—United States. 8. China—Ethnic relations. 9. United
States—Ethnic relations. 10. Kuo, Alexander—Criticism and interpretation. 11. Zhang,
Chengzhi, 1948–Criticism and interpretation. 12. Alameddine, Rabih—Criticism and interpretation. 13. Yan, Geling—Criticism and interpretation. I. Title.
 PN56.M8J56 2012
 810.9'8951073—dc23
                          2011044160

Paper (ISBN: 978-0-8142-5647-3)
Cover design by Mia Risberg
Text design by Juliet Williams
Type set in Adobe Minion Pro

♾ The paper used in this publication meets the minimum requirements of the American
National Standard for Information Sciences—Permanence of Paper for Printed Library Mate-
rials. ANSI Z39.48-1992.

To
Jin Yiyu
Zhou Huizhu
    With love and gratitude

CONTENTS

PREFACE

IN THE AFTERMATH of the July 2009 Uyghur riot in Xinjiang, the far northwest province of China with a large concentration of ethnic minority people, foreign correspondent Howard French suggested in a special column in the *New York Times* that the Chinese government take note of the Kerner Commission that President Johnson appointed to investigate the causes for the 1967 race riot in Detroit. Instead of clinging to the "fiction that areas where ethnic minorities have predominated . . . are 'autonomous regions,'" French argued, the Chinese government should openly acknowledge the magnitude of the country's ethnic tensions.[1] Only then would the social causes underlying the repeated riots in such areas as Xinjiang and Tibet start to be addressed. French's criticism of China's nationalities policy is certainly not unjustified, but his invocation of the Kerner Commission is ironic. The federal initiatives that the commission's final report recommended for improving educational and employment opportunities for urban blacks, after

1. Howard W. French, "Letter from China."

all, were implemented only in a partial and diluted way under Nixon and directly attacked during the Reagan years, and the commission has become a synonym, for many, of social goals not yet met. If the Chinese policy of ethnic autonomy is a fiction that consolidates national unity at the expense of minority interests, then the idea that the U.S. has set an example for other countries, especially China, in resolving ethno-racial conflicts through legislation and government policy can only be described as a competing fiction. The *Times* piece illustrates a common way in which China's ethnic policy and measures against ethno-racial tensions in the U.S. are compared in the American popular imagination.[2] It is a solipsistic kind of comparison, where the other country is used as a foil for one's own.

This mode of comparison, unfortunately, reproduces itself on the Chinese side. In reaction to the unfavorable coverage of the Uyghur riot abroad, the Chinese media quickly adopted a counter strategy, scolding the Western media for being tendentious toward the rioters, downplaying their violence, and, more important, failing to place ethnic riots in China in the context of presumably worse ones in Western countries, including the LA riots of 1992.[3] Such exchanges between the two countries have become a recurrent scene in the post–Cold War era, when the disintegration of the Soviet Union turned the U.S. and China into the world's two remaining multiethnic "empires."[4] The term "empire" is commonly invoked in cultural and political commentaries on both the United States and China in the current era to convey criti-

---

2. For a similar example, see Michael Wines, "A Strong Man Is China's Rock in Ethnic Strife." Wines compares the July 2009 Uighur riot in China to race riots in 1960s America. He argues that, while the latter led to the Civil Rights Movement, the former would likely further legitimize the government's hard-line positions on discontent minority groups, including accelerated economic development in minority regions, aggressive Han settlement, and cultural makeovers.

3. See Qin Feng, "Cong wulumuqi 7–5 shijian kan xifang meiti shuangchong biaozhun" [The July 5 Urumqi incident reveals double standards in Western media].

4. Many studies have emerged since the early 1990s that examine U.S. culture and history in relation to the country's imperialist expansion across the North American continent and beyond through military, territorial, legal, economic, and cultural means. This focus on American imperialism updates W. J. Pomeroy's argument in his 1970 *American Neo-colonialism* that U.S. activities in the Philippines and Asia constituted a nonterritorial kind of colonialism, or "neo-colonialism." Also see Donald Pease and Amy Kaplan, ed., *Cultures of United States Imperialism;* Chalmers Johnson, *Sorrows of Empire.* Pease and Kaplan lay down important conceptual frameworks for studies of the U.S. as a new kind of empire. Johnson surveys the history, since the early nineteenth century, of how the U.S. became an empire that "dominates the world through its military power" (1). For discussions of the Chinese side, see Ross Terrill, *The New Chinese Empire: and What It Means for the United States.* Terrill's basic argument is that the PRC is "an autocratic Chinese state ruling a land nearly half of which was historically inhabited by non-Chinese people" and can be seen as "an empire of our time" (3). This view is typical of those critical of the current Chinese state's policy toward its minorities.

cisms of the ways in which the two countries maintain order among their diverse populations at the expense of the interests of ethno-racial minorities, while expanding their influence and power globally. The U.S. government has largely ignored or suppressed such criticisms, disclaiming racial and ethnic tensions at home while projecting them onto non-Western countries deemed to be "authoritarian" or "dictatorial," including China, in particular. The Chinese government, for its part, has opted for a tit-for-tat strategy. Consequently, each side has frequently accused the other for perpetuating racial and ethnic inequality.

Following a major disruption due to the 1989 Tiananmen incident, U.S.–China relations returned to the general principle of "comprehensive engagement" in the early 1990s.[5] Nevertheless, the U.S. government, especially members of Congress, has consistently expressed strong condemnations of China's record on human and civil rights, including minority rights.[6] The State Department ritualistically castigates China for failing to ameliorate "racism against minorities" in such areas as Xinjiang, Inner Mongolia, and Tibet, in its annual reports on human rights in China.[7] Since 2000, the Chinese government has sought to rebuke such remarks with its annual reports on human rights in the U.S., where race relations invariably figure as a prominent target for criticisms.[8] The new millennium has witnessed a few turns in U.S.–China relations, ranging from the tactical alliance on the "War on Terror" that the two governments formed immediately after 9/11 to the expanded U.S.–China Strategic and Economic Dialogue following the global

5. Robert L. Suettinger, *Beyond Tiananmen,* 328. After the Tiananmen incident, the first President Bush sought to restore the U.S.–China relationship, "persevering against growing congressional hostility" (Suettinger, 93). Clinton continued this policy and "enthusiastically adopted the idea of improving relations with China as one of the key foreign policy goals of his second term" (Suettinger, 283).

6. As Suettinger points out, individual members in Congress took the lead on efforts to adjust the White House's policy of "comprehensive engagement." For example, Nancy Pelosi and Frank Wolf headed a congressional caucus called the Working Group on China, from 1997 to 2006. They "drafted letters, circulated information, and developed legislation" to pressure China into making significant improvements in its human rights (Suettinger, 328). Also, in the years following the Tiananmen incident, Congress voted every year on legislation disapproving of extending China's MFN (most favored nation) status; not until 2000 did Congress pass H.R. 4444 extending normal trade relations treatment to China, in anticipation of China to entry to the World Trade Organization. Also, the State Department sponsored a resolution critical of China's human rights practices at the annual meetings of United Nations High Commission for Refugees up until 1998, prior to President Clinton's China trip.

7. U.S. Department of State, *2008 Human Rights Report: China (includes Tibet, Hong Kong, and Macau).*

8. Information Office of the State Council of the PRC, *2008 nian meiguo renquan baogao* [2008 report on human rights in the United States].

financial crisis of 2007–9. Mutual accusations of minority rights violations, however, have remained a constant theme.

The solipsistic, accusatory mode of comparison that characterizes the political exchanges between the two countries is also mirrored in the sphere of popular culture, often in surprising and subtle manners. One good example is the Disney movie *Mulan,* released in 1998, which tells the story of a young girl in feudal China who enlists in the imperial army to protect her aged father from conscription. Very few were troubled at the time by the movie's portrayal of Shan Yu, the sinister head of the "army of the Huns" at war with China. Covered with an unnatural, gray tint, Shan Yu cuts a hulking, beastly figure, almost twice as big as the Han Chinese characters in the movie. For all his size, he comes across froglike, with a small head, a receding forehead, and beady eyes, surrounded by subordinates who are simply altered versions of him. One might see Shan Yu as just another typical Disney villain, but he is too closely based on real historical figures to be brushed aside as a fantastical embodiment of pure evil. Shan Yu, after all, is a phonetic transliteration of the title for the chiefs of the Xiongnu, a nomadic people on the steppes of central Asia who became such a threat to the early Chinese dynasties that the Great Wall was built to defend China. The movie refers to Shan Yu and his army as the Huns, who are sometimes believed to be descendents of the Xiongnu, to make its villains recognizable to the Western audiences. Attila the Hun pillaged the eastern and western Roman Empires during the fifth century A.D., and the Huns have served as a symbol of military and cultural threat to Western civilization ever since. Invoked during World War I and World War II as an epithet for the Germans, the Huns are not in a strict sense racial figures in the West. However, they pick up clear racial overtones in *Mulan,* complete with a different skin color and physiological abnormalities. Why did Disney get away with racializing the army at war with imperial China, when it would be pretty much unimaginable, for example, to portray the Native Americans in *Pocahontas* in the same way?[9] When *Mulan* first came out, much critical attention was drawn toward the staging of the Han Chinese (the ethnic majority in China) in the movie. To the delight of many, Mulan, a girl from feudal China, struck one as a credible embodiment of proto-feminism who defied the stock figures of submissive Asian women in Western cultures. Few, if any, however, took offense at the portrayal of the "Huns" in the movie.

9. *Pocahontas*'s romanticization of the Smith–Pocahontas relationship and, symbolically, the white–Indian relationship, is not without problems. Nonetheless, the difference between *Pocahontas* and *Mulan* remains clear. In the former, it is Governor Ratcliffe, leader of the English settlers in the movie, rather than the Native American figures, that is overtly caricatured.

One has to acknowledge that the figure of Shan Yu, as a throwback to the blatant racism characteristic of political cartoons of the World War II era, poses a few interesting questions. Did China provide Disney with an outlet to let loose, or at least leave uncensored, racialist sentiments that are culturally forbidden in the U.S.? Or was Disney simply trying to present Chinese history from a "native" point of view, with the implication that a racialist view of nomadic peoples on the borders of ancient China (some of whom were incorporated into PRC territories and identified as "minority nationalities") remained normative in contemporary China? I believe that the answer to both of these questions is yes. In other words, one can read the "Huns" in the movie *Mulan* as a revelation of the racialist attitudes lingering in American culture against a Chinese backdrop *and* as a (conscious or unconscious) hint at the ways in which Chinese culture remains in the grip of racial discrimination. In either case, the movie demonstrates that representations of ethno-racial issues in the two countries are intimately connected: A movie ostensibly about China can betray racialist sentiments in the U.S., while at the same time suggesting that China (ancient or modern), unlike contemporary America, is a place where racialist attitudes can be taken for granted. The political correctness mandated in the multicultural U.S. is both joyfully jettisoned and slyly bolstered (by being subtly contrasted against "Chinese" racism) in a Disney movie about China. *Mulan,* then, prompts us to reflect on the unconscious of American multiculturalism, the persistent racialist mindset beneath the "postracial" rhetoric that requires a Chinese background to simultaneously uncensor and purify itself. Just like the political exchanges between the two countries, *Mulan* reveals an unproductive and often unconscious pattern of comparison that reduces the other country to a foil onto which one's own can project the evil of ethno-racial prejudice.

What this book does is counter this negative, incriminating mode of comparison by offering a few alternatives. It not only critiques the limitations of both U.S. multiculturalism and China's ethnic policy during the post–Cold War period but also shows the unexpected continuities and connections between the two projects, placing them in a shared context of the global experiment in viable structures for multiethnic nations. The genesis of my thoughts on these questions lies primarily in my involvement with Asian American literary studies. Diasporic Chinese American narratives, including works by Maxine Hong Kingston, Alex Kuo, and Yan Geling, provide important material and viable conceptual models for a new form of transnational or comparative critique. Addressing both Chinese and American histories and literary traditions and at times obtaining an "afterlife" through actual translation into a different language, these narratives provide perspectives on U.S.–China connections that are rarely glimpsed in other forms of cultural production. They also comment suggestively on *how* these connections can be drawn. Kuo, in particular, ruminates on the conflicting implications of metaphor to propose a model of critical comparison that draws linkages between two disparate political and cultural contexts without positing an easy symmetry. Chinese American narratives, thus, enable me to construct the kind of comparative critique that I enact here. Grappling with such narratives, I contend, helps propel Asian American studies into more active collaborations with contiguous fields, including American studies and East Asian studies, thus furthering its transformation from a field organized around a group of embodied subjects into a loosely associated set of provocations in existing discourses about the conditions and implications of subjectivation and identity formation in different but related national contexts. The intellectual sizzle that comes from crossing Asian/Chinese American literary studies with comparative multiculturalisms is what my project seeks to capture.

A Note on the Text

Most Chinese names (not including Chinese American names) are given in the order of family name followed by given name. Exceptions include names of Chinese writers and scholars that customarily appear in the Western style. The pinyin Romanization system is used for all Chinese proper names. Unless otherwise noted, quotes from Chinese-language material are my own translations.

ACKNOWLEDGMENTS

M OST OF THIS BOOK was written at Columbia University, but the seeds for it were sown many years ago, when I was still a confused undergraduate. My most important mentors from that period of my life, Chu Xiaoquan of Fudan University and Donna Richardson of St. Mary's College of Maryland, introduced me to the life of the truly exceptional mind and the possibilities that life might open.

This book can be seen as a new version of the dissertation I completed at Northwestern University, even though most of the dissertation has been discarded or transformed beyond recognition. At its heart, this book addresses the central questions intimated, though not well formulated, in that earlier work. My dissertation committee—Dorothy Wang, Betsy Erkkila, Paul Breslin, and David Eng—placed me on a promising track. Dorothy, in particular, put much of herself into helping me adapt to graduate education and the academic job market. Many others at Northwestern, both faculty and fellow graduate students, shared time, friendship, and ideas with me and to this day evoke warm feelings in me. I can name only a few of them here: Brian Edwards, Christopher Lane,

Jules Law, Coleman Hutchison, Peter Jaros, and Katy Chiles. Special appreciation must go to Shuji Otsuka, whose companionship and wisdom were indispensable for my well-being in graduate school.

Since I started working on this book in my second year as an assistant professor, I have received consistent guidance and help from my wonderful colleagues at Columbia. Bruce Robbins's everyday cosmopolitanism—his open-mindedness toward everything global and unknown—added a well-needed dose of optimism to my teaching and research as a junior professor. Rachel Adams, Ross Posnock, Brent Edwards, Joey Slaughter, Marianne Hirsch, Nicole Horejsi, and many others also offered important advice.

Richard Jean So deserves a special place in my acknowledgments. An incredible interlocutor over many years, Richard has always inspired me with his devotion to intellectual rigor and ambition. I also benefited a great deal from the feedback I received from a reading group that James Kim organized over the years 2008–10, during which time I conducted workshops on parts of my manuscript. Jeffrey Santa Ana, Thuy Linh Tu, and Elda Tsou, along with James, tolerated and critiqued my earlier drafts. Xiao-huang Yin served as an informal mentor for me since I was a Ph.D. student. Sau-ling Wong kindly provided me with several of her insightful articles on Kingston, in addition to advice and support. My colleagues at other institutions, including in particular Steven Lee and Stephen H. Sohn, introduced me to resources and ideas of which I was not previously aware, giving me a warm sense of long-distance camaraderie. Thanks also to Evelyn Hu-dehart, Colleen Lye, Crystal Parikh, Allen Isaac, and Victor Bascara for giving me advice and support despite their own demanding careers. I shall not forget the inspiration I received from excellent graduate students, especially Brandon Ruben and Tim Gunatilaka.

I must also mention my colleagues in the Department of East Asian Languages and Cultures at Columbia, who sent along their work and conversed with me about their projects. Eugenia Lean invited me to the Modern China Seminar, an invigorating intellectual home outside my own department. Weihong Bao spent much time comparing notes with me on the process of writing academic books. Lydia Liu shared with me her thoughts on Chinese ethnic cultures, among many other topics. For me, she personifies the meaning of intellectual agility and expansiveness. Thanks also to her partner Li Tuo for scintillating conversations.

One normally does not need to acknowledge the labor of anonymous readers for one's work, but over the years I have really come to appreciate the generosity of many fellow academics, who always remind me of why I entered this profession in the first place. My readers at The Ohio State University Press were particularly exemplary in their understanding of productive criticism.

Even more unforgettable is my debt to the authors I write about in this book. Alex Kuo and his wife Joan Burbick graciously hosted me and granted me an extensive interview. They have continued their investment in me since then. Yan Geling also made time for me, even when I was myself unclear about what to accomplish through my questions for her. I also contacted Zha Jianying and Su Wei when researching my book. I was not able to write about them extensively in the end, and I hope they will forgive me for that failure.

A version of chapter 5 was originally published as "Transnational Criticism and Asian Immigrant Literature in the U.S.: Reading Yan Geling's *Fusang* and Its English Translation," *Contemporary Literature* 47, no. 4 (2006): 570–600. Part of chapter 3 was originally published as "Toward a U.S.–China Comparative Critique: Indigenous Rights and National Expansion in Alex Kuo's *Panda Diaries*," *American Quarterly* 62, no. 3 (2010): 739–61. I would like to thank the University of Wisconsin Press and Johns Hopkins University Press for the permissions to reprint my articles. I am also grateful for an NEH Summer Stipend (2010) and two Summer Research Grants from the Graduate School of Arts and Sciences of Columbia.

Finally, a personal note. My parents have never once told me what to do with my life, yet none of what I have done would have been possible without them. They not only have taught me to work hard and depend on myself but also have shown me what it means to practice the ethic of generosity. This book is dedicated to them. Liu Daxian proved that it is possible to combine intellectual stimulation and the simple matter of having a good time. For that, I remain deeply grateful.

INTRODUCTION

Whatever the explanation, Asia is witnessing the rise of "identity politics." People are mobilizing along ethnic, religious, racial, and cultural lines, and demanding recognition of their identity, acknowledgement of their legal rights and historic claims, and a commitment to the sharing of power.

—Baogang He and Will Kymlicka, *Multiculturalism in Asia*

A double critique, "an other thinking," would lead to the openness of the "unforeseeable diversity of the world" and of "unheard and unexpected" forms of knowledge, as argued by Glissant (1998).

—Walter D. Mignolo, *Border Thinking*

PLURALIST UNIVERSALISM provides a comparison of U.S. liberal multiculturalism and China's policy toward minority nationalities that does not ascribe a fundamental otherness to either side. It argues that U.S. liberal multiculturalism and China's policy toward minority nationalities are two increasingly intertwined components of contemporary multiculturalism, which we do well to conceive of as a global movement that draws upon different intellectual and political traditions and responds to different local conditions. They are two different but not entirely incongruous forms of pluralism that have increasingly come to bear on each other, through translation (with China at the translating end for the most part) and other kinds of discursive mediation, since the end of the Cold War. A number of historians and cultural critics have intervened in the Cold War discourse of the ideological rivalry between the U.S. and the Soviet Union by demonstrating that, throughout the twentieth century, notions of racial and ethnic equality in the U.S. were affected by

1

U.S.–Soviet relations and American perceptions of the Soviet nationalities policy.[1] The similar task of complicating the U.S.–China binary in the post–Cold War era, which inevitably requires different approaches, has not been seriously attempted.

Using the term "multiculturalism" to describe conceptions of racial and ethnic relations in both the U.S. and China does not flatten the differences between the two contexts; rather, it entails a plea for a globalized, nonnormative understanding of this very familiar idea. In political and social theory, "multiculturalism" has picked up different and sometimes conflicting meanings since the early 1970s, when it became the name for Canada's official policy of promoting immigrant languages and cultures. Most conceptions of multiculturalism in existing literature presume that it is a phenomenon peculiar to Western liberal democracies and are thus too narrow to accommodate the multiplicity of cultural pluralisms in the world. I detach multiculturalism from political ideology, defining it as a corrective to what one may call unitary nationalism, which predicates itself upon a homogeneous conception of national culture and interests. Embodied in state legislation, government policies, social programs, and cultural and political movements, multiculturalism promotes group-specific rights that aim to help ethnic and racial minorities sustain their societal cultures and counter the effects of their forced integration into the majority nation or, alternatively, exclusion from it. These rights often include, understood differently in different contexts, political autonomy, fair political representation, preferential treatment in education and employment, and institutional support for certain languages and cultural practices. Multiculturalism, to borrow from Bhikhu Parekh, can be seen as a form of "pluralist universalism"—it acknowledges simultaneously the importance of cultivating common values and practices as a basis for a functional national identity and that of addressing the particular needs of historically disadvantaged ethno-racial groups.[2] It is a profoundly political

1. See Mary Dudziac, *Cold War Civil Rights;* Kate Baldwin, *Beyond the Color Line and the Iron Curtain;* Steven S Lee, "Cold War Multiculturalism" and "Borat, Multiculturalism, Mnogonatsional'nost.'" Dudziac explains the way in which the Cold War both helped produce and placed severe limits upon the civil rights reform in U.S. from 1946 through the mid-1960s. Baldwin focuses on black American intellectuals' interactions with the Soviet Union between 1922 and 1963 to reassess at once the impact of Soviet internationalism on the political visions of black America and U.S. black modernism. Lee's work, still in dissertation form, proposes that U.S. multiculturalism experienced a turn away from internationalism in the era following the Civil Rights Movement in part because of the pervasive disillusionment with the Soviet nationalities policy.

2. Bhikhu Parekh, *Rethinking Multiculturalism,* 126–36. Parekh uses the term to define a conception of human cultures that departs from both hegemonic universalism and unprincipled relativism. I use it to describe an attitude toward cultural differences within a nation-state

project that serves to mediate between the imperative of national coherence and assertions of minority difference, so that their conflicts do not come to a head. Most states in the world today are multiethnic, via colonization and voluntary or involuntary migration, and many have been compelled, by the pressure of minority insurgences or the international promotion of group rights, to implement a certain form of multiculturalism, redefining national identity in a way that accommodates minority demands for autonomy or equality.

As it functions to counter, or at least contain, ethno-racial tensions, multiculturalism cannot simply be equated with narrow identitarianism or communitarianism.[3] That it oftentimes seeks to contain, rather than fundamentally confront, the political conflicts among different ethnic and racial groups subjects multiculturalism, not unjustly, to the criticism that it accords merely formal or symbolic recognition to minorities, masks structural inequalities, and distracts from the goal of social redistribution.[4] However, the limitations of certain configurations of multiculturalism should not be a reason for rejecting the entire idea. Even superficial forms of multiculturalism open the door to broad discussions, in scholarly circles as well as the public sphere, of multiple understandings of national solidarity—social democratic vs. culturalist, for example—and possible ways of making it compatible with the goals of equality and justice. This point is particularly important to emphasize, given that the victory of multiculturalism over the arguably bigger evil of overtly oppressive or exclusionary forms of nationalism is by no means clear. As Anne Phillips points out, there has been much talk of the "death of multiculturalism" in recent years in Britain and continental Europe, among other parts of the world.[5] Even though U.S. liberal multiculturalism

3. This view that multiculturalism equals communitarianism was more prevalent in the theoretical discussions of multiculturalism in the 1990s, and it remains a popular understanding in both conservative and radical quarters. See Slavoj Žižek, "Multiculturalism, or, the Cultural Logic of Multinational Capitalism," 26. The author warns leftist intellectuals against subscribing to the dominant fiction of group identity and modeling progressive movements upon the logic of communitarianism or popularism, which, for Žižek, always entails pernicious practices of exclusion and easily slides into ethnic fundamentalism. Instead he urges them to shift their focus from the cultural to the political, to offer a program for *égaliberté* that seeks to transform the public space of civil society and active responsible citizenship—the fight for human rights, ecology, and so forth. *Pace* Žižek, I do not reduce multiculturalism to a narrow particularism but instead emphasize the political, dynamic nature of contemporary multiculturalisms, defining them as discursive and political battles that continue to reshape the configurations of national identity and political universalism.

4. For two of the most oft-cited criticisms of multiculturalism's neglect of structural inequalities, see Iris Young, *Justice and the Politics of Identity;* Michael Waltzer, "Multiculturalism and Individualism."

5. Anne Phillips, *Multiculturalism without Culture,* 5. One can make a similar argument

and China's policy toward ethnic minorities are both severely constrained, working more often to conceal deep-seated social tensions than to openly address them, both have provoked or helped fuel alternative conceptions of pluralism in their respective context.

Canadian political philosopher Will Kymlicka, one of the most influential and prolific theorists of multiculturalism, has most consistently written about this subject in relation to nationalism, defining it expressly as a project integral to the process of "nation-building."[6] It is not a coincidence that Kymlicka and his collaborators are also major proponents of a global, comparative approach to multiculturalism. The understanding of multiculturalism as an instrument of nation formation both necessitates and enables a collection of case studies from states other than Western liberal democracies. As Jacob T. Levy points out, Kymlicka is an important practitioner of "contextualist political theory" who remains sensitive to the specific circumstances surrounding different instances of pluralism.[7] Kymlicka's work emphasizes the undiminishing urgency of the project of nation-building in the contemporary era of globalization, pointing out that states with drastically different histories and political systems, ranging from the post-Communist states in Central and Eastern Europe to the various postcolonial societies in Asia, Latin America, and Africa, share the task of forging national identities while addressing minority demands for autonomy and equality. Liberal multiculturalism has spread its influence around the world, especially among intellectual elites, but the actual policies addressing minority needs vary widely from country to country.[8] Kymlicka and his collaborators, among others, have produced a substantial amount of work that constitutes an emerging discourse on comparative multiculturalisms.[9]

---

for post-9/11 America as well, with renewed outcry against "political correctness" and the vaunted rhetoric of a "postracial" society.

6. Kymlicka, *Politics in the Vernacular*, 23–27. Kymlicka believes that academic debates around multiculturalism have undergone three stages. The first stage revolves around the merit of the perceived communitarianism of minority groups, the second stage focuses on the implications of multiculturalism for traditional political liberalism, and the third, current stage emphasizes the relationship between multiculturalism and nation-building. The three stages, of course, do not have to be seen as a linear sequence.

7. Jacob T. Levy, "Contextualism, Constitutionalism, and *modus Vivendi*," 183.

8. Will Kymlicka provides a vivid testimonial to this growing interest among global elites in liberal models of multiculturalism. See *Multicultural Odysseys*. The author has been participating in "seminars, workshops, and advisory groups" on the formulation of international norms of minority rights in "some two dozen countries, from Ethiopia to Estonia, from Syria to Sri Lanka, from Mexico to Moldova," where he watched the diffusion of liberal concepts and discourses "through academia, civil society, and the bureaucracy" (7).

9. See Grant H. Cornwell and Eve Walsh Stoddard, *Global Multiculturalism*; Ella Shoha

Extrapolating from this emerging discourse, I contend that, as a political project central to the process of nation-building, multiculturalism does not have to be grounded in liberal theories of rights and justice. Political liberalism provides a particular set of conditions and challenges for multiculturalism, but it does not define multiculturalism. The liberal emphasis on individual rights has been conceived as both a foundation for and impediment to the promotion of group rights in multiculturalism, but these rights can also derive from other political and cultural traditions.[10] As I point out in more detail later in this Introduction, although Kymlicka's work gestures clearly toward an expansive view of multiculturalism through his various case studies, it remains invested in using these case studies to test the feasibility of the global diffusion of conceptions of liberal justice. For Kymlicka, in other words, a global perspective on multiculturalism entails, to a large part, understanding the conditions for and means of transplanting liberal multiculturalism into various local contexts. By contrast, I see multiculturalism as an inherently global phenomenon with many interrelated components that compete with and influence one another. I elaborate in chapter 1 that U.S. and Chinese multiculturalisms can be seen, respectively, as a liberal and a socialist version of cultural pluralism that have come into increasing contestation and contact in the post–Cold War era. I adopt this expansive understanding of multiculturalism not to erase all distinctions between U.S. liberal multiculturalism and China's nationalities policy but to provide a conceptual basis for the comparative project that I undertake here, which aims to illuminate the different but related ways in which nation-building projects affect racial and ethnic minorities in the two countries, thus unsettling the habitual practice, espoused by both, of elevating one system over the other.

This is not to say, however, that my study *inaugurates* a way of mediating between U.S. and Chinese ethno-racial politics across a chasm of mutual misconceptions. Rather, it builds on the comparative perspectives articulated in the literary writings produced in the two countries since the early 1990s, including, in particular, Chinese American fiction (defined broadly, including texts written in both English and Chinese). These writings constitute a rare alternative to the common practice of pitting U.S. liberal multicultural-

---

and Robert Stam, *Multiculturalism, Postcoloniality, and Transnational Media;* Milan Mesic, *Perspectives of Multiculturalism.*

10. In regard to how multiculturalism both derives from and challenges the tenet of individual rights and that of the common rights of citizenship, see Joseph Raz, "Multiculturalism"; Yael Tamir, *Liberal Nationalism;* Kimlicka, *Multicultural Citizenship.* For forms of multiculturalism outside the liberal framework, see N. Ganesan's discussion of Malaysia's consociationalism and Chua Beng Huat's discussion of Singapore's communitarian model of multiculturalism.

ism and China's nationalities policy against each other by illustrating the interlinked social contexts to which they respond in the post–Cold War era and reflecting upon the political functions and structural limitations they share. If, as I have argued, it is both important and intellectually viable to study the two systems as two related components of the global movement of multiculturalism, this study must give a crucial role to fictional narratives from Chinese America. They provide a crucial but overlooked source of insights into the relations between U.S. and Chinese multiculturalisms. My book reveals, analyzes, and structures itself on the basis of the logic of these narratives.

Narrative fiction and fictionalized narratives, then, constitute a supplement to social science discourses, allowing us to question and dislodge the liberal biases built into normative definitions of multiculturalism. If multiculturalism's mediation of the conflicts between national unity and minority differences continuously changes the connotations of both terms, the ways in which this very mediation proceeds should not be a fixed matter either. As a form of pluralist universalism, in other words, multiculturalism is best reconceived in a way that simultaneously universalizes and pluralizes it. Multiculturalism, indeed, is itself in need of being "multiculturalized." Through an analysis of the narrative texts included in this study, I project a fluid conception of multiculturalism that is more encompassing *and* more accurate than the normative liberal conception. I do not subsume heterogeneous ethnic policies under one coherent model but instead make the idea of multiculturalism more accommodating to actually existing, competing modes of ethnic and racial integration. In the meantime, as I trace how multiculturalism has played out in related ways in Chinese American, and Chinese and American, narratives from the post–Cold War period, I offer a comparative, dual critique of the contemporary American and Chinese nations.

Strategic Doubling

In 2006, the prolific but underdiscussed Chinese American author Alex Kuo published his novel *Panda Diaries,* which he drafted in 1991 and 1992, when he visited China as a foreign teacher. In the novel, Kuo juxtaposes the Indian policies of the nineteenth-century U.S. with the Chinese government's efforts to integrate ethnic minorities into the project of socialist modernization during the Cultural Revolution. This comparison involves time–space configurations that are apparently distanced from the post–Cold

War moment in which the novel was written and published. It is, however, a comparison that can be read as a response to the later moment, when the U.S. and China both claim a genuine form of cultural pluralism, often over and against each other. Kuo's juxtaposition of the two unsavory historical moments throws these claims into question by highlighting the colonization of minority space that occurred in the process of national expansion in both countries. His comparison also intervenes in the emerging discourse in China that parallels the Chinese government's ongoing campaign to develop its western regions, which have a high concentration of minorities, with the American westward expansion, a parallel that largely serves as a justification for prioritizing the state's conception of economic and social development over minority interests.

Chinese immigrant writer Yan Geling, one of the best known of her generation, provides another example of a simultaneous critique of U.S. and Chinese multiculturalisms. Her 1996 Chinese-language novel *Fusang,* set in nineteenth-century San Francisco, portrays a Chinese prostitute as an embodiment of a new form of subjectivity by turning sexual slavery into a voluntary act that disturbs the regimes of race and gender in nineteenth-century America. Widely read among Chinese-speaking audiences in both the U.S. and China, this novel reached an English-speaking audience through a translation in 2001. The capacious, amorphous subjectivity embodied by the character of Fusang, thus, came into conflict with the logic of mainstream multiculturalisms in both the U.S. and China. The story of Fusang departs drastically from the familiar narrative of Asian American female empowerment that operates as a testimonial to the dissolution of racial barriers in the U.S. At the same time, the ambiguous characterization of the female protagonist also resists appropriations by Chinese readers and critics, who habitually read Asian American characters like Fusang as a symbol of a united, though ethnically diverse, Chinese nation grappling with the legacies of Western imperialism and racism.

The examples of Yan and Kuo, both of whom are studied in all their complexity in my book, demonstrate that Chinese American and Chinese immigrant fiction plays a crucial role in modeling a conceptual framework within which one can study U.S. and Chinese multiculturalisms as two comparable, interrelated processes of mediation between the imperative of national coherence and minority demands for autonomy and equality. The model, to borrow from Argentinian critic Walter Mignolo, can be called "double critique." Mignolo uses the term largely in relation to Moroccan philosopher Abdelhebir Khatibi's critique of both "the domain of Western metaphysics" and the "theological realm of Islamic thought."[11] It is a critique that grapples with the legacy of French colonialism in Maghreb and Arabic nationalism simultaneously. For Mignolo, Khatibi's double critique signals the practice of thinking from multiple discursive lineages and yet none of them, thus generating subaltern knowledge that did not previously exist before the very act of mediation. It does not constitute a transcendent vision, but a site of irreducible epistemic difference. The concept of double critique, along with its various critical cognates, resonates strongly with the logic of *Panda Diaries* and *Fusang*.[12] Studying these works helps illuminate the shared limitations of U.S. and Chinese conceptions of ethnic and racial difference and the connections between the two (for example, the relationship between China's official and popular nationalism and the translation of postcolonial theory from the U.S. to China). The logic of double critique in their works is naturally affiliated with the emerging discourse of comparative multiculturalisms in that it also engages in comparisons that are sensitive to both parallels and differences, but it challenges the latter by refusing to establish, even implicitly, a normative conception of ethno-racial justice against which others are measured. Kuo and Yan address both the U.S. and Chinese contexts so as to allow them to decenter and defamiliarize each other, holding up a distorting mirror to each other so that neither figures as a model or positive exception.

Double critique is not an idea extraneous to Chinese American writings. In 1943, Lin Yutang published a collection of essays titled *Between Tears and Laughter* with John Day. Having written a string of books, including *My Country and My People,* that made him the first best-selling Chinese author in America, Lin waded into international politics in the new book. In the essays, he critiques the Allies' neglect of struggles for decolonization and national liberation in Asia, pointing out that their wartime rhetoric of freedom contradicted their begrudging of freedom to their colonies in Asia. In contrast to lopsided, imperialist views of the world, Lin advocates for a "binocular vision," a comparative, transnational perspective that traces how such ideas as freedom pick up different meanings in different national contexts.[13] Lin's venture into political commentaries hurt his popularity in the U.S., but the idea of a "binocular vision" survived, re-emerging in Chinese American narratives of later eras.

Double critique does not assume that the two things being organized

---

11. Walter Mignolo, *Local Histories/Global Designs,* 68.

12. Mignolo cites Dubois's double consciousness, Anzaldúa's new mestiza consciousness, and Glissant's creolization, among others, border thinking as concepts akin to double critique. See Mignolo, 77, 84.

13. Lin Yutang, *Between Tears and Laughter,* 40.

into one critical framework occupy symmetrical positions in their respective cultural and political contexts. There are no such neutral grounds in any comparative projects. I do not assume, that is to say, that the question of race and ethnicity has the same resonance for readers on both sides of the Pacific. Instead, I consider double critique as a form of "strategic doubling," along the logic of strategic essentialism. Strategic essentialism reappropriates existing identity categories, including racial and ethnic ones, to transform the disciplinary force inherent in them into subversive energy. Likewise, "strategic doubling" responds critically to the conventional manners in which racial and ethnic issues in the two countries are compared, explicitly or implicitly, in popular culture and official political rhetoric.

I not only study how Chinese American authors such as Kuo and Yan mediate between two different national contexts but also extend the logic of "strategic doubling" embodied in their narratives. Comparative insights into U.S. and Chinese multiculturalisms can derive not only from transnational narratives that straddle different national spaces but also from the critical practice of juxtaposing and comparing narratives that emanate from within these spaces. Both U.S. and Chinese authors have addressed the relationship between national identity and minority difference in the form of fictional narratives, a genre that allows for more diverse and nuanced perspectives than the more overtly political genres. Some of them demonstrate that, over the past two decades, U.S. liberal multiculturalism and China's ethnic policy have been conceived and questioned in related ways. Clive Cussler's *Treasure of Khan* (2006, translated into Chinese as *kehan de baozang* in 2008) and Jiang Rong's *Lang Tuteng* (2004, translated into English as *The Wolf Totem* in 2008), both bestsellers when first published, illuminate some of the common denominators of the popular views of nation and ethnicity in the two countries. Hui Muslim writer Zhang Chengzhi's *Xinling Shi* (1991) and Arab American writer Rabih Alameddine's *Koolaids: The Art of War* (1998), on the other hand, call our attention to the ways in which these popular views are questioned in Muslim writings. Double critique, then, is a mode of critique embodied both in the Chinese American fictional narratives I study and in the connections I draw between previously unrelated Chinese and U.S. narratives.

Rereading *The Woman Warrior,* Yet Again

Authors like Kuo and Yan, of course, do not work in a vacuum. Double critique is not an exclusive product of the post–Cold War period, though it is particularly important for this period, one that has seen increased U.S.–China cultural relations, the ascent of both Chinese nationalism and U.S. global hegemony, and the resurgence of the question of ethnicity on a global level. This section studies Maxine Hong Kingston's *The Woman Warrior* as an earlier example of what double critique may look like as a literary practice. Kingston has often been thought of as one of the first to "create in literature a sui generis [Chinese American] reality."[14] She breaks the silence imposed upon Chinese in America not by acting as a cultural informant but by offering consciously subjective, personalized narratives of Chinese history and cultural traditions. In other words, Kingston disavows conventional notions of narrative authority that customarily deny access to marginalized social groups. I endorse this reading of Kingston but believe that more attention is to be paid to exactly *how* she handles her Chinese sources and how the descriptions of China and the U.S. interact in *The Woman Warrior*. If the book bodies forth a singularly Chinese American reality or consciousness, it contains surprising dimensions that are yet unexplored.

About thirty years before Disney's *Mulan* came out, Kingston drew upon Mulan's story in her 1976 work *The Woman Warrior*. Kingston's version of the story carries much more nuance than the one from Disney. Unlike the movie, Kingston's book interweaves the experiences of the protagonist-narrator, a Chinese American teenage girl, in the postwar U.S. and Chinese folklore and culture that the narrator reconstructs from a familial oral tradition. Whereas the Disney movie *Mulan* contains an expression of the unconscious of contemporary multicultural America, which requires China to uncensor and purify itself, *The Woman Warrior* is a much more conscious exploration of the formal and political implications entailed in juxtaposing notions of race and ethnicity from the two countries. Kingston's subtly presented critique of what is amiss in both countries' ethnic and racial dynamics foreshadowed the later Chinese American writings that I study, gesturing toward a history of Asian American critical comparativism that dates back to at least the Cold War era.

The Woman Warrior, the most widely read and taught work in Asian American literature, incited a long-standing debate in Asian American lit-

---

14. For the best-known article on this topic, see Sau-ling Wong, "Autobiography as Guided Chinatown Tour?" 48. Wong makes a case for the claim of artistic freedom, as we see in Kingston's imagining of China, as an antiracist narrative strategy. Also see Robert G. Lee, "*The Woman Warrior* as an Intervention in Asian American Historiography"; Mark Chiang, *The Cultural Capital of Asian American Studies,* chapter 3. Both Lee and Chiang argue that the anxiety of representation in *The Woman Warrior*, its constant move to question its rendering of Chinese history, constitutes a major impulse underlying much Asian American literature. Chiang ascribes the same impulse to Asian American literary criticism as well.

erature. The debate centers on the cultural work performed by the representations of Chinese history and culture in Kingston and Chinese American writings in general. As Colleen Lye points out in a recent essay, Chinese American literature, unlike other subcategories of Asian American literature, has been characterized by an "exoticist presentation of ancestral culture" since at least the 1930s.[15] This phenomenon, which Lye sees as a formal correlative of the "unevenness of Asian American panethnicity,"[16] has largely been discussed as either a symptom of U.S. orientalism, which authorizes a set of racial stereotypes that permeate the Asian American imaginary, or an effort to "displace" or undermine these stereotypes.[17] My reading of *The Woman Warrior* takes the discussion into a new direction.[18] I argue that Kingston's incorporation of redacted Chinese folklore into a narrative about growing up in the Cold War U.S. prefigured the comparative, doubly critical politics of post–Cold War Chinese American narratives, even as it attests to the bewilderment with which Chinese Americans struggle with the "mass of unexplained cultural data" about Chinese culture and customs transmitted from their parents.[19] Read closely, the novel that marked a watershed moment in Asian American literature turns out, surprisingly, to have heralded the project of comparative multiculturalisms undertaken in this study.

The second chapter of *The Woman Warrior,* "White Tigers," centers on an extended fantasy on the part of the Chinese American girl narrator, in which a Chinese girl follows a bird into the mountains and meets an old couple, who adopt her and train her in martial arts. After she returns to her birth village as a young woman, she protects her father from being conscripted by the imperial army and then leads an army of rebels toward Peiping, the capital, where they overthrow the emperor and install a peasant, one of their own, on the throne. Having accomplished the impossible, the warrior woman returns to her village to confront the baron who has been oppressing the villagers. She beheads him and metes out well-justified punishment to his family and servants who had been involved in evil deeds. Inspired by the Chinese folk-

15. Colleen Lye, "The Sino-Japanese Conflict of Asian American Literature," 43.

16. Ibid., 45.

17. David Leiwei Li, "The Production of Chinese American Tradition," 319.

18. One must qualify this statement by pointing out that Sau-ling Wong offers a useful discussion of how "a few traditional Chinese literary sources have been altered to serve as commentary on the narrator's Chinese American reality," though she does not touch on the issues I discuss here. See her "Kingston's Handling of Traditional Chinese Sources," 28. Also see Feng Lan, "The Female Individual and the Empire." Lan traces the permutations in the figure of Mulan through the several renditions of her story in Chinese literature, finding that Kingston's portrayal of the heroine embraces the Confucian and Communist doctrines about women's social position in some ways while deviating from them in others.

19. Sau-ling Wong, "Autobiography as Guided Chinatown Tour?" 45.

lore that the narrator's mother passes down to her as an oral tradition, the figure of the warrior woman is clearly the narrator's expression of her desire for empowerment, confronted as she is with socially debilitating injustices: prejudice against girls within the Chinese American community, racism against Chinese in America (which has gendered implications as well), and the Communist rule in China (which the narrator believes had robbed her family of their farm).

Critics have found this fantasy troubling for various reasons. Those familiar with the Chinese sources of the mother's stories that the narrator reinvents in the fantasy have pointed out that, in creating the figure of the young warrior woman, Kingston blends together two of the most beloved folk heroes in Chinese history. The more obvious one is Fa Mu Lan (Hua Mulan), whom the narrator refers to in the beginning of "White Tigers" as a figure she has heard about from her mother. Fa Mu Lan is a household name in China, the protagonist of the "Ballad of Mulan," commonly believed to have originated during the Northern Wei period (386–534 A.D.). Mulan is known for being in the imperial army for more than ten years disguised as a man to protect her aged father from conscription.[20] A less overt subtext for the narrator's fantasy is the story of Yue Fei (1103–42 A.D.), a general during the Southern Song Dynasty (1127–79 A.D.) celebrated for his unwavering loyalty to the emperor and his valiant but failed attempts to recover northern China from the Jin Dynasty (1115–1234 A.D.), ruled by the Jurchens. Although Yue Fei is more of a verifiable historical figure than Mulan, the lives of both have been mythologized in various stories and legends in China. The narrator's fantasy invokes Yue Fei with the detail that the swordswoman's parents carved words of resolve and revenge into her bare back before she leads the army of rebels to the capital. Yue Fei is known for having borne the tattoo "*Jinzhong baoguo*" [Serve the country with utmost loyalty] on his back. The conflation of the two unrelated folk heroes in Kingston seems simply disrespectful to some of her critics,[21] but more pernicious to others.

---

20. The date of the composition of the "Ballad of Mulan" is uncertain. Today it is most commonly introduced (to Chinese students and common Chinese readers) as a ballad from the Northern Wei Dynasty, composed in a folk style called "*yuefu.*" Some point out, however, that the ballad, like many folk songs, were collective creations. The basic form of the ballad we see today was most likely to have emerged during the Northern Wei, but it probably derived from earlier sources and continued to be revised through the subsequent dynasties. See He Yuping, "'Mulanci' chuangzuo shidai yu zuozhe zhi tanjiu" [A study of the composition and authorship of the "Ballad of Mulan"].

21. Zhang Ya-Jie, "A Chinese Woman's Response to Maxine Hong Kingston's *The Woman Warrior.*" As a Chinese professor who visited the U.S. at one point, Zhang writes that she first reacted negatively to the stories in *The Woman Warrior*, finding them "somewhat twisted" (17).

Frank Chin's famous parody of the fantasy section of "White Tigers" compares the liberties Kingston takes with Yue Fei, by fusing him with a female figure, to defiling Joan of Arc by portraying her as a lesbian to a Chinese audience.[22] For Chin, Kingston's disregard for the authenticity of Chinese history and folklore perpetuates the "Christian social Darwinist stereotype" of Chinese culture as despicably misogynistic, and additionally, the transmission of the deed of a male hero onto a female one promotes an Asian American feminist agenda at the expense of Chinese American men, who are deprived of a chance to connect with the powerful male archetypes in the Chinese folk tradition.[23] The Kingston–Chin debate sparked a series of critical responses, which mostly seek to establish a common ground between Chin's search for viable models for Asian American masculinity and Kingston's critique of the structural causes for the various challenges facing Asian American women.[24] Both, in other words, are seen as deeply concerned with the implications of racialization for the configurations of gender and sexuality in Asian America.

These responses, however, do not address directly Chin's argument for more authentic, faithful representations of Chinese culture and history. It is perhaps because the notion of authenticity, when understood as factual accuracy, sounds inherently naïve and unsupportable. For Chin, however, authenticity matters because Chinese folklore, understood in its own context, does not figure Chinese patriarchy the same way as Kingston does in her novel but instead contains a range of admirable male figures who can provide important cultural resources for Chinese American men as they struggle against exclusion from the prevailing model of masculinity in mainstream American society.[25] Chin's point will sound more interesting to Asian Americanists if one just reframes it slightly, as an argument against Asian American writers' employment of China as a source of cultural material that can be taken out of context and transformed at will to fit the themes at hand. Understood this way, Chin is calling for authenticity not in terms of

---

22. See Frank Chin, "The Most Popular Book in China."

23. Frank Chin et al., *The Big Aiiieeeee*, 29.

24. King-kok Cheung, "The Woman Warrior versus the Chinaman Pacific"; David Eng, *Racial Castration*. Cheung summarizes the debate as one that construes a dichotomy between "feminism and heroism," between "Chinese American women and men" (113). She believes that this dichotomy can be deconstructed when Chinese American woman writers "find a way to negotiate the tangle of sexual and racial politics in all its intricacies" (127), and Kingston, she argues, does just that not only in *The Woman Warrior* but in her subsequent works as well. Eng revisits this debate, agreeing that "Asian American activists and critics must refrain from seeking antifeminist solutions to predicaments of Asian American masculinity" (16).

25. Chin et al., *The Big Aiiieeeee*, 30–52.

mere factual accuracy but in terms of adequate contextualization. Implicit in Chin's critique of Kingston is an argument that, even as Asian American writers insist justly on the distinctions between Asia and Asian America and reject the demand for "authentic" representations of Asia, they need to avoid mystifying Asia in a way that perpetuates existing stereotypes in American culture. In light of Chin's challenge, then, how does one rethink Kingston's novel? Does she take the stories of Mulan and Yue Fei out of context and blend them together irresponsibly? Or does she recontextualize their stories in "White Tigers" according to a certain narrative logic? Reading carefully, we can see that Kingston is not simply using the story of the warrior woman to make a point about the empowerment of Asian American women; she also places the story within the context of the historical relationship between the Han Chinese and the nomadic peoples on China's northern borders, some of whom were eventually incorporated into the administrative structures of China and identified as "minority nationalities" after the founding of the PRC. Existing criticisms of *The Woman Warrior* completely overlook Kingston's representations of ethnic dynamics that affected both feudal and modern China, which are in fact intertwined with the author's commentaries on race relations in Cold War America.

In the passage right before her army scores its final victory over the emperor, the warrior woman surveys the capital from the top of a hill: "Between roads the woods and plains move too; the land was peopled—the Han people, the People of One Hundred Surnames, marching with one heart, our tatters flying. The depth and width of Joy were exactly known to me: the Chinese population."[26] The warrior woman's adoration for the Han people here is certainly at odds with the historical circumstances surrounding the figure of Mulan in Chinese folklore. The Northern Wei Dynasty originated from the nomadic Xian Bei tribe. While it was subsequently influenced by Han culture and eventually subsumed under the Sui Dynasty, ruled by the Han, the Northern Wei Dynasty was certainly non-Han in its origin. The original "Ballad of Mulan," in fact, contains both Han and non-Han elements as a result of the mutual penetration of different cultures during the Northern Wei. The draft call answered by Mulan is issued by *"ke han"* (khan), the title for the leaders of a number of nomadic peoples that destabilized China's northern frontiers throughout history. One can certainly argue that, by combining the story of Mulan and that of Yue Fei, Kingston erases an important distinction between the two figures in terms of their ethnic affiliation, as well as their gender. To be fair, this distinction has been all but erased even

26. Kingston, *The Woman Warrior*, 42.

within China. The Northern Wei was eventually incorporated into China and the Chinese today hardly remember the non-Han identity of the "khan" that Mulan serves in the ballad. Nevertheless, one may find Mulan's emphatic love for and identification with the "Chinese population" in "White Tigers" out of place.

One way of explaining this passage is that it fits well into a pattern of romanticization that runs through the entire fantasy section in "White Tigers." Kingston not only transforms Mulan from a loyal soldier of the khan in the original ballad into a leader of a peasant rebellion, a warrior against feudalism and patriarchy. She also diffuses the ethnic elements of the original story, suppressing not only the differences between Mulan and the Han and but also the war in which Mulan enlists to fight in the original ballad, a war that has been identified as a successful campaign against a neighboring confederation of nomadic tribes, the Rouran.[27] Kingston's Mulan, therefore, is cleansed of any involvement in violent encounters among the various peoples inhabiting China's northern borderlands. By extension, Kingston also alters the Han-centric tone of Yue Fei's story, distancing the general from the war against the Jurchens that makes him a celebrated hero in the Chinese national imaginary. We can argue that Kingston consciously merges Mulan into the "Chinese population" as a gesture toward rejecting rigid ethno-racial or cultural divisions. She recontextualizes Chinese folklore to stage a kind of romanticization, or critical romanticization, that challenges ethnicity-based, as well as gender- and class-based, hierarchies in Chinese history.

Kingston's critique of Chinese history, moreover, is also an implied critique of Cold War America. The narrator's fantasy in "White Tigers" contains an intriguing dream scene, where the Chinese girl, at the end of a survival test (part of her training under the old couple) that exhausts her, sees a vision of "two people made of gold dancing the earth's dances."[28] The dancers appear to be "Chinese lion dancers," but then morph into "African lion dancers in midstep," and their dance is accompanied by "Javanese bells," which deepen "in midring to Indian bells, Hindu Indians, American Indian."[29] At this point in the fantasy section, the Chinese girl becomes a conduit for an ideal form of cultural pluralism that the novel's Chinese American narrator derives from and wishes for Cold War America. This illogical detail can be read as an instance of deliberate conflation that punctures the fantastical nature of the entire middle section of "White Tigers" and the author's conscious disavowal

27. Zhong Jialian and Ye Xinyuan, "'Yanshan huji' dang zhishui?" [What does the "Yan Mountain Barbarian Calvary" refer to?], 147. Also see Feng Lan, 231.
28. Kingston, 27.
29. Ibid.

of factual accuracy. In light of the overall structure of *The Woman Warrior*—the girl narrator's memories of her and her family's experience of settling in America interwoven with redacted folktales from China—the easily missed detail hints at an emerging Chinese American consciousness that simultaneously rebukes the racial injustice that silences the narrator's "'chink' words" in the Cold War U.S. and the Han-centrism that motivates the lionization of Yue Fei at various points in Chinese history.[30] It suggests that both American and Chinese cultures are burdened with a history of racism or ethnocentrism that might be counterbalanced by imaginings of a fluid kind of pluralism, which allows all cultures to converge with and infiltrate each other.

Kingston amplifies this point at the end of the novel's last chapter, "A Song for a Barbarian Reed Pipe," projecting a full-blown vision of how the racial and ethnic boundaries might be made porous in both Chinese and American contexts. She presents an imaginary moment of ethnic amalgamation during imperial China as a comment on the possibility of racial reconciliation in Cold War America. Kingston ends the last chapter, and the entire text of *The Woman Warrior*, with the story of Ts'ai Yen (Cai Yan), a Han noblewoman who was captured by the Hsiung-nu (Xiongnu) in her twenties. Ts'ai Yen is a real historical figure, documented to have been born circa 177 A.D. She was eventually ransomed by the Han people, though forced to leave her two young sons behind. Upon return, she composed long poems based on the rhythm of the Hsiung-nu music with which she became familiar, expressing the sorrow of having had to choose between homeland and motherhood. As with all the other folk material she invokes, Kingston takes liberties with this story, rendering the encounter between Ts'ai Yen and the Hsiung-nu into a process of mutual understanding. Though Kingston refers to the Hsiung-nu as "barbarians," invoking the common English translation of *hu* (the epithet that the Han people used historically to refer to the Xiongnu), she works to deconstruct the self–other split entailed in both the Chinese term and its English translation. When Ts'ai stays with the "barbarians," she listens to the sound of their flute, eventually learning to imitate this sound in her own songs about her life back home. Although the "barbarians" cannot follow her words entirely, they catch a few "barbarian phrases about forever wandering" and become mesmerized by her voice.[31] Before too long, the "barbarians" join Ts'ai in an invented ritual of mourning, sitting in a ring around her as she sings to their music in a hybridized language. When Ts'ai returns to the Han people, she brings them an appreciation of a different culture by

30. Ibid., 53.
31. Ibid., 209.

composing songs in the "barbarian" style, the most famous of which is titled "Eighteen Stanzas for a Barbarian Reed Pipe" (a literal translation of "*Huqia shiba pai*," reputed to have been authored by Ts'ai). The song "translate[s] well," the narrator points out in the very last sentence of the novel, suggesting that Ts'ai had turned her experience of captivity into a condition for cultural mediation.[32] Kingston's reappropriation of Ts'ai Yen's story can certainly be read as a continuation of her romanticization of historical Han–"barbarian" relations in "White Tigers," but it also comments on contemporary American culture. The chapter concluded by the Ts'ai Yen story contains the oft-discussed passage where the girl narrator tortures another Chinese American girl at school and then falls mysteriously ill. If that passage emblematizes the psychic and physical symptoms of the racial trauma sustained and transmitted by Asian Americans, then the Han–"barbarian" reconciliation that Ts'ai Yen helps broker models an idealized solution to it.

We can argue at this point that, although Kingston does not address the political conditions in the PRC or its nationalities policy in significant ways in *The Woman Warrior,* she does present a few moments from an imaginary historical China, inherited by the PRC in 1949, that was shaped in the midst of continuous contact and conflicts between the Han and other peoples around them. Weaving together the ethno-cultural dynamics in imperial China and the experiences of racial minorities in the contemporary U.S. in her narrative, Kingston stages a critique of both histories while mining them for imperfect but valuable models of ethno-racial reconciliation. With *The Woman Warrior,* therefore, Kingston offers a uniquely Chinese American perspective on U.S.–China relations, a perspective that was unusual during the Cold War and remains so today. Although the novel has been canonized as *the* classic of Asian American literature, almost no attention has been paid to its impulse toward thinking about the issues of race and ethnicity in U.S. and Chinese contexts comparatively.

The comparative impulse in *The Woman Warrior* is continued in Chinese American writings that emerged in the 1980s, especially writings by Chinese students and intellectuals who came to the U.S. for study during the decade. Many of them articulate a kind of skepticism toward national identifications that results from their exposure to racial discrimination in the U.S. and disillusionment with official nationalism in China. They frequently invoke the sociological concept of the "marginal man" in explaining the social condition and literary sensibilities of new Chinese immigrants in the U.S.[33] Oftentimes,

32. Ibid.
33. In 1987, a number of PRC intellectuals and students based mainly at Columbia University formed a literary group, called the Morningside Society. Some of its members held a

their renunciation of the idea of a cohesive Chinese nation to which they owe their primary allegiance is accompanied by an understanding of the nation's internal ethnic and regional divisions. Zha Jianying's novella, *Congling xia de binghe* [The ice river in the jungle] (1988), for example, tells the story of a female Chinese student in the U.S. who slowly realizes the irreversible dissolution of her comforting, if blinkered, attachment to the idea of the Chinese nation, even as she navigates the well-concealed racial code in American social life. In a key part of the novella, the female protagonist returns to China for a vacation and goes on a trip to the northwest region to trace the footsteps of her former lover, who had chosen to work in the underdeveloped area upon graduation and died in an accident while there. The small northwestern cities that she visits have an ethnic and cultural mix that she finds alienating, forcing her toward a mental and literal diarrhea. Unable to fit in there, the protagonist feels as if she is stuck in a "neither–nor state," neither dead like D nor alive like the others around her.[34] This feeling of alienation replicates the tone of her experiences in the U.S., where she looks in vain for friendships and relationships that transcend racial and class barriers. The state of double marginality explored in writings like *Congling xia de binghe* can be seen as the affective corollary of the practice of double critique.

Asian American and East Asian Studies

To tease out the comparative insights in Asian American literature, one needs, as Kingston does in the structure of her narrative, to transgress a few borders and build a few bridges. The comparative approach that my book studies and employs is not simply an antidote to political and popular discourses that polarize the two countries; it is also a challenge to the traditional disciplinary divides that separate Asian American studies, and American studies in general, from East Asian studies. To fully understand the complex models of double critique that authors like Kingston, Zha, Kuo, and Yan engage in, it is imperative that Asian American critics reconstruct, and bring

---

roundtable discussion on the development of "overseas student literature" in New York City in 1987, and the transcript of the discussion was published in a 1988 issue *of Xiaoshuo jie* [Fiction world], a prestigious literary journal based in Shanghai. Yu Renqiu, a central member of the literary society, started the discussion by examining the historical positions of Chinese students in the West. The concept was also brought up in a parallel discussion held in Shanghai. See "Ninyue chenbianshe 'liuxuesheng wenxue' zuotan jiyao" [Minutes from New York Morningside Society's roundtable on "Overseas Student Literature"] and "'Liuxuesheng wenxue' zuotan jiyao" [Minutes from the Shanghai roundtable on "Overseas Student Literature"].

34. Zha Jianying, *Congling xia de binghe* [The ice river in the jungle], 68.

into dialogue, the various histories and literary and political discourses they address through robust collaborations with both American studies and East Asian studies. My study shows the critical possibilities that can be generated through such interdisciplinary work, mimicking the mediating role that many Asian American authors assume through their writings. In so doing, it argues that Asian American studies should be conceived, on an intellectual level, as a multiply located field, or a set of provocations in nation-based fields that have long been kept apart.

Asian American studies and U.S. ethnic studies in general have taken the critical examination of race and ethnicity into a comparative direction. It is important to note here that, as an invented category that did not exist prior to the 1960s, "Asian American" entails a comparative orientation inherently. By virtue of its inception, Asian American studies contributed significantly to a heterogeneous conception of race in the U.S. by disrupting the familiar black–white binary. The recent comparative turn extends the founding logic of the field, with a focus on the interconnected patterns of racialization in the U.S. and the resonance, as well as dissonance, among the oppositional political and cultural tactics that different minority groups employ to negotiate the "institution of citizenship" or "racial power."[35] Asian Americanists' venture into comparative racialization and comparative ethnic studies has borne much fruit.[36] My study, however, involves a type of comparison that is equally important but rarely attempted, namely, a binational comparison that places U.S. ethno-racial dynamics in the unfamiliar context of their counterpart in an Asian nation.

Although there has not been much critical attention to what might be called U.S.–Asian comparative ethnic studies, Asian American literature, as

35. Helen Jun, "Black Orientalism"; Claire Jean Kim, *Bitter Roots.* Jun argues that nineteenth-century black discourses on the "institution of citizenship" employed orientalism to ground black opposition to segregation (1049), and Kim argues that black–Korean conflicts in contemporary America is a symptom of and response to "racial power" (9).

36. Such comparative projects fall within a range of disciplines. In history, see Mae Ngai's *Impossible Subjects.* In literary and cultural studies, see James Kyung-Jin Lee's *Urban Triage,* Crystal Parikh's *An Ethics of Betrayal,* and Allan Punzalan Issac's *American Tropics.* Lee brings together Asian American, Latino, and white American novels in his discussion of the failure of multiculturalism's fantasy of a "parallel movement of more equitable representation and resources" during the Reagan era (xiv). Parikh juxtaposes Asian American and Latino narratives in her exploration of the ethics of betrayal in "emergent U.S. literatures and culture." Isaac sets out to "[supplement] the project of comparative ethnic studies" with a postcolonial perspective, by demonstrating the linkages between the various U.S. territorial acquisitions outside of the North American continent. The book brings together Filipino American, Puerto Rican, and Hawaiian writers who articulate a "postcolonial" consciousness, while comparing them with mainstream U.S. representations of the American empire in the first part of the twentieth century (19).

we have seen in the example of *The Woman Warrior,* has long been invested in bringing into dialogue the different ethno-racial politics of the U.S. and Asian countries. Chang-rae Lee's *A Gesture Life* juxtaposes the veneer of racial harmony in suburban America during the 1990s with the racial hierarchy constructed under the Japanese empire in East and Southeast Asia during WWII. Wendy Law-Yone's *Irawaddy Tango* opens and closes in a fictitious dictatorship (based on Burma) embroiled in ethno-religious conflicts (based on the Karen-led insurgency against the military dictatorship in Rangoon), with a middle section that lampoons American culture's obsession with capitalizing on the gruesome experience of Third World refugees and exiles. Meena Alexander's *Manhattan Music,* yet another example, interlaces the experience of Indian immigrants in the culturally volatile Manhattan of the 1990s with the history of East Indians in the West Indies and Muslim insurrections in contemporary India. These writings, like the work of Kingston, Zha, Kuo, and Yan, can be described as diasporic. Discussions about the meaning of "diaspora" in Asian American literary and cultural critique flourished throughout the 1990s and early 2000s.[37] I invoke this term here to describe a type of narrative text, as well as interpretative approach, that pays particular attention to the ways in which Asians in America, due to a history of exclusion from U.S. legal and cultural citizenship, occupy what

37. The cultural nationalist politics that locates Asian Americans fully within the domestic sphere of the U.S. started to share its stage with the critical framework of diaspora in the early 1990s. See Sau-ling Wong's "Denationalization Reconsidered." There, Wong analyzes a set of related frameworks that emerged in Asian American studies in the early 1990s, defining cultural nationalism and diaspora as two distinct discursive and political positions. Diasporic subjectivity is characterized by "a perpetual turning of one's gaze toward the lost homeland" while cultural nationalism focuses on the conditions of living in the place of residence (10). But her argument contains its own antithesis. She notably acknowledges that the longing for the "lost homeland" might be read as a correlative of the racialized exclusion of Asians from the U.S. mainstream, thus linking diasporic impulses to U.S. domestic issues. In the context of Asian American cultural politics, in other words, the diasporic approach should not be equated with being oriented toward Asia or defined as the binary opposite of the U.S.-centered cultural nationalism. It provides a set of conceptual tools with which to examine the formation of racial, ethnic communities within specific locales in relation to *both* national and transnational processes, including state racism, postcolonial migration, and global capital. See Oscar V. Compamanes's "Filipinos in the United States and Their Literature of Exiles" and David Palumbo-Liu's *Asian/American.* Campomanes's idea of "a literature of exile and emergence," which he uses to describe literature about Filipino nation-building by Filipinos in America, best captures the ironic doubleness (the displacement from and imaginary return to nation-states) characteristic of the concept of diaspora (Campomanes, 51). Palumbo-Liu uses the term "Asian/American" to suggest that the teleological narrative of Asian immigrants settling in the United States, symbolized by the U.S.-centered term "Asian American," is "yet incomplete and unsettled" (227). The hyphen and the slash symbolically disrupt the nationalist approach to Asian Americans and gesture toward an indeterminate map of diaspora.

David Eng refers to as a state of "suspension" between competing structures of citizenship, modes of belonging, and patterns of cultural experience.[38] The emphasis on diaspora in Asian American studies, however, has not translated into systematic reflections upon how Asians in America, in their cultural expressions or embodied experience, straddle and mediate between different conceptions of race and ethnicity in the U.S. and Asia. Critical interpretations of Chinese American diasporic writings, for example, have so far largely focused on how these writings present the condition of diaspora and complicate nation-based literary categories.[39]

To pave the way for projects in transnational ethnic studies, then, Asian American studies needs to further its collaborations with not only other fields in American studies but also Asian studies (or, more specific to this study, East Asian studies), where much of the knowledge of ethnic and race relations in Asian countries is produced. These collaborations do not simply involve gathering exotic knowledge. Their more profound implication lies in enabling and emphasizing a broad conceptualization of the intellectual location of Asian American studies.[40] Since its beginning at the end of the 1960s as a revolt against Cold War, exceptionalist conceptions of American history and culture, Asian American studies, along with other components of U.S. ethnic studies, has effected important paradigm changes within American studies.[41] While Asian American studies has played a subversively constructive role within American studies, standing apart while taking an active part in the transformation of the latter, the field's relationship with East Asian studies is much more tenuous and tense. Asian American scholars who began their careers in East Asian studies often tell stories of how their interest in Asians outside of Asia or Asian migration to the West was not

---

38. David Eng, *Racial Castration*, 211.

39. Sau-ling Wong, "The Stakes of Textual Border-Crossing"; Xiao-huang Yin, *Chinese American Literature since the 1850s*. Wong offers an important discussion of the position Chinese-language writings in the U.S. in relation to exiting literary taxonomies (modern Chinese literature, Taiwan literature, immigrant literature, world literature, etc.).

40. One should certainly add "institutional" here, but it exceeds the scope of the present book.

41. For a memorable discussion of how minority insurgence has unsettled American studies as an institutionalized discipline since its Cold War origin, see Donald Pease and Robyn Wiegman, eds., *Futures of American Studies*, 1–42. Their argument is that the various social movements in the 1960s played a crucial role in restructuring academic politics, including the politics of American studies, opening it to an uncertain, unbounded futurity. Ethnic Studies has also been instrumental in fostering the transnational turn in American Studies, which has recently been theorized. See the presidential addresses for the American Studies Association in 2007 and 2005, respectively, namely, Emory Elliott's "Diversity in the United States and Abroad" and Shelley Fisher Fishkin's "Crossroads of Cultures.

sufficiently supported. Asian American studies, therefore, has become the main intellectual home for an impressive array of studies, in the humanities as well as social sciences, that focus on Asian migration as a site for inquiries into processes of globalization and transnational patterns of power that link America to Asia.[42] More recently, however, East Asian studies has become more receptive to projects focusing on Asian subjects and Asian-language writings in the U.S., giving an impetus to research that speaks to Asian Americanists' concerns.[43] These developments make the current moment an auspicious one for more exchanges between Asian American studies and East Asian studies aimed at synthesizing, while transforming, the knowledge produced in both fields. Comparative Literature scholar Eric Hayot argues in his recent essay "The Asian Turns" that "the encounter between Asian American studies and East Asian Studies" through a mutual focus on "sub-national locations" and "ethnic matrices" can set in motion the "becoming that reconstitutes the fields," neither of which will return from this encounter unchanged.[44] Similarly, I propose that an active engagement with East Asian studies will allow Asian American studies, comparative and transnational all along, to broaden itself further into a field with multiple intellectual locations, consisting of not a bounded body of knowledge, but a series of provocations in the more established, nation-based fields.

Pursuing the kind of interdisciplinary encounter that I promote, my study draws extensively on the histories of China's minority nationalities constructed by scholars in Chinese studies. Chapter 1 provides a detailed account of the development of both U.S. and Chinese multiculturalisms

42. Eiichiro Azuma, *Between Two Empires;* Yong Chen, *Chinese San Francisco, 1850–1943;* Catherine Ceniza Choy, *Empire of Care;* Gayatri Gopinath, *Impossible Desires;* Madeline Hsu, *Dreaming of Gold, Dreaming of Home.*

43. See Shu-mei Shih, *Visuality and Identity;* Eric Hayot, Haun Saussy, and Steven G. Yao, *Sinographies: Writing China.* Shih theorizes the "Sinophone Pacific" in her study of the circulation of visual images between Chinese America and other sites of the Chinese diaspora. In 2007, this project gave rise to a three-day conference at Harvard, "Globalizing Modern Chinese Literature," where international scholars from both China and Chinese American Studies gave papers on Chinese-language writings across the Pacific. *Sinographies* brings together essays that deal with the perceptions of Chineseness in American culture and Chinese-language writings in the U.S.; both of these topics broaden the traditional concerns of the scholars of Chinese literature. One can perhaps go back a bit further. Also, in 2005, a two-day conference at Wesleyan University, "Traffic and Diaspora: Political, Economic, and Cultural Exchanges between Japan and Asian America," occasioned a dialogue between scholars in Japanese studies and Japanese/Asian American studies. Though not an entirely fruitful dialogue, it did signal that studies of Asian cultures and literatures were beginning to show interest in the extension of Asia in America.

44. Eric Hayot, "The Asian Turns," 910.

since the mid-twentieth century, but it is useful to offer a brief account of existing studies of the latter here. The ethnic policy in the PRC was fashioned after the Soviet model of a multinational federation, though it resisted explicit invocations of the term "federation".[45] During Republican China (1911–49), both the ruling GMD (Chinese Nationalist Party) and the CCP (Chinese Communist Party) ascribed paramount importance to the unity of the nation-state in formulating and implementing their respective policy toward minorities. While the GMD exercised only weak control over minority regions, many of which were ruled by semi-independent warlords, the CCP eventually seized and held on to these regions with a combination of military force and an appealing policy of minority autonomy. In the early 1950s, upon the founding of the PRC, a system of regional autonomy for ethnic minorities was established, consisting of autonomous areas at provincial, prefectural, and county levels. The 1952 *General Program for the Implementation of Nationality Regional Autonomy of the Chinese People's Republic* stipulated that these areas were "inalienable parts of the motherland."[46] Under the overriding principle of state sovereignty, the central government was to recruit cadres from minorities so as to increase their political representation in autonomous areas and on the state level, as well as encourage minorities to develop their own language scripts and cultural traditions. The 1954 Constitution reiterated that the state would "pay full attention to the full features" of minority groups in implementing its economic policies.[47] The ethnic policy has since then fluctuated in the degree to which it accommodates minority rights, in ways particular to the specific areas involved.

The 1990s and the first decade of the twenty-first century have seen a slew of anthropological and historical studies of one or more of the fifty-five officially recognized minority nationalities.[48] The past two decades has also witnessed important efforts to link China's minorities to Western conceptions of race and ethnicity. Pamela Crossley's important essays at the turn of the 1990s trace the meaning of *minzu* ("nationality" or "nation" in English)

---

45. Terry Martin, *Affirmative Action Empire*. Martin argues that the Soviet nationalities policy did not involve federation in a rigorous sense. Although the term "federation" was used in the 1922–23 constitution settlement, it "concentrated all decision power in the center" (13). Lenin's rehabilitation of this word in 1917, according to Martin, to "describe what amounted to a much more ambitious version of" ethno-territorial autonomy (14).

46. June T. Dreyer, *China's Forty Millions,* 105.

47. Ibid., 126.

48. Gru Gladney, *Muslim Chinese;* Stevan Harrell, *Way of Being Ethnic in Southwest China;* Louisa Schein, *Minority Rules;* Ralph Litzinger, *Other Chinas;* Katherine Kaup, *Creating the Zhuang;* Tsering Shakya, *The Dragon in the Land of Snows;* Uradyn Erden Bulag, *The Mongols at China's Edge;* Colin Mackerras and Michael Clarke, *China, Xinjiang and Central Asia.*

in contemporary China to multiple intellectual traditions, including the discourse on lineage that emerged during the Qing Dynasty (1644–1912), and notions of race and ethnicity developed in Western history.[49] Some of the more recent studies of minority nationalities in contemporary China have sought to borrow useful critical tools from critical race studies and postcolonialism. One approach is to rework the idea of orientalism, turning it into an analytical framework for understanding the power dynamics between the Han Chinese and non-Han minorities. Louisa Schein, for example, argues that the early 1990s saw a proliferation of "otherness" in China, with the feminization and fetishization of cultures in rural, ethnicized areas mimicking the structure of orientalism.[50] Schein's argument about what she calls "internal Orientalism" casts the PRC's incorporation of ethnic others, not implausibly, as a form of colonialism and racialization.[51] Another approach that has emerged is comparing the oppositional cultures of minority nationalities in China with those of racial minorities in the West. Steven Venturino explores this approach in a recent essay, which takes the initiative of linking the subversive tactics in Tibetan literature, produced both inside and outside China, with those found in African American literature.[52] The comparative approaches employed in studies of China's ethnic minorities have produced critical visions similar to those embodied in Chinese American diasporic narratives. They challenge, rightly, the fiction of a pluralist Chinese nationalism by implicating it in the enterprises of colonialism and institutional racism, suggesting that, while we must acknowledge the West's preponderance in constructing the social categories, including race, ethnicity, and nation, central to global modernity, it is also necessary to consider regional or local patterns of power that complicate Western-centric narratives of modern his-

49. Pamela Kyle Crossley, "Thinking about Ethnicity in Early Modern China," "The Qianlong Retrospect on the Chinese-Martial (*hanjun*) Banners." Crossley's early projects were extended later in a collected edition, which traces the vicissitudes of ethnic identities during the Ming Dynasty and Qing Dynasty through dynamic interactions between the imperial state and the human subjects of the state. See Pamela Kyle Crossley, Helen F. Siu, and Donald S. Sutton, *Empire at the Margins*. Studying the earlier meanings of ethnicity in China, the authors argue, is indispensable to integrating the investigations of "various frontiers" and minority nationalities in contemporary China (17).

50. Louisa Schein, "The Consumption of Color and the Politics of White Skin in Post-Mao China." Also see Schein's *Minority Rules;* Chih-yu Shih, *Negotiating Ethnicity in China.* Shih argues that some minority groups in China, such as the Miao, actively cash in on the Orientalized images created by "the dominant state and market forces," in a move that Shih calls "reflective Orientalism" (66–67).

51. Schein, "Consumption of Color," 478.

52. Steven J. Venturino, "Signifying on China."

tory.[53] To claim that we can find racial and ethnic politics outside of the West that do not result completely from Western colonialism and imperialism is not to espouse a reductive form of universalism that implicitly naturalizes race and ethnicity as inevitable givens, just as proposing a global perspective on multiculturalism does not indicate that there is anything natural to it. Rather, it is to promote a strategic, antihegemonic universalism that rebels against the safety of the conventional ideological and political mappings of the world as well as the traditional division of labor among different academic fields.

Multiculturalism and Comparative Multiculturalisms

Based on interdisciplinary work, my book provides a comparison of U.S. liberal multiculturalism and China's nationalities policy as interconnected, competing means of nation formation, both seeking to forge a coherent national identity by containing minority dissent from or revolts against structural inequalities. By organizing these two different systems into one conceptual framework, my argument both resonates with and departs from the emerging discourse of comparative multiculturalisms, founded by Will Kymlicka and his collaborators, among others. Having occupied a prominent position in the study of multiculturalism since *Liberalism, Community, and Culture* (1989), Kymlicka's work not only has played a frame-setting role for other scholars but also has displayed the eclectic character of the field as a whole. It registers a mixed theoretical impulse, wavering between a normative approach to multiculturalism and a contextualist one. He is clearly invested, as he puts it in *Multicultural Odysseys,* in examining and helping advance the efforts, on the part of international organizations, to promote "a distinct liberal form of multiculturalism and minority rights" on a global scale through the codification of international legal norms and the diffusion of best practices of liberal multiculturalism.[54] This normative commitment, however, is implicitly undercut by his acknowledgment of the

53. One can argue that this dual perspective arose from an encounter between Area studies and postcolonialism. Discussions of Chinese nationalism have been an especially fertile site for the development of such a dual logic. For a concise summary of these discussions and an argument for this dual perspective, see Timothy Brook and Andre Schmid, *Nation/Work.* The authors simultaneously recognize that the history of modern nations in Asia is "inseparable from the history of imperialism" and calls attention to "sets of fissures internal to Asian nations" (2–3).

54. Kymlicka, *Multicultural Odysseys,* 18.

historical circumstances and "larger field of power relations" in which liberal multiculturalism developed in the West and the implausibility of duplicating these conditions in other parts of the world.[55] The contextualist side of Kymlicka's thought is what my book emphasizes and amplifies. Multiculturalism assumes a different shape in each given context and should not be limited to its liberal manifestations. To be sure, non-Western nation-states, including China, have often borrowed consciously from Western liberalism, its concepts if not institutional apparatus, in articulating their official policies toward ethnic and racial minorities.[56] However, these articulations also hark back to theoretical traditions outside of liberalism, including, in the case of China, the Lenin–Stalinist conception of nationalities and Confucian ethics. The Chinese government's goal to build *"hexie shehui"* ("a harmonious society"), announced at the Sixth Plenum of the Sixteenth CCP Congress in 2006, borrows selectively from the Confucian attitudes toward cultural difference, especially the idea of *"he er butong"* [harmony without sameness], as well as the rhetoric of liberal multiculturalism from the West.[57] We see in chapter 2 the ways in which the notion of national harmony, and by extension that of world harmony, are echoed and promoted in a 2004 popular novel, Jiang Rong's *Lang Tuteng*.

Official or dominant formulations of ethno-racial policies, it must be noted, are not the only component of any particular multiculturalism. A case in point is minority challenges to the Confucian approach to cultural difference. Although the Chinese government's interpretation of Confucian ethics emphasizes its toleration of other cultures, Zhang Chengzhi's 1991 work *Xinling Shi* [A history of the soul] implicitly rebukes this view by offering a reconstructed history of Hui Muslim rebellions in eighteenth- and

55. Ibid., 109. Kymlicka clearly voices his opposition to imposing liberal multiculturalism on non-Western parts of the world, because, for one thing, theories of ethnic relations are under debate in the West and, for another, geopolitical and historical factors in other parts of the world (including paramount security concerns and the absence of a liberal tradition) also make applying Western principles inviable. See in particular chapters 6 and 7 of *Multicultural Odysseys*.

56. India is probably the most notable example. See Selma Sonntag, "Self-Government in the Darjeeling Hills of India." Sonntag offers a history of what she calls "linguistic federalism" in India upon its independence, as encoded in the Indian Constitution drafted by the Nehruvian liberals, and its contemporary manifestation in the 1988 establishment of self-government in the Nepali-speaking area in northern Bengal (181).

57. Some scholars in China have teased out the liberal echoes in the CCP's articulation of its vision of a "harmonious society." See Yin Wenjia and Yu Li, "Xifang duoyuan zhuyi ji dui zhongguo de jiejian yiyi—zai hexie wenhuaguan de shiyu zhong," 165–67. The authors offer an introduction to the history of multiculturalism as public policy in the West, especially white-settled countries, including the U.S., Canada, and Australia, since the mid-twentieth century, and argue that this liberal tenet of equality between different cultures is manifest in the Chinese government's plan for building a "harmonious culture" in a multiethnic context (166).

nineteenth-century China. Zhang's history critiques the ways in which the Confucian conception of social and cultural hierarchies failed historically to accommodate the resistance to secular political power among the Hui Muslims, an ethno-religious group, and continues to limit their spiritual expressions in the contemporary era. If, as I have argued, multiculturalism should be understood as a global movement with a fragmented basis and a shifting contour, each particular component of this movement is also a dynamic process, through which the power relations among, as well as within, different ethnic and racial groups in a particular nation-state are continuously reconstituted.

The complex dynamics of multiculturalism are articulated in the distinctions often drawn between its "official" and "critical" versions. Legislation and government policies providing for group-specific rights and compensatory, or preferential, treatment toward minorities are often referred to as official multiculturalism (as in Canada and Australia, and one might add China) or managed multiculturalism (as in the U.S.), which David Theo Goldberg critiques as a "centrist" strategy that the state employs to project an image of national solidarity without working concretely toward this goal by tackling the political, cultural, and psychic causes for the inequalities among different ethno-racial groups.[58] A competing version of multiculturalism, often prefixed with "critical," advocates for broad social recognition of the distinct histories and identities of minority groups as a means of advancing the larger struggle for an equitable distribution of economic, political, and cultural opportunities.[59] Critical multiculturalism assumes the form of an insurrection, diffused among the political initiatives of minority organizations, academic research, and cultural articulations, against the domination of majority cultures and interests. The official and insurgent versions of multiculturalism, always intertwined in any given context, encompass a range of competing perspectives on how national identity should be conceived so as to accommodate minority demands and how minority groups can enhance their social positions through what Goldberg calls a "transformative incorporation" into the "mainstream" of a national culture.[60] In each particular national context, therefore, multiculturalism should be seen as a series of political contestations that are manifest in and mediated by law, social policy, as well as cultural practices and production.

In his essay "Culture/Wars: Recoding Empire in an Age of Democracy,"

---

58. David Theo Goldberg, ed., *Multiculturalism*, 7.
59. Ibid., 19.
60. Ibid., 9.

Nikhil Pal Singh argues that it is unproductive to discuss "American plural-ism" as a "singular, embattled term," or a static set of values and public poli-cies that can be hijacked by various political forces.[61] For Singh, the history of U.S. liberal multiculturalism is the history of the various battles between dif-ferent conceptions of equality and justice in the U.S. since at least the 1940s, an era marked by the simultaneous "emergence of state-driven efforts to engineer a 'Second Reconstruction' within the United States" and "the mas-sive mobilization of anti-racist initiatives."[62] To paraphrase Singh, while this multiculturalism undeniably exhibits the tendency of "aestheticizing" power differentials, its more radical incarnations focus on structural inequalities and become a credible form of progressive politics that combats racism, colonial-ism, and capitalism as interlinked and mutually constitutive processes.[63] The understanding of multiculturalism as a process of change and an unceasing series of political battles pertains to the Chinese context as well. The official policy toward minority nationalities in China is profoundly state-centric, seeking to uphold the legitimacy and unity of the party-state through the rhetoric of ethnic amalgamation. The minority nationalities have responded to the official policy in different ways, ranging from active endorsement to violent resistance. The government has often changed its conception of amalgamation since the founding of the PRC, partly in response to minority reaction, oscillating between a hard-line position favoring a forced integra-tion, on both economic and cultural levels, of the various nationalities and a more liberal one allowing minority groups to preserve distinct economic, social, and cultural institutions.

Fiction of (Comparative) Multiculturalism(s)

Taken together, the fictional texts I study here capture the dialogic, constantly changing nature of particular varieties of multiculturalism, suggesting that the encounters and contestations between different conceptions of national identity and social equality unfold like an extended narrative consisting of competing impulses and patterns of meaning. They do not just allude the-matically to particular issues shaping or confronting the ethno-racial politics in contemporary China and America, but also illustrate, or propose concep-

---

61. Nikhil Pal Singh, "Culture/Wars," 471–72.

62. Ibid., 474.

63. Lisa Lowe argues, for example, that muliticulturalism, in its official or managed version, operates to "aestheticize ethnic differences as if they could be separated from history." See Lisa Lowe, "Immigration, Citizenship, and Racialization," 9.

tual alternatives to, the underlying logic of official or managed multiculturalism, which seeks to contain ethno-racial tensions without addressing the structural causes of these tensions. As a group, they encapsulate the instability of U.S. and Chinese multiculturalisms and are crucial to understanding their internal dynamics and interconnections in the contemporary era. They can therefore be loosely grouped together under the term "fiction of multiculturalism." I use this term to mean two things at once: what is normally thought of as "multicultural fiction"—fiction written by minority writers and/or focused on minority perspectives—and fiction that provides extensive reflections on multiculturalism as a political project.

Among the authors I study, Clive Cussler and Jiang Rong are aligned most closely with the logic of official or managed multiculturalism. Formally, they hew close to the conventions of certain genres of popular fiction in the contemporary U.S. and China. Cussler's *Treasure of Khan* continues his Dirk Pitt series, a typical product of the Cold War, that revolves around an antitotalitarian American superhero who spreads liberal-democratic and multicultural values around the globe. Jiang's *Lang Tuteng* builds on the familiar plot of the immersion of Han Chinese intellectuals in minority cultures in remote areas, which signals a form of ethnic amalgamation. Both authors modify the generic conventions that they appropriate, but their modifications, for the most part, function to salvage, rather than transform, these conventions and the particular variety of multiculturalism that they support. Their works are discussed first, therefore, setting a context against which the other authors studied here, Kuo, Yan, Zhang, and Alameddine, can be read as a revision or rejoinder.

All of these four authors draw our attention to the continuation of ethno-racial conflicts in the two countries, thus undercutting the logic of official or managed multiculturalism. Their narratives are invariably nonlinear, moving between the current post–Cold War moment and various points in the past, as a way of placing these conflicts in a deep historical context and suggesting that this history continues to bear on the present. In addition to invoking and reconstructing the past as a rebuttal to the rhetoric of national progress and harmony that official or managed multiculturalism generates, these authors also set out to locate in the past a few tactics for survival and subversion that can be reappropriated as tools of renewing the multicultural nation in the contemporary era. Based on these tactics, including "dissenting nationalism" (Kuo), oppositional faith (Zhang and Alameddine), and "impersonal intimacy" (Yan), they actively propose ways of mediating between national identity and minority demands for autonomy and equality without sacrificing the latter to the shibboleth of unity.

Taken together, then, these narratives are in conversation not only with Mignolo's concept of double critique but also with Homi Bhabha's theorization of the multicultural nation as a "double narrative movement," where the "people" are both the "historical 'objects' of a nationalist pedagogy" and the "'subjects' of a process of signification that must erase any prior or originary presence of the nation-people."[64] For both Bhabha and the authors I study, the multicultural nation moves in time like an internally fractured narrative in which the "signs of a coherent national culture" are continuously recreated by various elements of the "people," especially those inhabiting the margins of a projected national space, including ethno-racial and other minorities.[65] The process of narration that constitutes the modern nation can be captured metonymically in individual fictional narratives and in their mutual interactions. Bhabha's theorization of the nation as narration has long been criticized, rightly so, for eliding the material constraints upon and conditions for the formation of national identity.[66] One can argue, however, that the pervasive concept of doubleness in Bhabha can be read as a metaphor for the multiplicity of forces, material as well as symbolic, that intervene in the meaning and structure of a particular national identity at a given time–space conjunction. Bhabha's ideas remain useful for understanding the ways in which contemporary fictional narratives, including those studied here, both encapsulate and propel the process of becoming and transformation that is the multicultural nation.

Indeed, the conception of modern nationalism as a "double narrative movement" has had a strong impact on American studies. Amritjit Singh and Peter Schmidt describe the U.S. as the world's first "postcolonial and neocolonial" country.[67] This defining doubleness plays out in the inseparable intertwining of a nationalist pedagogy—the myth of a perennially inclusive national identity—and minority critiques of this pluralist myth. The two authors construct a long genealogy of cultural wars from the progressivists of the 1890s–1920s through the development of various minority social movements, along with their cultural articulations, since the 1960s, which have been fully invested *simultaneously* in struggles over civil rights in the U.S.

64. Homi Bhabha, *Location of Culture,* 145.
65. Ibid.
66. Pheng Cheah, "Given Culture." Cheah criticizes Bhabha's theory of historical agency as narrative energy (as well as Marxist theories of material dialectics) for projecting a notion of human freedom that can overcome the limits of material history. Instead he calls on us to assume our "responsibility to given culture" (321), arguing that the postcolonial national body is a "nontranscendable moving ground extending across the globe in which political, cultural, and economic forces are brought into relation" (324).
67. Amritjit Singh and Peter Schmidt, eds., *Postcolonial Theory and the United States,* 5.

and in antiracist and anti-imperialist struggles on the global scale.[68] These movements rarely aim to redraw the administrative structure of the U.S. state, and yet they offer a series of representational and political tactics for mobilizing minority communities around multiple political allegiances, over and beyond the nation, while advocating for their fuller integration into the institution of U.S. legal and cultural citizenship.

In China, in comparison, challenges to the official rhetoric of pluralism are more circumscribed and muted, as a result of the government's control over the nation's political and cultural life and the popular notion that China remains a developing, postcolonial country in need of uniting and strengthening itself against foreign sabotage and intervention. Nevertheless, minority writings and representations of minority cultures have often rebelled quietly against state power. Liu Daxian, a scholar of ethnic literature in China, points out that, since the end of the Cultural Revolution, minority writers have increasingly turned away from celebrating the unification of the Chinese nation under state socialism and toward constructing ethnic consciousness and identification. Liu describes their works as part of the many "little traditions" that have taken shape alongside of and under the shadows of "mainstream" contemporary Chinese literature.[69] Eminent critic Chen Sihe raises the same argument from a slightly different angle, theorizing that much of the Chinese literature since the 1980s has consciously accentuated the idea of *minjian*, which translates literally as "the sphere of the people." Part of this body of work excavates cultural forms and practices in ethnic areas that are submerged or marginalized under the official ethnic policy.[70] The Chinese writers included in my study, especially Zhang Chengzhi, engage in this work of excavation, and so does Chinese American author Yan Geling, from a different angle. U.S.-based Comparative Literature scholar Lydia Liu points out rightly that *minjian* was partially manufactured by the state—in fact, the Chinese government supported and sponsored the collection of ethnic and folk art during the 1950s and 1960s, in keeping with its liberal policy toward ethnic minorities during that period. The more recent upsurge of *minjian*, in light of this history, can be seen as a "sentimental turn" to state-sponsored

---

68. For an account of the internationalist commitment constitutive of the beginning of the Asian American Movement, see Sucheta Mazumdar, "Asian American Studies and Asian Studies"; David Eng, *Racial Castration*, 211–15.

69. Liu, Daxian, "Zhongguo shaoshu zuyi de rentong yu zhuti wenti," [Identification and subjectivity among China's minorities], 7.

70. See Chen Sihe, *Zhongguo dangdai wenxueshi jiaocheng* [A history of contemporary Chinese literature], 12–14. For a more detailed explanation of the notion of *minjian*, see chapter 5.

folk culture.[71] Nevertheless, the literary homage to *minjian* over the past three decades puts pressure on official conceptions of the folk, suggesting an eagerness on the part of Chinese cultural workers to reimagine the Chinese nation on eclectic, unstable grounds, as a "double narrative movement."

Organization of the Book

Before delving into the literary texts, I offer in chapter 1 a history of U.S. liberal multiculturalism and the policies and discourses around China's minority nationalities since the mid-twentieth century. The chapter first clarifies the meanings of *"minzu"* (the Chinese term for "nationality") and establishes a basic continuity between the concept and notions of race and ethnicity in Western traditions. It then argues that the two multicultural projects are integral to the construction of dominant forms of nationalism in the two countries—civic nationalism in the U.S. and official nationalism in China—while being constrained by the imperative of national identity. Both are contingent upon assigning contrasting meanings to the ideas of race and ethnicity (and their Chinese counterparts *zhongzu* and *minzu*). The mobilization of the notion of ethnicity, or *minzu,* as a repudiation of the politicization of genealogical and cultural differences (for either oppressive or subversive purposes), has facilitated, in both the U.S. and China, the project of casting what Goldberg terms a "racial state" into a multicultural nation.[72] The chapter then highlights a few specific ways in which the two multiculturalisms have intersected over the past two decades. The parallels and intersections between American and Chinese multiculturalisms reviewed in this chapter forecast the themes of the literary texts that the following chapters study.

The four chapters that follow analyze specific fictional texts with a focus on how they help bridge U.S. and Chinese multiculturalisms. Each places its central text(s) against a backdrop of popular, political, and critical discourses on the subject of ethnic and race relations in the two countries. These chapters show that, compared with the other discourses, the fictional narratives that they study encompass a much broader range of political perspectives and impulses, thus implying, collectively, an exceptionally sinuous argument about what limits the official or dominant modes of multiculturalisms in the two countries and what may enable them to change. They offer an indispensable supplement to the other discourses by mimicking, on a formal level, the process in which ethnic and racial issues are negotiated in the multicultural

71. Lydia Liu, "A Folk Song Immortal," 571.
72. David Theo Goldberg, *The Racial State.*

nation. More important, they offer a valuable alternative to the negative mode of comparison customarily employed between these two multiculturalisms, whereby one is invoked only to bolster or justify the other.

Chapter 2, "How Not to Be an Empire," juxtaposes two popular novels, one American and one Chinese, with converging themes and imagery. Clive Cussler's *Treasure of Khan* (2006) and Jiang Rong's *Lang Tuteng* (2004), translated into English in 2008 as *The Wolf Totem,* were bestsellers in their respective country when first published. They project an imaginary reconciliation between the two countries' pursuit of natural resources and political influence around the world and their commitment to protecting the weaker peoples both within and outside state borders. In so doing, the novels illustrate and reinforce the logic of official or managed multiculturalism, or what I term "conciliatory multiculturalism," as it manifests itself in the contemporary U.S. and China. They thus help deflect international criticisms over the imperialist excess of the two countries' domestic and foreign policies in the post–Cold War era. Cussler imagines a culturally diverse, energy-independent, nonexpansive America to re-elevate the country's moral standing in the world in the wake of its open embrace of expansionism after 9/11, solidifying it further by juxtaposing the fantasized America against an illiberal China where minority nationalities are exploited and deprived of their natural environments. Jiang Rong's call for the Han Chinese and the Chinese government to embrace a toned-down version of the military tradition of the historical Mongols, ancestors of the ethnic Mongols in contemporary China, projects a past and future of ethnic amalgamation that, for the author, distinguishes Chinese nationalism from Western, and in particular, U.S., imperialism. The popularity of the two novels is an indication of their rhetorical proximity to conciliatory multiculturalism in the two countries.

Chapters 3, 4, and 5 study authors who stage a conscious critique of conciliatory multiculturalism. All these authors rewrite particular histories of ethno-racial conflicts to recuperate from these histories the political, cultural, and psychic resources for building forms of nationalism that are more inclusive. They do not treat ethnic and racial conflicts arising from the historical workings of power and social formation as what needs to be contained, privatized, or placated but as an impetus for new ways of imagining national unity. They propose their own models of "pluralist universalism," to borrow from Bhikhu Parekh's term for multiculturalism again, by allowing the ideas of unity and difference to challenge and transform each other, rather than project a false reconciliation of the two.

Chapter 3, "Toward a Comparative Critique," offers a discussion of Alex Kuo's prose and poetic writings, especially the generically ambiguous *Panda*

Diaries (2006). *Panda Diaries* draws an analogy between the history of Native Americans and that of the Oroqens (a small minority nationality) in China. This analogy echoes the parallel that a number of Chinese intellectuals have recently drawn between China's campaign to develop its western regions in the new millennium and the U.S. westward expansion in the nineteenth century. While the Chinese intellectuals use the history of U.S. expansion as a rationale and a model for China's own modernization, Kuo launches a double critique through his analogy. He shows that both the U.S. and China have engaged in the construction of a modernized, integrated national space through the colonization of minority and indigenous space, a process with human as well as environmental implications. In conjunction with this double critique, Kuo also offers important reflections on the political implications of metaphor as a conceptual and rhetorical tool. While it comments explicitly on the conceptual violence entailed in metaphor, the novel proceeds metaphorically, yoking together disparate histories as inexact replicas of one other. In so doing, Kuo suggests that drawing comparisons between asymmetrical patterns of power is a productive hazard that must be embraced. The logic of metaphor also allows Kuo to serialize, in his various works, minority struggles to promote "dissenting nationalism" in different parts of the world, thus proposing an antidote to the impulse toward homogenizing national space that lingers in both contemporary America and China, despite the rhetoric of ethno-racial harmony that they espouse.

Chapter 4, "A New Politics of Faith," turns to one of the most glaring failings of the two multiculturalisms, namely, the racialization and suppression of Muslim communities in both the U.S. and China before and after 9/11. It juxtaposes Hui Muslim author Zhang Chengzhi's *Xinling Shi* [A history of the soul] (1991) and Arab American author Rabih Alameddine's *Koolaids: The Art of War* (1998). These works show the imbrication of religious and ethno-racial differences and the severe limits of conciliatory multiculturalisms by reconstructing little-known histories of Muslim and Arab communities in the two countries from the perspective of these communities. At the same time, Zhang and Alameddine set out to imagine, by reworking religious concepts, forms of pluralism that can accommodate radical ethno-religious differences. While Zhang recasts the Jahriya teaching of the autonomy of the soul as an ethical condition for fostering competing collectivisms in China, Alameddine points toward the potential of reworking the idea of universal love (as opposed to that of moral law) embodied in Christ as grounds for a kind of oppositional politics that mends, rather than exploits, ethno-religious divisions. Both authors, then, simultaneously puncture the myth of ethno-racial harmony or unity constructed in the popular novels discussed in chapter 2 and recuperate the idea of multiculturalism on renewed grounds. In dialogue with contemporary intellectual discussions in the two countries on religious activism and political religiosity, Zhang and Alameddine demonstrate that religion is not a divisive force that forecloses genuinely expansive multiculturalism, but a shifting constellation of values that should be allowed to participate fully in the discursive negotiation that constitutes the project of multiculturalism.

Finally, chapter 5, "Impersonal Intimacy," discusses a literary critique of the patronizing nature of conciliatory multiculturalism, which groups minorities under a number of somewhat arbitrary labels and turns them into beneficiaries of the majority state or culture. It offers a reading of Yan Geling's novel *Fusang* (1996), which depicts a Chinese prostitute in the nineteenth-century U.S., and its English translation in 2001, titled the *Lost Daughter of Happiness*. It argues that the novel resists symptomatic readings, often seen in existing criticisms of both versions of the novel, that identify its main character, Fusang, as a victim of the gendered workings of racialization. The English translation, through a form of bowdlerization (removing and shortening certain passages in the original), preinterprets the novel for the Western audience, anticipating and reinforcing the Anglo-American criticisms of the novel. *Pace* existing criticisms, I argue that the novel's depiction of Fusang's all-accepting resilience under sexual servitude constitutes a utopian statement of the possibility of a borderless and yet sustainable subjectivity that actively embraces the experience of being penetrated by difference. This conception of subjectivity provides a basis, as well as a model, for group identities (ethno-racial as well as national) that maintain a level of coherence without striving for uniformity. The novel, in other words, explores the psychic conditions for an ideal form of pluralist universalism. In defiance of the expectations of most segments of her audience, Yan reconstructs the experience of nineteenth-century Chinese American prostitutes not simply to reveal historical forms of racial injustice but also to picture a possible future for both U.S. and Chinese multiculturalisms. In so doing, she speaks to some of the most exciting psychoanalytical and cultural theories from both the U.S. and China, including Leo Bersani's theory of "impersonal intimacy" and Chen Sihe's conception of *minjian* as a quotidian web of relations that resists the disciplinary power of the collective identities constructed by the state.

This book does not attempt to provide an exhaustive study of U.S. and Chinese fiction of multiculturalism from the post–Cold War era. It selects a few absorbing moments from two deep repertories that illuminate their overlaps and interconnections. In Alex Kuo's short story "10,000 Dildoes," a Chinese American physicist navigates his transnational experiences as if he were "dancing in a tangled story."[73] And that may just be a fitting metaphor for the ways in which this study and the authors that it includes mediate between the two multiculturalisms.

73. Alex Kuo, "10,000 Dildoes," 263.

CHAPTER 1

Bridging the Chasm

A Survey of U.S. and Chinese Multiculturalisms

[The] major variants of pluralism are fundamentally assimilationist.

—Christopher Newfield and Avery F. Gordon,
Mapping Multiculturalism

Although the origins and histories of ethnic groups in China are different, the overall trend of their development was to form a unified, stable country with multiple ethnic groups.

—White Paper on China's Ethnic Policy (2009), Section I

THE FIRST PART of this chapter offers a survey of the histories of U.S. liberal multiculturalism and China's official ethnic policy. The survey extends back to the rise of racial minority movements in the U.S. in the 1960s and the institutionalization of the CCP's ethnic policy in the early 1950s, though it also touches on some of the relevant history prior to these two moments. Like all historical surveys, this one is not simply descriptive. It contains the argument that these projects can be seen as two interconnected, competing forms of conciliatory multiculturalism, which generate and contend with alternative visions of the relationship between national identity and ethno-racial differences in their respective context. The term "conciliatory" signals the myth of easy reconciliation that both projects promote and depend on, the idea that the conflict between the drive toward national unity and persistent racial and ethnic inequalities can be reconciled without radical interventions in the economic, political, and psychic conditions of these inequalities. The defining formal characteristic of conciliatory multiculturalism, therefore, is its simultaneous recognition and disavowal of ethno-racial tensions. Chapter 2 elaborates on this conciliatory logic as it is illustrated in popular fiction from both countries. The present chapter underscores a central component of this logic, namely, the ways in which race and ethnicity are assigned contrasting meanings. In the U.S. context, it is no news to point out that race and ethnicity are socially constructed categories, but it is important to remember that, in the mainstream and everyday political imagination, they signify two different modes of construction. While race is tied to a form of essentialization, the attribution of group differences to factors that are considered to lie beyond the realm of history, ethnicity has largely come to signal the construction of group identity on the basis of historical patterns of interaction and conflict, a mode of construction that entails an understanding of difference as situated, mutable, and adaptable to circumstance. The Chinese concepts of *zhongzu* and *minzu*, both with a particular, complex history, can be loosely mapped onto the notions of race and ethnicity in the contemporary United States. The construction of conciliatory multiculturalism in the two countries, a process integral to their nation-building practices, depends on collapsing race into ethnicity and confining racism—discrimination based on the essentialized category of race—to the past or other nations. This parallel, to be sure, should not obscure important differences between the two contexts, which I explain in detail in my survey. Nevertheless, without recognizing this loose continuity, we have no grounds for meaningful conversations about racial and ethnic politics across the pre-existing ideological and political lines that divide the two countries. These conversations, I believe, will ultimately make productive transformation more likely on both sides. The second part of this chapter discusses the ways in which U.S. and Chinese multiculturalisms have come into contact over the past two decades through translation and other forms of mediation.

The story of China's official multiculturalism begins, in part, in the nationalities policy of the Soviet Union. A metaphor that the Soviet state used to describe the result of this policy is a large communal apartment with separate rooms.[1] The various ethnic minorities under the former Russian empire were organized by the new state into culturally homogenous republics with "characteristic institutional forms of the nation-state."[2] When the

1. Yuri Slezkine, "The USSR as a Communal Apartment, or How a Socialist State Promoted Ethnic Particularism." She takes the phrase "communal apartment" from a Soviet publication from 1924 (415).
2. Terry Martin, *The Affirmative Action Empire*, 1.

Soviet Union dissolved in 1991, the republics' demands for independence were seen as the last straw on the unwieldy state teetering on the brink of collapse due to the simultaneous processes of marketization, democratization, and decolonization that occurred under Gorbachev.[3] The "earnestness of bolshevik efforts on behalf of ethnic particularism" and its delayed, alarming percussions triggered much heated discussion around Soviet ethno-politics in Slavic studies in the 1990s and early 2000s.[4] One might see the Soviet nationalities policy as the earliest and the most important form of nonliberal multiculturalism. With the passing of the Soviet Union, the PRC's ethnic policy has come to embody a major example of socialist multiculturalism.[5] Partially modeled on the example of the Soviet federation, the Chinese policy provides ethnic minorities—known until fairly recently as minority nationalities—with the right to regional autonomy. As many have pointed out, the definition of autonomy under the Chinese system differs significantly from standard liberal understandings of minority rights even as it overlaps with the latter.[6] As it was instituted upon the founding of the PRC, the policy of ethnic regional autonomy aimed to integrate minority groups into the administrative structures of the party-state without foisting upon them Han culture or the socialist ideology, but the idea of integration came quite close to assimilation during the period between the late 1950s and late 1970s, when the socialist state launched a series of radical leftist movements, including the Cultural Revolution, under which class took precedence over nationality

3. Ronald Grigor Suny, *The Revenge of the Past*. It is one of the earliest post–Cold War surveys of the history of the "nationality problems" in the USSR.

4. Slezkine, 415. For two diverging perspectives on this issue, see Francine Hirsch and Terry Martin. Hirsch describes the Soviet approach to nationalities as "state-sponsored evolutionism," which believes that the state should take the lead in amalgamating clans and tribes into nationalities so as to, ultimately, "usher the entire population through the Marxist timeline of historical development" (7–8). Martin makes the similar argument that the Soviets considered national identity an unavoidable stage to "be passed through before a mature international socialist world can come into being," although he also emphasizes the belief that the nationalism of the non-Soviet people are "legitimate grievances against the oppressive great-power chauvinism of the dominant Russian nationality" (8). However, while Martin applies the concept of affirmative action to the Soviet nationality policy, Hirsch disagrees, arguing that affirmative action implies the promotion of national minorities "at the expense of 'national majorities'" (8). This is not a good place to adjudicate between these two arguments, but I do believe that it is impossible to draw an absolute line between the illiberal ethnic policy of the Soviet Union and the idea of affirmative action in Western liberal multiculturalisms. This position is consistent with my argument U.S. and Chinese multiculturalism should be studied comparatively, not as two unrelated species but as paralleled, interconnected, though quite distinct, processes.

5. For an introduction to the minority policy in the communist Laos, see Vatthana Pholsena, "A Liberal Model of Minority Rights for an Illiberal Multiethnic State?" 80–109.

6. See Baogang He's explanation of both sides of the issue later in this chapter.

and ethnicity. Since the beginning of the 1980s, the ethnic policy has largely swung back to a more liberal mode, although it has moved in the opposite direction in Tibet and Xinjiang in response to waves of pro-independence demonstrations and riots in these provinces.[7] The contradictions and limits of this policy, of course, do not deter the government from asserting that ethnic minorities are the "masters of their own house," evoking the communal apartment metaphor that has been used in describing the Soviet policy.[8] It is not yet clear whether the government's emphasis on central control in political and cultural matters and its circumscription of ethnic autonomy will effectively ensure stability in the long run. But even if stability is more or less maintained, we still need to consider the cost that the official ethnic policy exacts from the country's 100 million members of minorities.

Mainstream U.S. multiculturalism can be construed as a highly circumscribed version of liberal multiculturalism, which, in its normative formulation, supplements classical liberalism with the tenet of ethno-cultural justice.[9] Having originated in the racial reforms and popular mobilizations of the 1960s, U.S. multiculturalism is often associated with polychromatic metaphors—for example, the "mosaic" and "salad bowl"—that symbolize its conscious opposition to racial segregation and coercive assimilation. Unlike Canada's official multiculturalism, U.S. multiculturalism was from its very beginning motivated by an awareness of racially based political and economic inequalities.[10] Since the Reagan era, however, conservative reactions against government policies and programs assisting racial minorities and the rollback of the welfare state in general have imposed important limits on U.S. multiculturalism.[11] Meanwhile, U.S. multiculturalism departs sharply from

7. Colin Mackerras, *China's Minorities*, 145–66; June T. Dreyer, *China's Forty Millions*, 63–276.

8. Gardner Bovingdon, *Autonomy in Xinjiang*, 14.

9. Will Kymlicka, *Politics in the Vernacular*, 42; *Can Liberal Pluralism Be Exported?* 21.

10. The Canadian federal government announced its policy of multiculturalism in 1971, reversing the earlier emphasis on assimilation. The Canadian Multicultural Act was passed in 1988, providing financial and institutional support for racial and ethnic minorities and French-speaking Canadians. It is beyond the scope of this book to discuss the debates around Canadian multiculturalism, but, as Irene Bloemraad recently shows, Canadian multiculturalism has laid much emphasis on immigrant political incorporation through an active promotion of citizenship and has therefore consisted of more public policies and programs toward helping immigrants to overcome linguistic and cultural barriers. See Irene Bloemraad, *Becoming a Citizen*, 1–16, 102–37. This emphasis on culture, as Bloemraad points out, was initially adopted to counter Quebec nationalism as well as to fulfill the country's economic needs (in a way parallel with the economically driven encouragement of immigration in the nineteenth-century U.S.) (136).

11. For an account of the contradictions between "the dream of multiculturalism" incubated in the racial reforms of the 1960s and its deterioration during the Reagan era, see James

the model of the multination federation practiced in parts of Europe (Spain, Belgium, Switzerland, etc.) and Canada. Apart from a few exceptions (Native Americans, Puerto Ricans, and Native Hawaiians, etc.) ethno-racial minorities in the U.S. are immigrant groups that do not espouse aspirations toward state-building and thus do not fall under the category of "national minorities" established in standard liberal theories of multiculturalism.[12] The absence of a tradition in minority state-building has been noted by Kymlicka as a key feature of U.S. multiculturalism, which carries the potential consequence of being exploited by majority nationalists in other parts of the world to "justify suppressing minority nationalisms."[13] The term "nationalism" has been used in reference to the political militancy and cultural radicalism among African Americans, Chicanos, and Asian Americans during the 1960s and 1970s, though none of these groups has been given legally recognized rights for political autonomy.

Before launching into a detailed historical account, we can attempt a few preliminary remarks about the ways in which the two multiculturalisms are central to the project of nation-building in their respective context. Nationalism, of course, has very different meanings in the two countries. In the U.S. context, I am using the term to refer to what is often perceived as a kind of civic nationalism, the drive toward national identity and unity based on a set of commonly embraced, albeit frequently conflicting, political values, including democratic universalism and liberal individualism, that are incarnated in the nation's legal and political institutions. This civic ideology of nationalism can be seen as a nonaggressive version of American exceptionalism, the belief that the American nation embodies a unique array of principles, the American creed, that enables it to play the indispensable role of a "civilizational empire" in the world.[14] This dominant civic nationalism,

---

Kyung-Jin Lee, *Urban Triage,* xv, xvi. Also see Howard Winant, *Racial Conditions.* Howard Winant criticizes the Clinton administration for "borrow[ing] extensively from the right" in race-specific initiatives (35).

12. Will Kymlicka, *Politics in the Vernacular.* He defines national minorities as ethno-cultural groups that challenge majority nation-building by "fighting to maintain their own societal culture" or "engaging in their own nation-building" (28). One may add that Puerto Ricans can be seen as a national minority, but they largely count as part of the pan-ethnic group of Latinos in the U.S. context.

13. Will Kymlicka, *Politics in the Vernacular,* 273; *Multicultural Citizenship,* 58–69.

14. See Anatol Lieven, *America Right or Wrong,* 41, 49. Lieven defines American nationalism in relation to exceptionalism, offering a sophisticated view of the different moral and political implications of this exceptional nationalism. He argues that the popular version of U.S. exceptional nationalism, the belief that American culture is unique and worthy of pride, is in fact comparable in its intensity to the nationalism one finds in the "contemporary developing world," including India, Mexico, and the Philippines, reminiscent of "Europe before 1914" (20).

as many have noted, is continuous with the more overtly imperialist aspects of exceptionalism, consistently undermined by ethno-religious articulations of American identity that engender or exacerbate economic, political, and cultural inequalities within and outside the nation.[15] Liberal multiculturalism provides a crucial means through which the civic nationalist ideology is renewed and sustained, as it mediates between the promise of liberal democracy and historical injustices experienced by racial and ethnic minorities. It enables a vision of the U.S., to borrow from David Hollinger, as "a democratic nation-state that is commodious enough to sustain diversity yet cohesive enough to guarantee rights and provide for welfare."[16] Although Hollinger is known for rejecting multiculturalism in favor of cosmopolitanism, this understanding is rather misleading. Hollinger is critical of multiculturalism's tendency to fix racial and ethnic identities, but he is certainly not questioning the project's centrality to upholding the "civic character" of American national identity or, in other words, the civic nationalist ideology.[17] Hollinger's cosmopolitanism, which champions the "principle of affiliation by revocable consent," is in fact a continuation of an important strain in traditional American pluralism, one that counters the presumably divisive effects of particularized identities with an emphasis on the "dynamic mixing" of cultures and demographics and the primacy of national loyalty.[18] This form of pluralism, as we will see, can very well be seen as the foundation of U.S. liberal multiculturalism, rather than a critical alternative.

In comparison, Chinese national identity has been defined as "a relationship of 'identification' between nation and state."[19] The authority and interests of the party-state, rather than a set of abstract political values, are at its core. Suisheng Zhao, in particular, argues that a kind of state-centered "pragmatist nationalism"—the understanding of the party-state as the embodiment of the nation's will and fundamental interests and the sovereign center of the collective loyalty of its citizens—has remained the most potent form of Chinese nationalism since 1949.[20] However, just as American civic national-

15. Anatol Lieven discusses a host of imperialist symptoms of American exceptionalism, including white nativism, Jacksonian nationalism, and evangelical fundamentalism. For a discussion of the more pernicious aspects of American exceptionalism, also see Donald Pease, "Exceptionalism."

16. David Hollinger, *Postethnic America,* 143.

17. Ibid., 14.

18. Ibid., 13, 94.

19. Lowell Dittmer and Samuel S. Kim, "In Search of a Theory of National Identity," 30.

20. See Suisheng Zhao, *A Nation-State by Construction;* James Townsend, "Chinese Nationalism." Zhao argues that the CCP united various social classes and "claimed a mandate to rule China" by assuming leadership in the industrialization of the country (210). While this nation-

ism has long been undercut by the darker strains of exceptionalism, China's state nationalism is inseparable from ethnocentric or racialist conceptions of the nation, which first emerged at the turn of the twentieth century, when the notion of a unitary Han race was invented and mobilized as a rallying point for struggles against the invading European powers and the decaying Manchus (rulers of the Qing Dynasty).[21] This Han-centered conception of Chinese identity, however, threatened to alienate the non-Han peoples formerly under Manchu control and fuel separatist movements. Both the GMD and the CCP, then, were compelled to espouse a conception of national unity predicated upon a strong, centralized state rather than identifying the Chinese with the Han, though Han-centrism by no means disappeared. The ethnic policy established at the beginning of the PRC sought to rein in Han Chinese ethnic nationalism and integrate ethnic minority communities into the administrative structures of the communist state, thus securing the state's territorial integrity and legitimizing the CCP's leadership. This policy has undergone several different phases since then. As Zhao points out, to contain minority dissent from the assimilationist phase of the policy during the 1960s and 1970s, the government introduced in the 1980s "a dizzying array of preferential treatment in political representation, economic development, and social benefits" for ethnic minorities.[22]

In juxtaposing U.S. and Chinese multiculturalisms, I do not intend to offer a systematic comparison of the two countries' political systems or traditions. My aim, instead, is to tease out formal parallels between the two projects and, subsequently, the ways in which they are entangled in narrative texts from both countries. Literary studies can engage and supplement comparative politics by shedding light on the underlying continuity and connections between two disparate sets of ethno-racial policies. Both contemporary America and China practice a conciliatory form of multiculturalism that is simultaneously necessitated and delimited by the imperative of national unity. Conciliatory multiculturalism wields tremendous power

---

alism was initially "shrouded" by Mao's "utopian communism" (210), it became a pragmatic tool after the Cultural Revolution consciously employed by the government to fill the ideological void resultant from its shift toward market economy. Townsend argues that "[s]tate nationalism portrays the state as the embodiment of the nation's will, seeking for its goals the kind of loyalty and support granted the nation itself and trying to create a sense of nationhood among all its citizens" (18).

21. Suisheng Zhao, 21–22. Other forms of Chinese nationalism have been identified, especially popular nationalism, and cultural nationalism. State nationalism often coopts or competes with these other forms.

22. Ibid., 31.

in both contexts, even as it is challenged by competing proposals for ethno-racial relations. If each room in the cozy Chinese communal apartment is subjected to close supervision by a controlling central power, the dazzling America "mosaic" often obscures the distinct patterns of dissent emerging from within it.

Consent, Descent (Dissent)

In the U.S. context, the concept, if not the very term, of multiculturalism took shape in the racial reforms of the mid-1960s, which worked to "gradually and partially [transform] the [civil rights] movement into a constituency for the new program its efforts had won."[23] While racial desegregation and civil rights legislation (the Civil Rights Act of 1964 and the Voting Rights Acts of 1965) extended formal equality to all citizens, other policies and programs were explicitly intended to reverse the material effects of racism, even as they were couched in the language of universal rights and equal opportunity. In addition to a greatly expanded social welfare system, the affirmative action policy was implemented through a series of executive orders and government plans under the Kennedy, Johnson, and Nixon administrations.[24] The passage of the Bilingual Education Act in 1968 (terminated in 2001 upon the passage of the No Child Left Behind Act), as another example, made federal funds available to school districts for the establishment of educational programs for students with limited English. Although the racial minority movements had become fragmented by the late 1960s, they generated a veritable cultural revolution on college campuses, in public schools, and in the cultural mainstream. Curriculum changes at various levels of the educational system increased the representation of non-European cultures within and outside the U.S., in a way that addressed the needs of evolving student bodies and furthered their diversification. The federal government also institutionalized and expanded a few initiatives to recognize ethnic histories and cultures, which then trickled down to the level of public schools, colleges, and workplaces.[25]

23. Michael Omi and Howard Winant, *Racial Formation in the United States*, 99.

24. Since the 1970s, it has been subjected to constant scrutiny due to the conservative perception that some affirmative action policies contradict the equal protection clause of the Fourteenth Amendment. *Regents of the University of California v. Bakke*, 438 U.S. 265 (1978), a landmark decision of the Supreme Court of the United States on affirmative action, for example, bars quota systems in college admissions but affirms the constitutionality of affirmative action programs giving equal access to minorities.

25. For example, the Asian American Week was instituted in 1978 and later expanded into

These policies and changes became a flash point of the cultural wars of the 1970s and 1980s.[26] They were criticized by both sides, for either "disuniting" America, permanently dividing it on the basis of group membership and identification or for projecting false hope for racial reconciliation.[27] In his 1975 book *Affirmative Discrimination,* Nathan Glazer insisted that the U.S. was the "first great nation" to combine the principles of Republican citizenship with "a considerable concern for whatever is necessary to maintain group identity and loyalty."[28] While ethnicity in American held "great meaning" for individuals' lives, it had traditionally been given "no formal recognition."[29] A new "American ethnic paradigm," however, emerged in the mid-1960s as the nation entered into an "unexampled recording of the color, race, and national origin of every individual in every significant sphere of his life."[30] This new paradigm, for Glazer, overturned the valuable consensus that was reached over race and ethnicity through the Civil Rights Act of 1964, which wrote into law the principle that the Constitution is "color blind."[31] This argument followed logically from Glazer's ambivalence, since the 1960s, about the state's responsiveness to racially based rights, which, as Richard H. Thompson has pointed out, misread the function of the modern state as that of a "neutral referee" in social, economic, and cultural matters.[32] Glazer's neoconservative view of American history and society was openly challenged in the very beginning of the 1980s, when ethnic studies came of age as an intellectual enterprise dedicated to the study of racial and structural inequalities in the United States. In his 1982 essay "Reflections on Racial Patterns in America," Ronald Takaki argued against the premise that America had had a long history of racial inclusion, pointing out in particular that the democratic tolerance experienced by white "ethnic" groups had not been extended to "racial groups."[33] Michael Omi and Howard Winant's now-classic *Racial Formation in the U.S.* raises a similar argument that race should be studied as "an autonomous field of social conflict, political organization, and cultural/ideological meaning" without being conflated with

---

the Asian Pacific American Heritage Month, and Hispanic Heritage Month was instituted in 1968 and expanded in 1988.

26. Resistance to civil rights for blacks, in fact, developed alongside the Civil Rights Movement. See Omi and Winant's discussion of the "backlash" politics in the middle-1960s (96).

27. Arthur Schlesinger, *The Disuniting of America.*

28. Nathan Glazer, "The Emergence of an American Ethnic Pattern," 9.

29. Ibid., 19.

30. Ibid., 21.

31. Ibid.

32. Richard H. Thompson, *Theories of Ethnicity,* 97.

33. Ronald Takaki, "Reflections on Racial Patterns in America," 27.

ethnicity, class, or nation.[34] They offer a critique, in particular, of the old ethnicity paradigm that emerged in the 1930s, with the advent of the New Deal and antifascism and became coopted post 1965 by neoconservatives and the emerging Republican majority to reverse the civil rights gains made by racial minorities. This debate over the racial reforms of the 1960s, what Glazer called the "new American paradigm," represents the beginning of a long-lasting war between two visions of American pluralism. On one side is constitutional color blindness, the credo that no individual can be excluded from basic civil rights on the basis of their "race, color, religion, or national origin," which, for Glazer and many others to follow, provides a recipe for a genuine "national consensus" that an emphasis on racial difference threatens to undermine.[35] The principle of color blindness, furthermore, is temporally stretched back to the beginning of American history, such that it figures as a fait accompli, albeit tainted by a history of racial exclusion and segregation, rather than an uncertain ideal. In opposition to that is a growing critical race discourse contending that the ideal of color blindness, part and parcel of the civic nationalist ideology, works to perpetuate the existing racial order, under which people of color are expected to model their experiences on those of European immigrants while being confronted with structural inequalities precluding that possibility. These competing visions, both containing many variations within, underlie the two major forms of multiculturalism in the U.S., namely, liberal multiculturalism and critical multiculturalism.

While critical race scholars consider the premium placed on racial difference as a form of political dissent from civic nationalism, it is sometimes interpreted as a retrograde fixation on biological and cultural *descent.* The 1980s rearticulations of the old ethnicity paradigm, developed in the works of Gunner Myrdal, Milton Gordon, Glazer, and Patrick Daniel Moynihan, among others, insisted on using the rubric of ethnicity as a unifying category for both dominant and disadvantaged groups, with the rationale that it would facilitate the thriving of all different cultures in America without fracturing national consensus or identity. In his 1986 work *Beyond Ethnicity: Consent and Descent in American Culture,* Werner Sollors refines, and largely affirms, the traditional ethnicity paradigm, as opposed to the critical race paradigm that surfaced in the 1960s, reframing this tradition via Josiah Royce's idea of "wholesome provincialism," which projects an image of "diverse provincialities in harmonious cooperation."[36] Sollors makes a point

34. Omi and Winant, 52.

35. Glazer, 7.

36. Werner Sollors, *Beyond Ethnicity,* 179, 187. Sollors traces the lineaments of Joycean vision through Horace Kallen, Randolph Bourne, and W. E. B. Dubois, arguing that all three

of supplementing Royce's idea by acknowledging that large power structures, which he vaguely calls "cultural dominance," preclude some racialized groups from striving for their own political and cultural ideals in cooperation with others.[37] Ultimately, however, he proposes considering race as "one aspect of ethnicity," so as to reconcile the concept with the tradition of individualism, which emphasizes what can be achieved over what is ascribed through lineage.[38] Opposing "primordialist and even old biologist" conceptions of group formation, Sollors reappropriates the idea of ethnicity to signify presentist, constructionist approaches to localized identities, which allow these identities to enrich and enhance, rather than undermine, the "symbolic kinship" that unites all Americans.[39] While Sollors does not explicitly associate the primordialist notions of group identity with racial minority movements, his insistence on subsuming race under ethnicity implicitly rejects one of the founding rationales for these movements, the argument for a "profound distinction" between people of color and European ethnic immigrants in the "mode[s] and consequences" of their incorporation into the American body politic.[40] Sollors's argument for a consensus-based pluralism is echoed in a few other works in the 1980s and 1990s.[41] This trend reached a kind of apotheosis in Hollinger's *Postethnicity*, which takes Sollors's understanding of pluralism so far that it abandons the term "pluralism" altogether in favor of "cosmopolitanism," even though, as I pointed out earlier, "cosmopolitanism" connotes something strikingly familiar in this context—the rejection of any emphasis on identities considered to be based on descent (which include, for Hollinger, racial categories aside from African Americans) as a force that corrodes civic nationalism.[42]

Sollors's mediation between consent and descent does not touch on the question of whether the state has an active role to play in shaping and reshaping ethno-racial identities, a question that concerned Glazer and other critics of the new "American ethnic paradigm." Political theory started to engage this

---

share a set of ideas regarding ethnicity and race. All three, though with significant differences among them, embraced a form of pluralism that emphasizes the importance of preserving organically grown ethnic cultures while calling for the harmonizing of different cultures. See Sollors, 179–91.

37. Ibid., 191–95.

38. Ibid., 36.

39. Ibid., 21, 7.

40. Alan Wald, "Theorizing Cultural Difference," 23.

41. Mary V. Dearborn, *Pocahontas's Daughters;* William Q. Boelhowever, *Through a Glass Darkly: Ethnic Semiosis in American Literature;* Sacvan Bercovitch, *Rites of Assent.*

42. Hollinger explains his indebtedness to Sollors in the 2005 Postscript to *Postethnicity.* See 221.

question in the late 1980s and late 1990s, when scholars like Amy Gutman, Charles Taylor, and Jürgen Habermas formulated models of multiculturalism that do not give the state a powerful role in determining the boundaries of minority groups or the rights to which they are entitled. Their views largely constituted a political theory corollary of Sollors's argument for an updated version of "wholesome provincialism" as an individual and group attitude. They sought, in different ways, to extend traditional liberalism's focus on individual rights into respect for group rights without jettisoning the liberal tenet of the state's neutrality in cultural affairs. In his discussion of multicultural policies, what he refers to as the "politics of recognition," Charles Taylor questions both the practice of adhering strictly to the principle of formal equality, which would exclude the recognition of group-specific rights, and the top-down codification of these group rights.[43] Instead, he argues for a kind of "nonprocedural liberalism" that predicates itself upon an assumption of the equal value of different cultural traditions without proceeding to codify this assumption in a way that reifies ethnic and racial boundaries.[44] Habermas refutes Taylor's argument that there is a contradiction between procedural liberalism and the politics of recognition, arguing that a liberal state, in its normative configuration, is inherently multicultural, in the sense that civil rights are conceived and actualized on the basis of ethico-political discussions involving conflicting perspectives shaped within specific cultural horizons, discussions that oftentimes escalate into "cultural battles."[45] These battles do not have to render a nation fragmentary, however, if its citizens insist on the "inclusive character of their own political culture," thus expanding the parameters within which common constitutional principles can be interpreted.[46] For Habermas, then, the integration of a national community through a "consensus on the procedures for the legitimate enactment of law and the legitimate exercise of power" and the integration of subnational communities on an ethical-cultural level can and must be treated as two separate processes in liberal democracies.[47] This is probably the most refined and influential argument for a strictly liberal version of multiculturalism that does not disturb the principle of state neutrality vis-à-vis subnational communities, while seeking to alleviate social inequality.[48] The argument

43. Charles Taylor, "The Politics of Recognition."
44. Ibid., 63.
45. Jürgen Habermas, "Struggles for Recognition in the Democratic Constitutional State," 25.
46. Ibid., 139.
47. Ibid., 135.
48. Andrew Mason, "Political Community, Liberal-Nationalism, and the Ethics of Assimilation"; Anna Stilz, *Liberal Loyalty*. Like Habermas, Mason also advocates for a purely liberal

is certainly not without problems. It not only naturalizes and universalizes liberal values but also substitutes the construction of a normative model of liberal multiculturalism for a discussion of how multicultural policies should respond to actual configurations of power and hierarchy in a given society.

The consensus-based, liberal vision of multiculturalism in the U.S., to be sure, has a more centrist version, which supports a limited number of government or institutional policies and programs that promote the interests of racial minorities, but its main impulse remains clear.[49] It attributes to American history an *always and already* existing equilibrium between a unified national identity and a fluid pluralist tradition, neither of which needs to be drastically changed. For this impulse, it can be aptly described as conciliatory multiculturalism. Discontent with conciliatory multiculturalism prompted some quarters of the Left to raise the idea of "critical multiculturalism," which rebuffs, rather than answers, the call of nationalism. In an essay from the early 1990s, the Chicago Cultural Studies Group critiques the liberal underpinnings of U.S. multiculturalism, especially the ways in which it constructs ethno-racial cultures as merely particular to shore up the nation's claim to transcendence from local, culturally transmitted practices and values.[50] One way in which one can help counter this claim, for the Chicago Group, is to relativize the American nation through "international comparativism."[51] Doing that can transform liberal multiculturalism into "critical multiculturalism," namely, an expanded version of leftist cultural studies capable of crossing the "enormous gulf between different styles of identity politics" and generating a fully contextualized understanding of the figure of the "subaltern" in places like India and China.[52] The critical multiculturalism that the Chicago Group calls for, however, might have already been part of the American past. In *Black Is a Country*, Nikhil Pal Singh goes back to this past to offer an answer to the conservative backlash against multiculturalism that extended into the 1990s, which witnessed "a sweeping rollback of civil rights–era jurisprudence" under both Republican and

---

conception of national solidarity grounded in the distinction between a sense of "belonging to a polity" and a sense of "belonging together" (272). Stilz makes a similar argument based on Habermas's notion of "constitutional patriotism," which Stiltz interprets as collective democratic participation through "ethical-political reasoning," in adherence to the legal and political traditions of particular constitutional democracies (163).

49. For a theoretical expression of this centrist view, see Amy Gutman, ed., *Multiculturalism*, 3–24. As Gutman puts it, at its best, liberal democracy can be identified with "both the protection of universal rights and public recognition of particular cultures" (12).

50. Chicago Cultural Studies Group, "Critical Multiculturalism," 114–39.

51. Ibid., 135.

52. Ibid., 124.

Democratic administrations.[53] He attributes the frailty of mainstream liberal multiculturalism to a kind of historical amnesia, the forgetting of the most important lesson that can be drawn from black social movements throughout the long civil rights era, from the 1930s to the 1970s. Revisiting this era, Singh argues that the advancement of equality must "[pass] through the politics of race," defining political universalism broadly in both anticapitalist and anticolonial terms, which often entails "imagining coalitions and thinking and feeling beyond the nation-state."[54]

Singh's argument, like many others by those in U.S. ethnic studies and critical race studies, counters the widely propagated myth that multiculturalism erodes the politics of redistribution in the United States. It has long been argued that the struggles for civil and political rights on the part of racial minorities crowd out concerns for economic and social equality and distract from the development of class-based politics, and the racialization of welfare politics has limited the support among the larger population for TANF (Temporary Assistance for Needy Families) and AFDC (Aid to Families with Dependent Children) policies.[55] More recently, it has been suggested that multicultural policies and discourses have exacerbated the purportedly deleterious impact of race by further dividing "an already fractured polity" that would "otherwise support a strong welfare state."[56] Empirical analysis, however, has tended to find this claim about multiculturalism groundless.[57] More important than employing an empirical method is to point out that this criticism of multicultural policies is largely predetermined by the perception, expressed in the classic liberal critique of the "disuniting" function of multiculturalism during the cultural wars of the 1970s–90s, the belief that the pursuit of ethno-cultural justice can be reduced to narrow parochialism. The more recent critics of U.S. multiculturalism sow much confusion by blaming the neoliberal resistance to redistribution since the Reagan era on multicultural discourses that, in their most robust version, struggle against this very force. Multiculturalism's alleged role in eroding civil solidarity, as Singh suggests, is in fact an effort to combat the persistent expressions of exceptionalist, Jacksonian nationalism that are exploited, and at times fanned, by conservative movements in the era of neoliberalism.

53. Nikhil Pal Singh, *Black Is a Country*, 11.

54. Ibid., 218, 224.

55. For a summary of these arguments, see Rodney E. Hero and Robert R. Preuhs, "Multiculturalism and Welfare Policies in the USA," 122–29.

56. Ibid., 121. For sources often cited in this argument, see Todd Gitlin, *The Twilight of Common Dreams;* Brian Barry, *Culture and Equality;* Walter Benn Michaels, *Trouble with Diversity.*

57. See Hero and Preuhs, 129–51.

U.S. multiculturalism, as we have seen, is a dissonant chorus constituted by competing perspectives on how political, economic, and cultural equality can be best achieved for historically disadvantaged peoples, and how the ideal of national unity relates to that of political universalism. The liberal, conciliatory formulations of multiculturalism argue for allowing the state a limited activist role in overcoming past inequalities and broadening the definition of the American nation to accommodate different ethno-racial groups. The more critical formulations do not oppose the liberal position; they urge for its deepening, proposing alternative nation-formations that can more powerfully decenter, as well as reconfigure, the darker, imperialist dimensions of U.S. civic nationalism.

The Many Faces of *Minzu*

Chinese multiculturalism, as we will see, is also a complex, shifting process. The Chinese equivalent of ethnic or racial minorities in the American context is *shaoshu minzu,* commonly, and literally, translated into English as "minority nationalities." According to the fifth national census, conducted in 2000, the Chinese state recognizes 55 minority nationalities, their numbers accounting for less than 10 percent of the national population.[58] A majority of the minority population reside, often in close proximity with members of other minority nationalities, in autonomous areas (minority-governed administrative units), though a significant part of this demographic is spread out across the country.[59] The meaning of *minzu* in contemporary China largely derives from the Soviet definition of nationality, which descended in a large part from Western theories of ethnos, while drawing upon the notion of *zu* (denoting lineage, race, or ethnicity, depending on the context) developed during late imperial China. Over the past ten years or so, however, the Chinese government has abandoned the archaic-sounding "minority nationalities" and adopted "ethnic minorities" instead as an official translation of *shaoshu minzu,* in an apparent effort to conform to current international norms and avoid the unintentional or intentional conflation of "nationalities"

---

58. *Zhongguo minzu nianjian* (2009) [Yearbook of Chinese ethnicities (2009)], 603.

59. By the end of 2003, China had established 155 ethnic autonomous areas. Of these, five are autonomous regions, 30 autonomous prefectures, and 120 autonomous counties (banners). Of the 55 ethnic minorities, 44 have their own ethnic autonomous areas. The population of ethnic minorities practicing regional autonomy accounts for 71 percent of the total population of ethnic minorities, and the area where such regional autonomy is practiced accounts for 64 percent of the entire territory of China. See *Zhongguo minzu nianjian* (2009), 600–603.

with independent nations. On many levels, China's official ethnic policy is quite different from the conciliatory, liberal version of U.S. multiculturalism. In *Beyond Ethnicity,* Sollors finds it amusing that a 1785 pamphlet imagined the future U.S. as a union of ethnic valleys, an aggregate of separate regions assigned to different ethnic groups.[60] The system of autonomous regions in China would perhaps also draw some laughter from a casual American observer. It converges with U.S. liberal multiculturalism, however, in serving a particular kind of nationalist ideology. Both U.S. and Chinese multiculturalisms are highly constrained in how they construct minority difference and the terms of national integration. To proceed with this argument, however, we first need to clarify the meaning of *shaoshu minzu* in relation to a few Western and Soviet terms. What follows explains the multiple genealogies of this term, while outlining the main contour of the PRC's official ethnic policy since the early 1950s.

It is commonly argued that the immediate antecedent of the Chinese communists' notion of *minzu* is the Lenin–Stalinist understanding of *natsia,* a historically formed and stable community of people that has emerged on the basis of a common language, territory, economic life, and psychological makeup.[61] When combined with *shaoshu,* meaning minority, *minzu* does not denote a full-blown nation but can be equated with *natsional'nost'* or *narodnost'* in Russian, which refer to "ethnic communities that have survived through the period when tribal communities had disintegrated but no nations were yet formed."[62] Although, in the early 1930s, the Communist

60. Sollors, *Beyond Ethnicity,* 174–75. The particular pamphlet in question is *The Golden Age, or, Future Glory of North-America Discovered by an Angel to Celadon in Several Entertaining Visions,* published under the pen name "Celadon."

61. Stalin defined the term *natsia* for the Bolsheviks in his seminal 1913 article, "Marksizm i natsional'nyi vopros." A *natsia,* for Stalin, "is not a racial or tribal [*plemennyi*]" group, but a "historically evolved community" formed "from people of diverse races and tribes." A *natsia* is united by "a common language, territory and economic life"; its members share a "common mentality" (or consciousness), which is the result of shared experiences and is manifested in their culture." See Hirsch, *Empire of Nations,* 43.

62. Julian Bromley and Viktor Kozlov, "The Theory of Ethnos and Ethnic Processes in Soviet Social Sciences," 431. For a survey of theoretical efforts to gloss and flesh out Stalin's definition of a nation (*natsia*), see 426. In part, this history of theorization revolved around the question of whether a common territory and a common economy are prerequisites for the identification of an ethnic community. Bromley had argued in his work from the 1970s that the possession of common territory marks the difference between ethno-social organisms and what he calls "ethnicoses," which he correlates with the terms "*natsional'nost'*" and "*natsia*" (or its spoken version *narod*), respectively. The authors point out here that "*natsia*" has been used as the term for ethnicities in capitalist and socialist countries that make strong claims for statehood while "operating as a single economic organism" (Bromley and Kozlov, 431). Hirsch explains the term "*narodnost',*" documenting that "[w]hereas the ethnographers sometimes

Party endorsed the Soviet model of multinational federalism and Lenin's policy of self-determination for minority nationalities, he soon abandoned them in favor of an alternative model of regional autonomy, which allowed for the designation of areas with a high concentration of a certain minority nationality as autonomous regions, prefectures, counties, or banners. The Inner Mongolia Autonomous Region was established in 1947, the Xinjiang Uyghur Autonomous Region in 1955, and the Tibet Autonomous Region in 1965. Baogang He provides a useful account of the grounds on which Mao rejected federalism, including the argument that Lenin's theory of self-determination applied only to "oppressed nations casting off the rule of imperialism and colonialism" but not to "minorities within a socialist state."[63] Mao's rhetoric constructs the communists' ascent to power in China as a process through which the Han Chinese and the various peoples in China's borderlands converted animosity and distance into revolutionary camaraderie. This rhetoric notwithstanding, the move away from the Soviet model was motivated, to a large degree, by concerns with foreign designs on Chinese borders (the Soviet Union's on Xinjiang, for example) and the suspicion, as June T. Dreyer puts it, that minorities "would probably not choose to join China voluntarily."[64] While U.S. liberal multiculturalism necessitates the construction of a tradition of consent-based pluralism, balanced perfectly with national cohesion, the official ethnic policy in China predicates itself upon the myth of a symbiosis between the foundation of the party-state and the forging of irrevocable interethnic ties (in addition to China's prior claims to these areas during the long imperial era).

In the early days of the PRC, the communist leaders outlined the vision of the "gradual, unforced 'growing together' of nationalities under socialism."[65] In the words of Ralph Litzinger, author of a study of the Yao in contemporary China, throughout the 1950s, "minorities everywhere, across the expanse of China, were seen to move and advance through the stages of primitive communism, slave ownership, feudalism, capitalism, until they finally arrived, in the revolutionary present, in the space of state socialism."[66] Many ethnic peoples were considered by the state to belong to a certain stage of history

used *narodnost'* to refer to the common folk (such as the Russian peasantry) and sometimes to refer to 'a people' in the generic sense, the Bolsheviks usually used it to connote 'backwardness'"—that is, a people "at the precapitalist or early-capitalist stage on the historic timeline who had not yet formed a 'bourgeois-democratic nationalist movement'" (Hirsch, *Empire of Nations*, 43).

63. Baogang He, "Multiculturalism with Chinese Characteristics," 61.
64. Dreyer, *China's Forty Millions*, 69.
65. Ibid., 93.
66. Litzinger, *Other Chinas*, 84.

behind what the Han people had achieved. The establishment of autonomous governments in the early 1950s, therefore, consisted of a series of com-
promises between minority elites and communist cadres sent to minority
regions on a mission to "instill a consciousness of being Chinese" without
forcing socialism upon traditional cultural and social structures.[67] In regard
to the minority nationalities, therefore, the government pursued a policy of
ronghe [amalgamation] somewhere between the policy of *tonghua* [assimila-
tion] favored by the GMD and the Soviet model of federalist integration.[68]
The 1954 Constitution interprets *ronghe* as unity in diversity, promising
that the various nationalities would be given time to think over socialist
reforms and "make their decisions in accordance with their own desires."[69]
This gradualist, conciliatory policy was interrupted in the late 1950s, when
the political pressure of the Great Leap Forward forced minorities to form
communes and discard traditional cultures that may hinder their economic
and social advancement and was not reinstated until after the Cultural
Revolution. A draft constitution circulated at the end of 1970 noticeably
curtailed the rights made available in the 1954 document, making no mention of "retaining [minority] customs and habits."[70] The vision guiding the
nationalities policy between the late 1950s and 1970s was the eventual dissolution of ethnic and national differences. As Dreyer puts it, the state asserted
that "in socialist states, as the construction of industry increases, a common
proletarian culture [would] gradually emerge and the similarities (*tonghua
xing*) among peoples [would] become greater and greater as the differences
[became] smaller."[71]

The early 1980s saw the government return to an emphasis on minority difference. The Constitution of 1982 returns to the stance codified in
the 1954 Constitution, elaborating on the policy of autonomy to a degree
unmatched by previous constitutions. Baogang He's study of the document
finds that minority rights in China contain elements of three major categories of minority rights recognized in Western liberal democracies, including
(1) self-government rights, (2) special representation rights in the legislature
or bureaucracy, and (3) accommodation rights, providing legal recognition
to particular customs or practices.[72] These rights, for He, remain highly circumscribed, firmly subordinated to a unified state leadership, more so in

67. Dreyer, 136.
68. Ibid., 118.
69. Ibid., 126.
70. Ibid., 233.
71. Ibid., 157.
72. He, "Multiculturalism with Chinese Characteristics," 67.

volatile areas like Tibet and Xinjiang that are central to China's national security. He lists several ways in which the Chinese notion of ethnic autonomy falls short of normative definitions of the concept in liberal theories, including the lack of a "democratic verification mechanism for minorities" (the absence of an independent court to check the Communist Party's control over decision making in minority matters, for example) and the restriction of ethnic organizations with political agendas.[73] He's comparison, detailed as it is, remains beholden to a monolithic understanding of minority rights and multiculturalism. It might be more illuminating to stress the peculiarities of the Chinese policy that cannot be accounted for within the liberal framework.

The PRC's policy of ethnic autonomy has had a materialist basis since its inception, under both the socialist ideology during the Mao era and the mandate of economic reform in the post-Mao era. The amalgamation of the different ethnicities in the Chinese nation is believed to be a function of the level of their economic and social development. Economic and material progress in minority regions, therefore, is the standard that the government most frequently invokes as a measurement of the efficacy of its ethnic policy. A series of infrastructure and development projects in Tibet since 1994 and the expansion of cotton and crude oil production in Xinjiang over the past two decades both attest to this logic.[74] In *China's Ethnic Policy and the Common Prosperity and Development of All Ethnic Groups,* the government's white paper on the ethnic policy released in 2009, much effort is devoted to detailing the government's measures in promoting economic development in minority areas, especially since 2000, when the government launched a campaign to accelerate economic progress in western regions, home to around 60 percent of China's ethnic minority members.[75] China's materialist approach

73. Ibid., 67, 8.

74. Colin Mackerras, *China's Ethnic Minorities and Globalization,* 60–61. Also see Melvyn C. Goldstein, "Tibet and China in the Twentieth Century." As Goldstein argues, the Chinese government's efforts to develop its hinterlands in the west, especially Tibet, which often entail the increased "influx of non-Tibetan laborers and businessmen into Tibet," have frequently come in conflict with Tibetans' demand for autonomy (207–11).

75. See *Zhongguo de minzu zhengce yu ge minzu gongtong fanrong fazhan baipishu* [China's ethnic policy and the common prosperity and development of all ethnic groups]. Section V, "Accelerating the Economic and Social Development of Ethnic Minorities and Minority Areas," outlines the "preferential measures" and key "infrastructure projects" carried out since 2000, including the "projects for transmitting gas and power from the west to the east," the extension of the Qinghai-Tibet Railway to Lhasa, the tapping of oil and gas resources in Xinjiang, with particular attention paid to "their effects in stimulating local development," as demonstrated in the West–East Gas Transmission project, which "alone can bring in over one billion yuan in revenue to Xinjiang every year."

to ethnic difference forms an interesting contrast to the polarization of recognition and redistribution in the U.S. context. This approach, as many have argued, is very flawed, though not necessarily in the ways in which it fails the test of liberalism. Large-scale Han migration to both Tibet and Xinjiang and the persisting inequalities between Han Chinese and ethnic minorities in their access to political and economic power have exacerbated the deepseated ethnic divisions shaped in the historical struggles over the political status of these areas.

Emphasizing the peculiarities of the Chinese case, of course, does not mean disavowing any continuity between Chinese and American multiculturalisms. Even though "*shaoshu minzu*" was for a long time translated into minority nationalities, the word "*minzu*" has complex genealogical ties with conceptions of race and ethnicity in the West. Prior to the adoption of the Lenin–Stalinist idea of *narodnost'* or nationality, China had its own histories of descent-based and culturally based group identities, which also powerfully shaped the idea of minority nationalities in the PRC. In her important work from around 1990, Pamela Crossley critiques the troubling tendency of undertheorization in earlier scholarship on China's minorities, which often took the different nationalities in China as natural givens rather than political and cultural constructs. In "Thinking about Ethnicity in Early Modern China," Crossley locates the Chinese equivalent of Western notions of race and ethnicity in *zu,* the second component of the term *minzu.* She points out that the Chinese term "*zu*" originally indicated "a small group of people within a locality or a larger organization," but over time became the preferred term for "established, historical peoples" during the Qing Dynasty.[76]

Significantly, Crossley maps the meanings of "*zu*" onto both race and ethnicity. By the turn of the twentieth century, "*zu*" had been used to connote shared bloodlines and physical traits, as in the case of *manzu,* the Manchus (those genealogically connected to the founding population of the Qing). The emergence of identities based on "genealogical descent," as Crossley argues, signals an indigenous concept of race.[77] At the same time, Crossley claims that, when coupled with "*min*" (people), the word "*zu*" also dovetails nicely with ethnicity. Though directly translated from the Japanese term "*minzukuo*" at the end of the nineteenth century, the Chinese term "*minzu,*" insofar as it is used in the PRC, finds important cognates in the Soviet terms "*natsia*" [nation] and "*narod*" [ethnos, people], which, in turn, grew out of Western ethnology.[78] As Crossley points out, the PRC's official criteria

---

76. Crossley, "Thinking about Ethnicity in Early Modern China," 20.
77. Ibid., 20.
78. Hirsch attests that Russian ethnology in the late nineteenth century, which heavily

for classifying ethnic minority groups, or *shaoshu minzu*, in the early 1950s invoked the traditional criteria established in the Morgan–Engels tradition, namely "language, religion, economic life, and consciousness," even though all the criteria were bent at certain points in the actual classification process.[79] Overall, then, Crossley associates the Chinese term "*zu*" with both a descent-based understanding of identity (race) and a culturally based understanding of identity (ethnicity and nationality) in Western traditions. Combined with "*min*," "*zu*" denotes a historically grounded, as opposed to an essentialized, collective identity. An interesting implication of her argument is that value-laden distinctions are made between different modes of group identity formation in the modern histories of both the West and China. In the Western context, race denotes a positivist view that humans can be categorized on the basis of physiognomy and lineage, while ethnicity, despite being frequently associated with a shared primordial origin, has largely functioned to denote group differences arising from the "tensions existing between ethnies and the polities by which they are framed."[80] In the Chinese context, the bifurcation of the word "*zu*" can be seen as a parallel to the race-ethnicity division.

For many in the West, indeed, racial discourses came about on the basis of the rise of modern science, in the nineteenth century, that sought to correlate biological and cultural differences. Kenan Malik points out that, in *We Europeans* (1935), Huxley and Haddon opposed the political uses of race under Nazi, suggesting that the term "race" should be replaced by "ethnic group" so as to "allow social distinctions to be studied in a neutral, value-free fashion."[81] The terms "ethnic" and "ethnicity" gained prominence in postwar America, as Malik puts it, precisely because "the discourse of race became very properly self-conscious about the employment of its central terms during the 1930s and 1940s."[82] The term "ethnicity" can of course be synonymous with "race" when used to indicate "primordialist" identities

---

influenced Lenin and other Bolshevik theorists, was shaped by British and American cultural evolutionists, including in particular Lewis Henry Morgan and Edward B. Tylor. Russian ethnologists were also influenced by such German romanticists as Herder (*Empire of Nations*, 44). But while the ethnographers "drew on the work of British and American cultural evolutionists to understand the connections between 'modern' cultures and their 'primitive' antecedents," the Bolsheviks "were most interested in understanding the socioeconomic conditions that gave rise to different types of national movements" (45). Also, as Bromley and Kozlov point out, "the general theory of ethnos in Soviet social science was developed mainly by ethnographers and ethnologists" ("The Theory of Ethnos and Ethnic Processes in Soviet Social Sciences," 425).

79. Crossley, "Thinking about Ethnicity in Early Modern China," 21.
80. Ibid., 14.
81. Kenan Malik, *The Meaning of Race*, 174.
82. Ibid.

transmitted through biological descent.[83] That is why postwar proponents of the ethnicity paradigm made a point of recasting ethnicity as a process of "invention" responding to the "specificity of power relations at a given historical moment."[84] It is neither in the West nor in the United States, one must note, that distinctions are drawn between "immutable and mutable differences," tied to the terms "race" and "ethnicity," respectively.[85] We can chart a parallel, though very different, history in China from the turn of the twentieth century onward.

Largely concurring with Crossley, Frank Dikötter argues that, racial categories emerged in China on the basis of "indigenous modes of representation," including folk notions of shared kinship and court conceptions of lineage groups, which the reformers at the Qing imperial court bolstered by borrowing aggressively from Western evolutionary theories during the last decade of the nineteenth century.[86] Dikötter interprets the idea of *huang-zhong* (yellow race), a key racialized identity that formed during this period, as largely an extension of the logic of *zu*—the word "*zhong*," which literally means "seed" or "breed," can be seen as a variation on "*zu*" that fuses the indigenous notion of lineage (all Han Chinese descend from the Yellow-huang-Emperor) with Western racial taxonomies.[87] Others have revised Dikötter's important but partial argument by placing the construction of race in China after 1895 in the context of Western colonialisms, which precipitated among Chinese intellectuals and reformers a notion of the yellow race that encompassed not just China, but other colonized peoples in Asia and the Pacific, who were grouped under the same *zhong*, or *tongzhong* (the same *zhong*).[88] The idea of *minzu* developed within the same global colonial context, when the ruling Manchus were seen as precursors to the Western powers threatening to colonize China and defined in opposition to the Han

---

83. In postwar America, this view is often associated with Andrew Greeley, Michael Novak, and Pierre Van den Berghe.

84. Werner Sollors, ed., *The Invention of Ethnicity*, xvi.

85. Ibid., 174.

86. Frank Dikötter, "Racial Discourse in China," 14.

87. Ibid., 15.

88. Rebecca Karl, *Staging the World*. See the Introduction, chapter 6, and, in particular, 166–68. The anti-Manchu discourse overlapped with the discourse of "Asian solidarity" at the turn of the twentieth century, demonstrating the proximity between *zhong* and *zu* in China at that moment (167). The overall point of Karl's study is that new concepts such as *zhongzu* and *minzu* enabled China to conceptually organize and strategically position itself within the "uneven global spatiality" at the turn of the twentieth century, so neither of them grew out of an essentialist logic in the beginning, though they could easily be naturalized for political purposes (16).

as a unified nation, or *minzu*.[89] The terms *"zhong"* (which often becomes combined with *"zu,"* hence *"zhongzu"*) and *"minzu,"* therefore, were not clearly differentiated from each other in the early twentieth century. However, the interpretation of *minzu* as a culturalist and historical approach to identity and its separation from *zhongzu* became emphasized in the Ethnic Classification Project (1954–83) that laid down the framework of fifty-six ethnicities (Han + 55 minorities) in effect today. This project, according to a dissertation completed in 2006 by Thomas S. Mullaney, can be traced back to the debates over how to define *"minzu"* in the 1930s and 1940s, which involved the nationalist authorities, the communists, Chinese ethnologists, and Chinese physical anthropologists. Mullaney finds that, by the end of the 1930s, "Chinese ethnologists and their system of language-based ethnic categorization had prevailed over physical anthropologists and their biometric approach to *minzu*."[90] After 1949, this culturalist interpretation of *"minzu"* "meshed well" with the communist government's conception of the term, which in turn echoed the Lenin–Stalinist definition of *"natsia."* *"Minzu,"* thus, has acquired a historically oriented, nonracial meaning.[91]

It is certainly right to argue that the Communists' approach to *minzu*, as reflected in the 55 + 1 taxonomy produced by the Ethnic Classification Project, is of a deeply instrumental nature. It propagated a descent-based notion of *minzu* by organizing the incredibly complex ethnoscape that the PRC inherited from imperial and republican China into "mutually exclusive, ethno-linguistic units . . . serviceable to the requirements of modern statecraft."[92] However, we should also take note of the ways in which the state has, in recent years, consciously modulated this instrumental approach by acknowledging the instability of ethnic identities in Chinese history. We can find a few telling signs of this shift in the 2009 white paper on China's ethnic policy. At the end of section I, the report states that "[t]he Chinese *minzu* has become an overarching name that all individual *minzu* recognize and identify with."[93] The word *"minzu"* performs double duty in this sentence, denoting both the Chinese nation as a whole and the individual ethnic groups that constitute it. The larger *minzu* is a heterogeneous collection of the smaller *minzu*, rather than a homogeneous group, and the glue

89. Ibid., chapter 5, especially 117.

90. Shawn Thomas Mullaney, "Coming to Terms with the Nation," 27. Mullaney published a book based on the manuscript, *Coming to Terms with the Nation.* In the book, however, Mullaney excised the parts containing these quotes.

91. Ibid., 123.

92. Ibid., 35.

93. See *Zhongguo de minzu zhengce yu ge minzu gongtong fanrong fazhan baipishu* [China's ethnic policy and the common prosperity and development of all ethnic groups].

that binds the different smaller units resides solely in history, especially the "anti-colonial, anti-separatist struggles" in which they had all participated.[94] The invocation of a shared revolutionary past is well-rehearsed rhetoric, the rationale, in fact, for abandoning the Soviet-style federalism in favor of a system of circumscribed ethnic autonomy in the 1940s and so is the explicit description of the Chinese nation as a nonunitary construct that transcends the Han majority. What *is* interesting, however, is that, in the same section, the individual ethnic groups within the nation are also described as having been "shaped by local conditions," intermingling with each other "through continuous migration, living together, intermarriage, and communication."[95] The significance of this emphasis can be seen in its conspicuous absence from the two previous white papers on the state's ethnic policies, released in 1999 and 2005, respectively. This new rhetorical move signals the government's effort to radicalize, on a rhetorical level at least, the differences between *minzu* (correlated with ethnicity or nation) and *zhongzu* (correlated with race), the latter of which has become associated with the practices and legacies of Western colonialism and imperialism solely. The campaign to cultivate *minzu tuanjie* [ethnic unity] in contemporary China, as we can see, requires a fluid, nonessentialist conception of *minzu* just as much as it requires an instrumental, descent-based one.

In their own ways, then, both the United States and China have had to confront the issue of unmeltable ethnicities. Since the mid-twentieth century, multicultural policies and discourses in both countries have consisted of a delicate dance between recognizing and containing ethnic and racial differences. Discursive negotiations over the meaning of "ethnicity" or "*minzu,*" therefore, have become central to this balancing act. What I referred to as conciliatory multiculturalism manifests in both contexts as emphatic rearticulations of ethnicity, or *minzu,* as a fundamentally mutable and open category, which work to delegitimize race, or *zhongzu,* as an essentialized and flawed category, thus downgrading group tensions to a level where they seem nonthreatening to the ideal of national consensus or unity. Rearticulations of ethnicity, or *minzu,* in other words, have *taken the place of* (rather than supplemented) concrete policies or programs for addressing minority demands for equality or increased autonomy. My idea of conciliatory multiculturalism is not far from what many others have termed "superficial" or "weak" multiculturalism, but I believe "conciliatory" more aptly captures the political function and rhetorical features of what I am critiquing.

94. Ibid.
95. Ibid.

In China's case, the issues of how to maintain territorial sovereignty and national unity are as pressing today as they were in the early days of the communist government. The successive waves of popular revolts and pro-independence activities in Xinjiang and Tibet, which have become thoroughly intertwined with international politics, most vividly illustrate minority challenges to China's state nationalism. Concerns with national security and sovereignty, coupled with economic calculations (many minority areas are rich in resources), continue to inform the official ethnic policy, as can be seen in the tightening of security in unrest-prone areas and the continued emphasis on economic development and patriotic propaganda. Minority groups are allowed to maintain, in part, their distinct cultural identities, but are also portrayed in official rhetoric as inextricably intertwined with the Han Chinese since times immemorial. This official, conciliatory multiculturalism, of course, has not completely supplanted racialist perceptions of group difference. As many have pointed out rightly, racism toward blacks often asserts itself in contemporary China and one can reasonably infer the existence of racialist attitudes and practices toward certain ethnic minority groups within.[96]

The U.S. situation is different yet similar. The unmeltable nature of ethno-racial differences was brought to the fore in the Civil Rights Movement and the intense theorization of race as a major sign of structural inequalities in the following decades. This emphasis on race, as I pointed out previously, is sometimes confused with the reification of cultural difference. This conflation is as often espoused by racial minorities eager to establish an inhabitable, distinct identity as by supporters of the ethnicity paradigm. The misunderstanding of and resistance toward the increasing focus on race are the driving forces behind the rhetoric of going "beyond ethnicity" and "postethnicity," which in fact is not a rejection of ethnicity but an insistence on a particular, nonracial conception of it, that is, as a flexible, shifting form of identity equally available to all. It is a conception that functions to equalize different social groupings and tame the group conflicts threatening to unbind the American nation. Indeed, the insistent repudiation of race has

96. See, for example, Frank Dikötter, *The Discourse of Race in China*. In the epilogue, Dikötter contends that those in the PRC periodically display racist prejudice against blacks in and outside China despite the idea of Third World solidarity to which the country officially subscribes. For a discussion of an anti-African protest in China, see Michael Sullivan, "The 1988–89 Anti-African Protests." Although there have not been rigorous studies of this issue, Uyghurs are often racialized in China, stereotyped as criminals or even terrorists. There are no easy linkages one can draw between different strains of racism in contemporary China, but they shared an underlying biological understanding of difference and are likely to share a connection to the surge of China's nationalism in the post-Mao era.

often been read as a way in which the majority nation "[acts] out" the trauma of being challenged by racial minority movements.[97] Liberal multiculturalism, hinged upon collapsing race into (a particular conception of) ethnicity, must be distinguished from critical multiculturalism, which foregrounds race and racialization not to exacerbate existing political and social divisions but to deepen our understanding of the mutual imbrication of these divisions and the operation of power and capital. In the words of Antonia Darder and Rodolfo D. Torres, a critical approach to race sees it as "one of the primary ideologies by which material conditions in society are organized and perpetrated."[98] A further twist to the U.S. case is the re-securitization of the state after 9/11 and the ensuing curtailment of civil rights, which refueled the culture wars of the 1970s–90s. The heightened tensions between, on the one hand, increasingly multiplied modes of attachment among America's ethnically diverse citizens and residents and, on the other, the cementing of American exceptionalism into a fervent patriotism have oftentimes given rise to efforts to further consolidate conciliatory multiculturalism. As Evelyn Alsultany documents, a few nonprofit advertising campaigns, for example, were launched after 9/11 to "deconstruct the binary opposition between American citizen and Arab Muslim," with the effect, however, of reproducing "restrictive representations of diversity."[99] While the U.S. government launched public relations campaigns in the Middle East seeking to "conceal the blatant discriminatory practices it enacts" on a daily basis, nonprofit organizations and civil rights groups also produced public service announcements that portrayed Muslims in the United States as model citizens who embrace American values as well as military and other public services while practicing a nonviolent form of Islam.[100] These efforts, though motivated by different concerns, converge in seeking to contain the politically charged friction between Muslim and white, Christian values, revalorizing the image of a perennially inclusive U.S. national identity.

From Parallels to Intersections

My preceding survey casts official Chinese multiculturalism and American liberal multiculturalism as two contemporaneous and parallel processes

---

97. Carl Gutierrez-Jones, "Color Blindness and Acting Out."
98. Antonia Darder and Rodolfo D. Torres, *After Race,* 101.
99. Evelyn Alsultany, "Selling American Diversity and Muslim American Identity through Nonprofit Advertising Post-9/11," 595–96.
100. Ibid., 618.

through which concepts of ethnicity, race, and nation are negotiated in relation to one another. Establishing structural and formal parallels between these very different processes, however, is not the endpoint of my study, the bulk of which focuses on the various ways in which the two multicultural projects are increasingly connected in fictional narratives and other related discourses in the post–Cold War era. The following is an overview of the discursive bridges that link them. Not all these bridges take the same shape or have the same effect in diminishing the chasm of mutual misconceptions that lies in between.

As pointed out, liberal, conciliatory multiculturalism underwent a period of theoretical legitimization in the United States throughout the 1990s and was further consolidated in the beginning of the twenty-first century. In China, the same period opened the country to Western liberal multiculturalism, which came to be regarded by some Chinese intellectuals as a useful model that can complement China's own ethnic policy without replacing it. The term "multiculturalism," often translated into "*wenhua duoyuan zhuyi*," has made steady appearances in China's academic journals since the 1990s, mostly in studies of the history of American multiculturalism.[101] Will Kymlicka's 1995 work *Politics in the Vernacular* (2001) and *Liberalism, Community, and Culture* (1989) were both translated into Chinese in 2005, giving rise to further theoretical elaborations of the history and principles of liberal multiculturalism for Chinese audiences.[102] Western liberalism theories have been invoked as a way of rethinking the pragmatic, politically driven approach to minority rights in China. At a 2001 conference cosponsored by the Chinese Confucius Society and Yunnan Nationalities University, a number of scholars explicitly appropriated Western discourses on individual and group rights to argue that the Chinese government should help preserve endangered minority cultural traditions and foster cultural diversity as ends in themselves. He Shaoyin, for example, discusses several cultural and natural conservation programs in Yunnan (home to several minority groups) launched in the beginning of the twenty-first century in comparison with multiculturalisms in white-settled countries, including the United States, and countries in Southeast Asia. She attributes an extraeconomic significance to the Yunnan programs, contending that their "ultimate goal" is generating an

---

101. Wang Xi, "Duoyuan wenhua de qiyuan, shijian yu juxianxin" [Origins, practices, and limits of multiculturalism], 54; Qian Hao, "Meiguo minzu lilun kaoshi" [On American ethnic theories], 13; Gao Jianguo, "Shilun meiguo minzu duoyanxing he wenhua duoyuan zhuyi" [Comments on ethnic diversity and multiculturalism in the U.S.], 3–4.

102. See, for example, Zhu Lianbi, "Duoyuan wenhua zhuyi yu minzu-guojiao de jiangou" [Multiculturalism and the construction of nation-states].

understanding of "the other."[103] The Yunnan examples, for her, are an integral part of a global effort to "create mutual understanding and communication among different cultures, dissolve cultural conflicts, and enable all cultures in the world to 'co-exist in peace.'"[104] The last phrase alludes to China's long-standing foreign relations doctrines—the Five Principles of Peaceful Coexistence—forged first in the Non-Aligned Movement of the 1950s, but the idea of coexistence is reinvigorated in this phrasing by being blended seamlessly with the principle of liberal tolerance.[105]

A competing idea is that the policy of regional autonomy in China, along with its Soviet predecessor, is already compatible with liberal models of multiculturalism in Western countries. The privileging of the "state will" and the central government's administrative control in the Chinese model can be justified by the fact that a shared set of civic values are not yet in place in China, still a developing country, thus precluding a nonstatist national identity, and that foreign interventions continue to pose a threat to China's multiethnic harmony.[106]

A more orthodox position, meanwhile, takes the liberal premise of individual freedom to task and, unsurprisingly, finds it fundamentally at odds with the goal of social justice. Those holding this position rehearse a semi-Marxist approach to ethnic difference, arguing that state socialism works more effectively than the free market in minimizing the material and cultural inequalities between different ethnicities and thus securing interethnic harmony, if not the ultimate elimination of ethnicities. This position exalts the importance of national cohesion and, at times, borrows indiscriminately from criticisms of liberalism within Western political traditions. One scholar, for example, strings together, without irony, Huntington's argument about the balkanizing effect of liberal pluralism in *Who Are We: The Challenges to America's National Identity* and the standard Marxist critique of liberalism's capitalist underpinnings.[107] China's encounter with U.S. liberal multicultur-

---

103. He Shaoyin, "Quanqiuhua yu haiwai minzu wenhua duoyuan fazhan de qishi" [Globalization and lessons from multiculturalisms in foreign countries], 66.

104. Ibid.

105. The Five Principles were formed in 1954 in a series of documents between the newly decolonized China and India. These principles include (1) mutual respect for each other's territorial integrity and sovereignty, (2) mutual nonaggression, (3) mutual noninterference in each other's internal affairs, (4) equality and mutual benefit, and (5) peaceful coexistence.

106. Guan Kai, "Duoyuan wenhua zhuyi yu minzu quyu zizhi" [Multiculturalism and ethnic regional autonomy], 51.

107. Chang Shiyan, "Minzu hexie yu ronghe: shixian minzu yu zhenzhi yiti de guanjian" [Ethnic harmony and amalgamation: The key to the unity and political integration of the nation], 69–71.

alism, of which we only catch a glimpse here, is a complex dynamic that involves rhetorical appropriations (respect for the marginalized "other," for instance), affirmations of the American model, as well as reassertions of the merit of the Chinese way. These are not separate attitudes but are often intertwined in each specific moment of this encounter. We see one such moment in chapter 3, which, in part, discusses the analogy that Chinese scholars and policy makers have recently drawn between the development of China's western regions, dense with ethnic minorities, in the contemporary era and the American westward expansion of the nineteenth century. This comparative move shows a mixture of the attitudes or impulses that I enumerate here.

If U.S. liberal multiculturalism has come into contact with China's ethnic policy through the work of translation, a particular site of translation is central to the linking of the two. Chinese American writings, as I argue, and figures as an important form of cultural translation by drawing connections between multiple national histories and cultures. These often become objects of translation as well, traveling on a textual level between the national spaces they address in their writings. The works of familiar Chinese American authors, including, among others, Kingston, Frank Chin, Amy Tan, and Gus Lee, and their Chinese translations have given rise to numerous academic articles and books in China, stoking among common readers and academics alike a strong interest in American social and racial history.[108] Academic discussions of the various theoretical issues in Chinese American literature have lent much currency to some of the themes central to the study of ethnic cultures in the United States and around the globe, including racialization, cultural hybridity, and diaspora. Meanwhile, Chinese American authors who write primarily in Chinese have prompted challenges to homogeneous constructions of Chinese literatures and cultures. In China, Chinese-language writings in the United States have long been considered to be part of *shijie huawen wenxue* [world literature in Chinese], a concept that emerged in the early 1980s and was formerly institutionalized as a field of study in the early 1990s.[109] This field has generated many inquiries into the ways in which

---

108. The earlier translations include all three novels of Kingston, Siu Sin Far's *Mrs. Spring Fragrance and Other Writings,* David Louie Wong's *Pangs of Love,* Gish Jen's *Typical American,* Frank Chin's *Gunga Din Highway,* Gus Lee's *Honor and Duty,* Fae Myenne Ng's *Bone,* Jade Snow Wong's *Fifth Chinese Daughter,* and Yung Wing's *My Life in China and America,* among others. In addition to the Chinese translation of works by individual writers, anthologies of Chinese American literature has also appeared in China. See Xu Yingguo, *Meiguo wenxue xuandu* [*An anthology of Chinese American literature*].

109. The term "overseas literature in Chinese" first emerged in the early 1980s. The Association of World Literature in Chinese was established and approved by the Ministry of Civil Affairs in the early 1990s, signaling the institutionalization of this field. See Rao Pengzi. "Haiwai

ethnic Chinese writers all over the world have transplanted, translated, reimagined, or repudiated Chinese literary and cultural traditions.[110] Even as Chinese American writers help reconfigure American literature and identity in multicultural, multilingual, transnational terms, then, they increasingly destabilize what it means to be Chinese. Chapters 3 and 5 of this book highlight the doubly critical role that Chinese American writings, in both English and Chinese, have played, while adding significantly to our understanding of this role.

In some instances, discursive mediation between the ethno-racial politics of the two countries responds to their "actual" relations. In the post–Cold War era, the most prominent example of such "actual" relations is the ambiguous, cautious alliance over the "War on Terror" that the two countries formed after 9/11. The U.S. projection of military power into Central Asia in the wake of 9/11 created a paradoxical effect. While raising new security concerns for China, it also lent more impetus and political legitimacy to the Chinese government's campaign against the pro-independence movement among the Uyghurs (Turkish-speaking Muslims) in the Xinjiang province and abroad.[111] As Mackerras documents, in the immediate aftermath of 9/11, the Chinese tied Uyghur separatists in Xinjiang to al-Qaeda and other Islamic organizations in Central Asia, and the U.S. State Department helped lend credence to this assertion.[112]

The Chinese government's campaign against Xinjiang separatists, of course, started well before 9/11. Resistance to Chinese control of the province on the part of the Uyghurs and other Muslim minorities and the movement for an independent Islamic republic started as early as the late 1950s.[113] Agitations for separation were stepped up in the early 1990s, when

---

huawen wenxue zai zhonguo xuejie xingqi de jiqi yiyi" [The development of studies in world literature in Chinese and its implications].

110. Rao points out that Chinese-language writings from outside of China contribute to an "integrated" conception of modern and contemporary Chinese literature and culture that emphasizes the unevenness of their interactions with different locales around the globe ("Haiwai huawen," 7). Rao's argument flows from a large number of studies of how Chinese-language writings outside the PRC speak to their specific contexts.

111. See Robert Bedeski, "Western China: Human Security and National Security," 43; Michael Dillon, *Xinjiang*, 159.

112. In 2002, the U.S., followed closely by the UN, formally classified ETIM (East Turkestan Independent Movement) as a terrorist organization after repeated lobbying from China. It, however, refused to recognize ETLO (East Turkestan Liberation Organization) as a terrorist organization in December 2003. Also, as Dru C. Gladney points out in "Islam in China," the U.S. exercised pressure on Pakistan to return a Uyghur activist to China (458).

113. Micheal Dillon provides a documentation of the major incidents of resistance in Xinjiang from the Khotan rising of December 1954 to the unrest in the mid-1990s. Bovingdon also documents several riots in the 1980s ("Autonomy in Xinjiang," 7). Mackerras offers an account

the independence of the former Soviet republics (especially Kazakhastan, Kyrgyzstan, and Tajikistan), along with the rise of Taliban in Afghanistan, precipitated the surge of militant Islam in Central Asia.[114] Since then, the Chinese government has grown more concerned with the stability of the province for both political and economic reasons.[115] No more than one month before 9/11, alleged incursions of Talibans into Xinjiang across the Afghanistan–China border drew many Chinese security forces.[116] The consensus that the two governments reached over the importance of fighting terror served to legitimize the criminalization and de facto racialization of Muslims occurring in both countries, each with a long history of wrestling with the religio-political tensions surrounding the presence of Islam. While the PRC has had to grapple with Uyghur secessionist activities since its earliest days, the United States engaged in military and political interventions in the Middle East throughout the Cold War, which culminated in the first and second Iraq War, laying the seeds, at least in part, for 9/11. The collapse of the Soviet Union in 1991, which destabilized Central Asia and enabled a period of American unipolarity, served as a catalyst for the convergence of these two histories in the beginning of the new millennium. It is important, therefore, to examine the two histories in conjunction with each other. Chapter 4 does this by juxtaposing two writers who help us form a comparative perspective on the ways in which Muslim communities challenge the secular configurations of multiculturalism in the two countries, while endowing the notions of terror and sacrifice stereotypically associated with Muslims with new, transformative meanings.

This overview does not cover all the ways in which U.S. and Chinese multiculturalisms intersect in the contemporary period through translation and the work of fictional narratives. It does show, however, that they are

of the Uyghur revolts since 1990 (*China's Ethnic Minorities and Globalisation,* 49–52). For a history of Xinjiang prior to the founding of the PRC in 1949, see Dillon, 8–22. Chinese control over what is today Xinjiang dates from the eighteenth century. During republican China, the GMD maintained weak control over the area through officials who virtually seceded from China and cooperated with Russia and then the Soviet Union. Attempts at independence during this period resulted in the proclamation of an independent Islamic republic in two separate incidents and locations (Dillon 20–22).

114. See Meckarras, *China's Ethnic Minorities and Globalisation,* 165–67.

115. Gladney explains that Uyghur separatism has serious consequences for the economy of the region, in the areas of oil production, foreign investment, and trade with China's Central Asian neighbors ("Islam in China," 458–59). Politically, Uyghur separatism continues to cause international pressure on China, eroding the credibility of the country's claim to cultural pluralism ("Islam in China," 460). Bovingdon reports a "political tightening" in the 1990s toward Xinjiang, which includes the yearly "strike hard" campaigns, periodical sweeps, and international offensives aimed to pressure China's neighbors to crack down on Uyghur separatists (23–46).

116. Gladney, "Islam in China," 458.

connected in complex ways that call for scholarly engagement. It also reveals the political stakes of comparing or translating between two different sets of ethno-racial politics, which can operate either as a mechanism of self-legitimization or as an instrument of comparative critique, namely, the practice of intervening critically in more than one national context at once. The following chapters flesh out my account here by examining a specific set of narrative texts that shuttle between U.S. and Chinese multiculturalisms.

CHAPTER 2

How Not to Be an Empire

On Conciliatory Multiculturalism

> Whatever it is, paperback fiction is of our time: it is ours. . . . Whatever we say about these books, in the whole stretch of time between the big bang and the final whimper these are some of the only stories that will ever have understood us.
>
> —Thomas J. Roberts, *The Aesthetics of Junk Fiction*

> Historically, China has eschewed the route taken by classical colonial powers. It has not sent its armies to distant countries, but has focused instead on regions it considered as part of its territory, including Tibet and Taiwan. In this regard, China is imitating the United States.
>
> —John Perkins, *The Secret History of the American Empire*

A N IMPORTANT GLOBAL publishing event in 2008 was the release of *The Wolf Totem,* in North America, Europe, and the Asia Pacific simultaneously, Howard Goldblatt's English translation of Chinese author Jiang Rong's novel *Lang Tuteng.* As of now, the translation rights for the book have been agreed for more than 30 languages.[1] A literary sensation in China when it came out in 2004, the novel fictionalizes the experiences of a small group of ethnic Han Chinese living in Inner Mongolia during the Cultural Revolution. In the novel, the affiliation they cultivate with the local Mongols allows them to develop a critique of the Chinese government's irresponsible economic policies in Inner Mongolia, designated as the Inner Mongolia Autonomous Region in

---

1. Shu jinyu, "Jiemi Lang Tuteng banquan shuchu shenhua" [Decoding the successful handling of publishing rights for *Lang Tuteng*].

1947.[2] What makes the novel a global bestseller seems to have much to do with its political ambiguity. The *New York Times* reviewer Pankaj Mishra marvels at the "indictment of Chinese imperialism" left intact in both the original and the English translation.[3] In China, by contrast, the wildly popular book has often been read as a cry for a muscular Chinese nationalism that borrows from the history of the thirteenth- and fourteenth-century Mongol empire, which ruled China for almost a hundred years. The novel's ambiguous relationship with imperialism has no doubt helped it gain acceptance from readers across a broad political spectrum. What is less noticed about this book, but equally important, is its comparative dimension, especially its invocation of the kind of naturalist, racialist discourse often associated with the writings of Jack London, an author alluded to in the novel as a favorite for the Han Chinese characters. The London allusions, as we will see, implicitly construct American parallels to some of the problems in contemporary China that the novel explores.

The Mongol empire and its modern "descendants," Mongolia (Mongolia People's Republic until 1992) and Inner Mongolia, are also the subject of an American novel published around the same time. Clive Cussler's 2006 adventure novel *Treasure of Khan* features Dirk Pitt, a marine engineer and adventurer, who defeats a present-day Mongolian mogul scheming to control world oil prices. Both China and the United States, along with Mongolia, Russia, and Middle Eastern Arab nations, figure as important players on global energy markets in the novel. While the United States is portrayed as particularly efficacious in tackling the threat of a looming energy crisis, China is criticized for having sought, though in vain, to secure oil and other natural resources through policies that are exploitive toward its ethnic minorities. In the middle of the novel, the protagonist and his sidekick take a significant detour into the Gobi Desert, running into a local Mongol who had been forced to cross the border from Inner Mongolia, where overdevelopment had ruined the environment and the locals' traditional livelihoods. Just as *Lang Tuteng* invokes London (and other references) to suggest historical precedents for the novel's proposal for reinvigorating Chinese nationalism,

---

2. It was the first provincial-level autonomous government to be established. Inner Mongolia had been incorporated into Chinese provinces under the Qing Dynasty. According to Mackerras, the Japanese attempt to set up puppet regimes in the eastern parts of the region came to an end with their defeat in World War II. Soon afterward, the CCP out-maneuvered the other political players in the region, declaring that Inner Mongolia would be reunited on the basis of "autonomy of equality," which "could be realized only with the leadership and help of the CCP (Mackerras, *China's Minorities*, 103). The new autonomous region was set on July 1, 1947.

3. Pankaj Mishra, "Call of the Wild."

Treasure of Khan juxtaposes China and the United States in its comments on how big states should conduct themselves to compete for resources without incurring charges of imperialism. *Treasure of Khan* was translated into Chinese in 2008, the fifth of the Cussler novels to be introduced to Chinese readers.

That the two novels appeared around the same time says something significant. As they both compare how contemporary America and China relate to the historical Mongol empire, *Treasure of Khan* and *Lang Tuteng* underscore the parallel ways in which the two countries figure in post–Cold War discourses of empire. The idea that the United States should be understood as an empire since its inception started to take hold in academic and popular discourses in the early 1990s, at a time when China began to be perceived as a key threat to U.S. power.[4] The prominent roles they play in the global competition for natural resources in the beginning of the twenty-first century, an issue that grounds both novels, has further fueled perceptions of the two countries as competing empires. Rodrigue Tremblay, for example, used the stark phrase of the "new American Empire" as a rubric under which to study "the explosive links between religion, partisan-politics, and oil" that formed in the United States after the Cold War.[5] He traces the roots of the Iraq War, in a large part, to the 2001 Bush–Cheney energy policy, which "aimed to stabilize the Middle-East, militarily, and sought to insure the control of enormous crude oil reserves, both known and unexplored, not only in Iraq but also throughout the Middle-East."[6] Michael Klare concurs, condemning the same policy for endorsing America's "prodigious oil habit" and "perpetual dependence on Persian Gulf oil," an endorsement that necessitated identifying Saddam Hussein as the biggest threat to American national interest in the Persian Gulf and the 2003 Iraq War.[7] The United States is certainly not the only country under heat for embarking on imperialist practices in search of energy and other natural resources. China has been increasingly criticized for engaging in a kind of "global activism" to ensure access to oil, which often entails offering loans and aid to governments of oil-rich developing countries without the conditions that Western countries often attach to such packages.[8] As Klare points out, China recently entered the race for energy in the Persian Gulf and other areas against the United States and Russia, in a

4. See, for example, Bill Gertz, *The China Threat*. For more on the discourses of the U.S. and China as two competing empires in the post–Cold War era, see the Preface.

5. Rodrigue Tremblay, *The New American Empire*, 12.

6. Ibid., 90.

7. Michael Klare, *Blood and Oil*, 74.

8. Joshua Kurlantzick, "Beijing's Safari," 2.

way that revives the geopolitical competition—power politics exercised for control over territory, natural resources, and other economic and military advantages—characteristic of the Cold War years.[9] The Chinese government has also been criticized for extracting resources, not just oil, from minority regions in the country's borderlands, including Inner Mongolia, a location featured centrally in both of the novels discussed here. Evan Osnos, a foreign correspondent of the *Chicago Tribune*, wrote an award-winning three-part series, titled "China's Great Grab," for the paper in 2006.[10] Aside from predicting a "coming fight for oil" that will embroil China and the United States in a new "Great Game of global strategy," Osnos detailed the environmental consequences of decades of irresponsible development in Inner Mongolia since the Mao era, which had culminated in the almost unregulated mass production of cashmere. Chinese environmental authorities started to stem overgrazing and desertification, but the belated effort may well fail to undo the damage.[11]

With all the echoes of contemporary political discourses in them, *Treasure of Khan* and *Lang Tuteng* belong to the kind of fiction that, as Thomas J. Roberts believes, derives its value from being "time-bounded."[12] The fiction that Roberts refers to, of course, is "junk fiction," his name for genre fiction or popular fiction. He believes that this body of fiction unfolds like a net that catches bits and pieces of everyday speech and the ongoing concerns and obsessions of a nation, and its deliberate allusions to and invocations of the present convey a deep understanding of the age that produces it, thus offering a vast number of readers a comforting image of themselves. This argument, to be sure, captures an important feature of popular fiction, a label, as I discuss more extensively later, that is apt for both *Treasure of Khan* and *Lang Tuteng*. However, since almost all fiction addresses a kind of newspaper reality, "an image of reality we put together from all the sources reporting on events we do not actually see for ourselves," to point out the time-boundedness of popular fiction does not quite explain the particular cultural work that popular fiction performs and the distinct pleasure it generates.[13] This chapter does not seek to address these questions in a systematic manner, but it does offer a few new clues to possible answers by examining the ways in which popular fiction speaks to the related questions of empire, nationalism,

9. Klare, 147.

10. Evan Osnos, "China's Great Grab." The Asia Society in New York City awarded Osnos the Osborn Elliott Prize for Excellence in Journalism on Asia in April 2007. See "Asia Society Awards Osborn Elliott Journalism Prize to Evan Osnos."

11. Osnos, December 16, 19, 2006.

12. Thomas J. Roberts, *An Aesthetics of Junk Fiction*, 11.

13. Ibid., 13.

and multiculturalism. The two novels studied here, I argue, demonstrate that popular fiction has a crucial role to play in mediating the relations among these concepts in a given national context.

Cussler and Jiang acknowledge the imperialist undertones of the domestic and foreign policies espoused in contemporary America and China, respectively. At the same time, however, they disavow the same observations by attributing an idealized pluralist tradition to the two nations. The two novels' extensive invocations of the Mongol empire and its various premodern and modern analogues serve as convenient foils for the legitimacy of the U.S. and Chinese nationalisms that they imagine. Cussler repudiates modern equivalents of the Mongol empire while distancing the contemporary United States from them; in comparison, Jiang articulates the belief that the Han Chinese have been historically influenced by Mongol culture and will continue to draw upon the latter, in a way that will forge a strong, culturally hybrid Chinese nationalism without perpetuating the imperial legacies of Genghis Khan. The two authors are strikingly similar in their politics. I argue that the narrative politics of these novels illustrates the formal logic of conciliatory multiculturalism (a term, as I argue in chapter 1, that can encompass both China's official multiculturalism and U.S. liberal multiculturalism), which functions to create national unity through largely rhetorical or symbolic means, projecting an image of ethno-racial harmony without striving concretely toward this goal by tackling the political, cultural, and psychic causes for the inequalities among different ethno-racial groups. Both the Chinese and American varieties of conciliatory multiculturalism depend on casting ethno-racial tensions within a state and, by extension, cultural and ideological conflicts between states, as having *always and already* been reconciled under a form of liberal or measured nationalism, which is posited as naturally distinct from imperialism. Conciliatory multiculturalism, then, is poised somewhere between recognizing and disavowing ethno-racial tensions, between engaging in cultural and political critique and justifying existing power structures. Its ambiguous logic is encapsulated in the formal and political oscillation that we will see in Cussler and Jiang. In the meantime, they also show that the sustainability of this logic depends profoundly on comparative narratives. The juxtaposition of American and Chinese histories in the two novels is constitutive of the ways in which they reconcile the political and social tensions internal to the two countries. Allusions to China play a key role in Cussler's project of reimagining America as a restrained moral power in the world, just as interpretations of American history and culture are integral to Jiang's portrayal of China in a similar light. In other words, U.S.–China comparisons allow the two authors to uphold the political legitimacy of contemporary American and Chinese nationalisms *without* a thorough critical examination of their imperialist excess. Both novels, therefore, reconcile social critique with endorsing the status quo, marked by a pattern of political and formal vacillation that gives them a broad, centrist appeal. In fact, we can argue that their popularity is an index to their formal and political proximity to conciliatory multiculturalism.

I start my analysis that follows by situating the two novels within U.S. representations of ethnic issues in China and Chinese representations of race relations in America, to show that Jiang and Cussler, in interweaving two national contexts, at once continue and update the pattern of comparisons found in these other texts. I then offer a reading of the two novels, with a focus on the relationship between the U.S.–China comparisons they engage in and their conceptions of multiculturalism and nationalism.

An Impulse for Comparison

Treasure of Khan and *Lang Tuteng* are not two isolated texts. They are preceded by many popular texts, from both China and the United States, that concern themselves with ethnic and racial issues in the *other* nation. These texts do not engage in explicit comparisons of the two countries, as do Cussler and Jiang and a few other authors discussed in this book. However, many are covertly comparative in that they criticize one nation without reflecting on the other, thus implicitly holding up the latter as a standard. It is these implicit comparisons that, in most cases, more powerfully shape the cultural unconscious of the two nations. They constitute a variation on the pattern of accusatory comparisons that, as I point out in the Introduction, functions to polarize the two countries in terms of their ethnic and racial policies. We can very well say that Cussler and Jiang, by interweaving the United States and China in their narratives, bring to surface the comparative impulse inherent in many post–Cold War cultural representations.

The end of the Cold War era was punctured by a few dramatic developments that thrust China into the center of media attention in America. Coverage of the Chinese government's suppression of the student protests in 1989, accompanied by images of ordinary Chinese confronting army tanks, portrayed an authoritarian style of government oddly impervious to political reform. Criticism of the government's treatment of ethnic autonomous regions came to a head around the same time, as a series of violent anti-Chinese protests erupted in Tibet between 1987 and 1989, prompting the government to impose martial law in Lhasa in mid-1989. The year 1989 is also when the Dalai Lama won the Nobel Peace Prize, marking a high point in his international campaign since the 1980s for greater autonomy for Tibet. The ensuing decade, not surprisingly, saw a consistent cultural offensive in the United States in support of the Dalai Lama. The Franco-American film *Seven Years in Tibet* (1993) is based on the eponymous memoir, first published in 1957, by Heinrich Harrer, an Austrian mountaineer who was imprisoned by the British while mountaineering in India in 1939 and escaped across the border to Tibet in 1944.[14] In a significant departure from the book, the film shows Harrer evolving emotionally under the influence of Tibetan culture, while playing up the level of violence involved in China's invasion of Tibet in 1950. The film became the first of a series of controversial cinematic representations of Tibet to receive angry reactions from the Chinese government. Martin Scorsese's *Kundun,* a biographical film of Dalai Lama spanning between 1937 and 1953, came out a few months afterwards, eliciting the same response from the Chinese government, which banned the director and scriptwriter from entering China.[15] Paul Wagner's *Windhorse* (1998) is set in a more recent Tibet, depicting three young Tibetans who sacrifice their careers and lives in protesting against the Chinese government.[16] Even though only *Seven Years in Tibet* is explicitly narrated from the perspective of a foreigner, with all three of these films, the process of filmmaking itself came to figure as a form of humanitarian intervention. The official website for *Windhorse,* tellingly, carries a story about the making of the film, which involved one week of secret filming in Lhasa.[17] The filmmakers pretended to be tourists to fool the Chinese secret police and the spies working for the Chinese government, who would suddenly swoop down on anyone looking even slightly suspicious. The making of the film, thus, became a kind of counterspying, an act of humanitarian heroism.

The righteousness of the Western "spy," while frequently assumed, does not go unquestioned. After the most recent riots in Lhasa on March 14, 2008, the Western media (CNN included) found itself faced with pointed criticism launched from the Chinese blogsphere and YouTube, where instances of misreporting and inappropriate image editing were cited as evidence that the Western media had stooped to political propaganda in its eagerness to support the Tibetan exile government's claim that the riots began as a response to the Chinese military police's attack on monks protesting peacefully outside a monastery in Lhasa and that the police fired guns at the rioters. These

14. Jean-Jacques Annaud, John H. Williams, and Iain Smith, *Seven Years in Tibet.*
15. Barbara De Fina, *Kundun.*
16. Paul Wagner, *Windhorse.*
17. "About *Windhorse.*"

criticisms prompted Nicholas Kristof to write a column in the *New York Times* that invited readers to air any grievances they might have over the U.S. media coverage of the event. He refused to fully endorse these criticisms, however, pointing out that the Chinese, not unlike Americans, tend to be oblivious to "how [their] own country is perceived abroad" and how their nationalism negatively impacts ethnic others.[18]

Kristof's statement is not unfair. Chinese-language writers are not immune from one-sided criticism. Their comments on race relations in the United States are hardly ever placed in the context of race relations in China. Writings by new immigrants from the PRC, which started flourishing in the mid-1980s and quickly reached Chinese-speaking audiences on both sides of the Pacific, often center on the problem of racial discrimination in the United States, a theme also explored in many of the Chinese American writings that have been translated into Chinese (Kingston, Chin, etc.). While Chinese immigrant writings from the 1980s and early 1990s tended to focus on the vicissitudes of immigrant struggles to survive, since then we have seen a slew of more assertive writings that consciously explore and critique the politics of race in American culture.[19] Shi Yu's novella *Daofeng xia de mangdian* [The blind spot beneath the scalpel], published in 2006, is set in Dallas, where a female immigrant Chinese plastic surgeon is scapegoated in an inexplicable surgical accident.[20] The novella shows that both her race and gender make her an easy target for the false accusation of medical malpractice, cranked up to protect the real culprits, who turn out to be powerful political figures. It devotes a few passages to making the point that the female doctor's experience illustrates the various symptoms of the marginalization of the Chinese in American society, which has contributed to the development of an ethnic Chinese consciousness. The film *Guasha*, which became one of the best-received films in China in 2001 and was adapted into an eponymous novel in the same year, depicts a Chinese immigrant couple in St. Louis who find themselves at the center of a lawsuit after an American doctor mistook a traditional Chinese treatment, *guasha*, performed on the couple's child, for a form of physical abuse.[21] The couple's American dream is

18. Nicholas Kristof, "Calling China."

19. The most influential work in the early type of Chinese immigrant writings is Glen Cao's novel *Beijing Ren zai Niuyue* [A Beijinger in New York]. It was adapted into a TV drama in China in 1993 and translated into English in the same year), which tells of a Chinese musician couple trying to striking it rich in New York. The novel offers a formulaic message that pits the East against the West, family stability against individualistic struggles for business success, social status, and sexual gratification, which reinforce familiar narratives about divides.

20. Shi Yu, *Daofeng xia de mangdian*.

21. Xiaoping Wang, *Guasha* [The guasha treatment]; Wang Zhongjun, *Guasha* [The guasha

put on hold as they grapple with cultural prejudices against Chinese notions of medicine and family. These popular narratives, among many other examples, commonly feature an enterprising or accomplished Chinese immigrant trying to penetrate the higher echelons of American society. If American representations of minority issues in China, especially those in Tibet, construct the image of the American humanitarian spy, Chinese American and Chinese immigrant depictions of racial discrimination in the United States proffer a Chinese counterpart. The Chinese spy is of course a prominent figure in American politics,[22] but in popular Chinese-language writings and films about the Chinese experience in the United States, the trope of the Chinese "spy" takes the alternative form of a struggling immigrant who uncovers the hidden prejudices and racial barriers in American society in a process of voluntary or forced assimilation. These popular representations are not unrelentingly critical, as they often portray the United States as a veritable land of freedom and opportunities; the film *Guasha,* for example, ends with the American prosecutor's realization of his mistake and the reversal of a court order separating the child from his father, signaling the possibility of cross-cultural understanding. Nevertheless, disaffection with anti-Asian and other forms of racism in these texts seldom leads to a broader critique of the workings of racial and ethnic difference in China or other national contexts.

Treasure of Khan and *Lang Tuteng* have much in common with the popular texts just listed and, by openly juxtaposing the United States and China, make explicit the impulse toward a negative mode of comparison that underlies the other texts. This impulse registers in the two novels in a modulated form, for neither simply reduces the other nation into a foil for one's own. They instead express certain ambivalence toward both the United States and China for the way they handle ethnic and international relations in pursuing economic and national security interests. This modulation, however, is carefully circumscribed. Ultimately, the novels neutralize their own critique by detaching the object of their critique from imperialist excess, while projecting it onto the other nation. The U.S.–China comparisons staged in the novels remain shackled in unproductive negativity. Both authors deserve a close look in this chapter for their complex, though perhaps unsophisticated, maneuvers.

---

treatment].

22. The most widely known case is that of Los Alamos physicist Wen Ho Li, who was accused of espionage in 1999 but eventually pleaded guilty to the lesser charge of mishandling computer files. In 2005, a federal judge threw out charges against Katrina Leung, another high-profile Chinese American, for taking classified documents. Also see Gertz.

Treasure Unwanted

Clive Cussler has authored more than thirty-six adventure novels, most of which appeared on the *New York Times* bestseller list when first published. *Treasure of Khan* was the nineteenth installment of a popular series that centers on the heroic deeds of Dirk Pitt, a marine engineer and adventurer. The Dirk Pitt series blends several subgenres that fall under adventure, frequently interweaving political intrigue, treasure hunting, wreckage excavation, exploration of exotic locales, and male romance. In a way, it bears out the worldly tradition of American genre fiction. As Bruce Robbins has argued, it is in such popular genres as the adventure novel, science fiction, and the political thriller that "the planet as a totality has become widely perceptible" to American readers.[23] Pitt, the protagonist, often finds himself triumphing, through daring and technological acumen, over villains bent on diabolical, world-harming schemes. The series, however, is notable among American adventure novels for its unapologetic political overtones that betray the surprising endurance of the East–West opposition as a dominant cultural trope. Several parts of the series have Pitt defend American national security against the threat posed by rogue regimes and terrorist or criminal organizations originating in East Asia. They parade a set of orientalist figures and narrative conventions that can be traced back to the pulp fiction and comic strips of the 1930s, including, in particular, Buck Rogers's struggle to rid the future world of Han/Mongol hordes and Flash Gordon's battles with warlord Ming the Merciless on the planet Mongo. In *Dragon* (1990), for example, Dirk Pitt defeats a group of terrorists seeking to restore Japan's imperial glory and destroy the U.S. economy by planting nuclear bombs on American soil. *Flood Tide* (1997) has Pitt rescue illegal immigrants from a Chinese tycoon based in Hong Kong and race against the Chinese government to locate the fictional sunken ship containing the lost bones of the Peking Man (an example of the *Homo Erectus* excavated in Zhoukoudian, China, during the first half of the twentieth century), which can purportedly be used to bolster the chauvinist view that the human race originated in China rather than Africa. *Black Wind* (2007), the installment immediately preceding *Treasure of Khan*, revolves around Pitt's battle with a North Korean secret agent who, with the help of a Japanese communist terrorist group, plots to wage a biological war on the United States as a way of pressing for the reunification of the Korean peninsula.

Treasure of Khan exemplifies this political strain in Cussler, but also

23. Bruce Robbins, "The Worlding of the American Novel," 15.

places an interesting twist on it. Pitt has defended American interests not only against foreign threats but also against what the novel implies as the compromising of the nation's claim to a liberal tradition in both domestic and international realms. Published at a critical juncture, when American power and moral status in the world were both undermined, I argue, the novel registers an eagerness to restore the nation, as well as the adventure genre, to a former state of moral certitude. The seasoned American hero who frequently intervenes in the politics of other countries while defending his own is subjected in the novel to some scrutiny, the legitimacy of his actions implicitly challenged but ultimately affirmed as they are distinguished from the imperialist quests that his antagonists, including a fictional China, engage in.

In *Treasure of Khan,* as in Cussler's earlier novels, Dirk Pitt works for a government agency named the National Underwater and Marine Agency (NUMA), which has an eponymous real-life counterpart that depends mostly on royalties from Cussler's books. Having recently been promoted to head the agency, Pitt now appears in Siberia, on a Russian research vessel, involved in a joint Russian–American scientific survey of Lake Baikal's uncharted current flows. Pitt and his American and Russian colleagues detect an underwater landslide that sends huge killer waves across the lake toward the fishing village on the shore. Pitt and his friend Al Giordino rescue from the waves the occupants of an oil survey vessel, employed by a Mongolian oil company called Avarga Oil Consortium. During the night following the rescue, however, the members of the oil survey team are abducted by mysterious agents working for the owner of Avarga Oil, Tolgoi Borjin. After some detective work, Pitt and Giordino find their way to Borjin's headquarters and discover that Borjin has been using a German device that creates sound waves to produce seismic waves deep underwater, which can then be "recorded and processed by computer modeling to develop a subsurface image."[24] It is revealed that Borjin uses this technology to do two things: first, search for oil-trapping geographical formations under the sea; second, induce artificial earthquakes to destroy major terminals of crude oil, such as Ras Tamura in Saudi Arabia, so as to raise the value of his own oil export. Eventually, Pitt and Giordino infiltrate Bjorjin's palace for the second time, destroy the earthquake device along with the palace, and succeed in rescuing surviving members of the oil survey team. In a final one-on-one showdown, Pitt kills Borjin after luckily dodging death at the hands of his enemy, therefore averting a "global depression" that can result from the oil panic that Bjorjin sought to create.[25]

24. Clive Cussler, with Dirk Cussler, *Treasure of Khan,* 403.
25. Ibid., 539.

Walter Nash points out that every action-packed thriller involves a problem "big enough" for the hero to solve.[26] I would argue, however, that it inevitably presents itself with an even bigger problem, namely, how to prevent the hero from turning into a villain in the process of solving a specific problem.[27] In *Treasure of Khan,* where the specific problem confronting the hero—how to stem the perpetuation of the evils of empire in the contemporary period—is a deeply political one, and the accompanying meta-problem has particularly higher stakes. How does Dirk Pitt avoid, in the process of fighting the oil tycoon Borjin, turning into a de facto agent for the American quest for foreign sources of energy? The novel accomplishes this task in two related ways. First, it presents the hero as only partially representative of the U.S. government. Second, it defends the U.S. government itself against the charge that it engages in imperialist practices motivated by energy needs by imagining an alternative, foreign-oil-independent America and distinguishing it firmly from the various forms of empire imagined in the novel. The construction of an alternative America is simultaneously a critique of the real America and a reassertion of America's claim to liberal political ideals.

In its real-life version, NUMA is not affiliated with the U.S. government. As advertised on its website, NUMA is a "501C3 non-profit, volunteer foundation" specializing in "preserving [the American] maritime heritage through the discovery, archaeological survey and conservation of shipwreck artifacts."[28] The foundation's projects include identifying shipwrecks and other historically significant artifacts (including cruise liners, passenger liners, freighters, gunboats, ironclads, and downed aircraft lost in wars, including the Civil War and World War II, among others), usually off the east coast of America and along transatlantic routes. The fictional version of NUMA, as we see in *Treasure of Khan,* extends its arms not only across the Pacific but into central and northern Asia as well. As a government agency, the fictional NUMA embarks on maritime projects that are shown to be central to the American national interest. Its members, however, act as often on their own counsel as on government orders, symbolically maintaining a certain critical distance from the various evils and inefficiencies associated with the government. Pitt and Giordino, for instance, decide to enter Borjin's palace

---

26. Walter Nash, *Language in Popular Fiction,* 68.

27. The best existing studies of popular fiction present their subject as formally innovative narratives that address in complex "serious" literature and surrounding cultural discourses through intense intertexuality. See Roberts, Nash, and Harriett Hawkins, *Classics and Trash.* For studies of the psychological and sociological dimensions of the experience of reading popular fiction, see Janice Radway, *A Feeling for Books.*

28. "About NUMA."

for the second time without contacting the local American embassy because they believe that "[d]iplomacy ain't going to work in this case."[29]

If the novel's heroes are NUMA and the U.S. government, its "bad guys" are outmoded or disintegrating empires and weak states hijacked by oligarchic power. The novel opens with a long prologue that juxtaposes two historical vignettes. The first is a description of the Mongols' attack on Hakata Bay, Japan, in 1281, when the Mongol empire reached its zenith. The Mongols were defeated by the Japanese counterattack, miraculously aided by a sudden storm, to which the Japanese would later refer as *"kami"* (the divine wind). The crushing defeat that led to the decline of the Mongol empire in the opening vignette is followed by a tale that symbolizes the resurrection of this imperial legacy. It is set in the 1930s, during the early stages of the Sino–Japanese war. A fictional British archaeologist, Leigh Hunt, is heading an excavation project in the city of Shang-du (in northern China), the location of the relics of Genghis Khan's Palace of Great Harmony. Hunt literally stumbles upon the long-lost map for the treasure buried at the tomb of Genghis Khan. Although Hunt seeks to take possession of the map, it is stolen by his local Mongol assistant Tsendyn, which Hunt does not realize until right before his death in a plane crash on his way from Shang-du to Ulanbataar (Ulan Bator). Tsendyn, as it turns out in the novel, passed the secret map on to his son, none other than the evil Borjin. The unearthing of the secret map sets in motion the main plot of the novel, serving clearly as the novel's metaphor for the persistence of empire into contemporary times.[30] The death of Hunt sounds an ironic elegy to British colonialism in Asia, while Tsendyn and his offspring, the genealogically "legitimate" heirs of Khan, appropriate and extend the heritage of the Mongol empire in what the novel portrays as a perverse manner. We learn later in the novel that the excavation of Khan's treasure enables the rise of Borjin's oligarchic power in present-day

---

29. Cussler, *Treasure of Khan*, 405.

30. How to define empire has become an unavoidably contentious matter in the contemporary academy. For a useful overview of premodern empires, see Susan Alcock et al., eds., *Empires.* The edited volume allows for diverging definitions of empire, which may or may not take the Roman polity of the first century C.E. as the archetype of all empires (Alcock, 125). Some of the contributing authors, however, prefer a more detailed, narrower definition. See Barfield and Schreider, for example, who define empires in terms of specific attributes, including being "organized to handle [cultural] diversity" and "[maintaining] sovereignty over all people and territories in their realms" (Alcock, 71). Empire, of course, has continued on from premodernity. Modern, or capitalism, imperialism of the late nineteenth and early twentieth century gave way, after the age of decolonization, to the American empire and what Hardt and Negri, in their work *Empire,* describe as the deterritorialized, post–Fordist Empire that cannot be equated with the power of one sovereignty state. China, in the meantime, is often seen as an anomalous relic of premodern, territorial empires that has lurched into the post–Cold War era.

Mongolia, allowing him to go as far as controlling Mongolia's foreign policies. Borjin had discovered the precise location of Khan's tomb and had built the headquarters of Avarga Oil, or his "palace," at the site. He has been selling parts of the treasure to foreign buyers to finance his oil exploration. Coveting oil reserves in Inner Mongolia, an ethnic autonomous region in present-day China that was divided from Mongolia, or the Mongolian People's Republic, when the latter achieved independence from Republican China (with the aid of the Soviets) in 1921, Borjin utilizes the German device to destroy major oil terminals in the world to create a severe pinch on China's oil import. Having achieved that, Borjin claims to have access to rich oil reserves that he is willing to sell to the Chinese if they allow Inner Mongolia to secede from China and reunite with Mongolia. In an unlikely turn of the plot, Borjin acts as a "broker" between the Chinese and Mongolian governments, arranging for the "Mongolian Autonomous Republic"—Cussler's name for the "Inner Mongolian Autonomous Region"—to rejoin "its rightful place as part of the greater Mongolia."[31] The Chinese, then, are virtually giving up a vast territory for oil that will come from this very place. The novel attributes a kind of ironic justice to Borjin's shenanigan. After their first encounter with Borjin, Pitt and Giordino narrowly escape his palace and wander unknowingly into the Gobi desert surrounding it. They become acquainted with migrants from Inner Mongolia, pushed out by the "Chinese bureaucrats" who had commandeered all the Mongolian land "without regard to its natural balance."[32] Through Pitt and Giordino's observations, the novel critiques the PRC's policy toward Inner Mongolia, for the insufficient autonomy it offers and its disrespect for the nomadic culture of the Mongols. It is only fair that they lose Inner Mongolia. Within the same sequence, Pitt and Giordino also take a jibe at the Soviets, mentioning that Russia dominated Mongolia's cultural and ideological identity for most part of the twentieth century.[33] China and the Soviet Union are both presented in the novel as outmoded empires that have disintegrated or are doomed to fall apart.

Significantly, *Treasure of Khan* does not present Borjin as someone righting modern colonial wrongs committed by both the West and Mongolia's neighboring empires. Borjin, the villain, clearly uses the rhetoric of Mongolian nationalism as a cloak for his own pursuit of power. Punishing both Borjin and his opponents, the novel attacks what it perceives as contemporary forms of empire (modern China, the Soviet Union, and Borjin's nonstate oil empire) for their pursuit of economic and cultural dominance, both symbol-

31. Cussler, *Treasure of Khan*, 275.
32. Ibid., 321.
33. Ibid., 334.

ized in the novel by the images of drilling and archeological excavation. The power struggle between what the novel considers to be lingering territorial empires and organized criminal networks that take root in weak states, represented by Mongolia in this case, may very well be read as a projection of the post-9/11 American obsession with global terrorism unto China.

Juxtaposed with the evil empires of the novel's post–Cold War world is the perfect liberal nation represented by the fictional America. At the end of the novel, the president of Mongolia extends his gratitude to Pitt and the rest of the NUMA team for "rescuing Genghis for all posterity."[34] The president also takes Pitt's advice that, once the government starts to collect revenues from the new oil fields developed in Inner Mongolia, which China has irreversibly acceded to Mongolia, the profit should "go to the people who need it most."[35] As the president puts it, "Indeed, we've taken a lesson from your own state of Alaska. A portion of the revenues will be distributed to every man, woman, and child in the country. The remainder will support the state's expansion of health, education, and infrastructure. Borjin has taught us that not a dime of profits will end up in the hands of an individual, I can assure you."[36] The president's speech here projects an idealized image of American nationalism as a template for Mongolia to follow. The fictional America here reconciles a New Deal era commitment to social welfare with the more socially conservative belief in small government. It is a perfect blend, in other words, of pre- and post-Reagan America.[37] It is an ideal embodiment of liberal nationalism, underlined by a state of equilibrium between justice and equality on the one hand and freedom and individual rights on the other. It has figured out, miraculously, how to employ state power to the benefit of the redistribution of wealth while containing the power within certain limits. The oil drilling in Alaska, unlike Borjin's plans to drill in Inner Mongolia, is romanticized in the novel, presented as a condition for this liberal nationalism. It is an alternative kind of drilling that enhances, through the mediation of the government, the well-being of the entire nation rather than special interests. We can see that, even as the practices of excavation and drilling figure in the novel as

34. Ibid., 536.
35. Ibid., 537.
36. Ibid., 537–538.
37. It is commonly agreed upon that the modern U.S. welfare state was established with the passage of the Social Security Act in the 1930s. See Joel Blau, *Dynamics of Social Welfare History in the United States.* New Deal liberalism gave way to a more muted form of liberalism in the Cold War era, reinvigorated through the Great Society programs in the 1960s. Since 1969, however, reactions against the Great Society programs have largely prevailed, and, as a result, "the potential for an activist social welfare policy and an expansive social work practice has shrunk" (Blau, 274).

metaphors for the continuation of the legacies of a premodern empire in the contemporary period, they become something else when associated with the operations of NUMA, the various levels of government in the U.S, and U.S. allies. The same operations come to signify scientific research, the exposure of historical "truth," and, as we have seen, the redistribution of resources, thus indicating substantial differences between contemporary configurations of empire and what NUMA and the United States stand for in the novel.

The question of drilling for oil in Alaska is directly addressed in earlier parts of the novel. After the destruction of several key oil terminals in the world at the hands of Borjin's minions, the novel moves to a Goldman Sachs conference room, where a few analysts discuss the impact of a possible "oil shock" on the American economy.[38] Oil markets specialist Jan Clayton lauds the previous administration's approval of drilling in the Arctic National Wildlife Refuge (ANWR), which had been allowed to "[run] at full capacity."[39] He expresses the belief that, along with an expanded Strategic Petroleum Reserve, oil drilling in ANWR helps defend the country from fluctuations on the world oil market, which the novel presents as vulnerable to disruption by criminal and terrorist networks. Through the Goldman Sachs passage, the novel takes a questionable stand on the thorny issue of access to oil reserves in ANWR. Drilling for oil in Alaska's wilderness preserve has remained a political controversy since the 1979 oil shock, and, as of today, no plans for drilling have actually been approved. The novel, as we can see, justifies its implicit advocacy for opening ANWR for oil drilling by exaggerating its importance for national security. The president in the novel is a "no-nonsense populist from Montana," aided by a wise vice president who had formerly headed NUMA.[40] Upon hearing the news of the destruction of several oil terminals in the Middle East (all as a result of Borjin's sabotage), the president immediately decides to call for voluntary gas rationing and announce the possibility of instituting mandatory fuel rationing, besides raising the terrorist threat advisory for all U.S. ports. The vice president, in the meantime, points out confidently that the fully operating "Alaska pipeline" will relieve the impact of oil shortage on the domestic market even though it cannot affect the global price of oil significantly.[41]

The novel's proposal for strengthening the ability of the United States to defend itself against global oil crises closely follows the Bush energy policy, announced in May 2001, which included a proposal to increase domestic

38. Cussler, *Treasure of Khan,* 175.
39. Ibid., 176.
40. Ibid., 366.
41. Ibid., 367.

oil production by initiating oil drilling in ANWR.[42] It also echoes a statement that President Bush issued later in 2001 that directed the Department of Energy to fill the Strategic Petroleum Reserve to its 700 million barrel capacity.[43] As Michael Klare points out, however, these measures had an almost negligible role in increasing America's independence from foreign oil and its ability to weather massive disruptions of the supply flow. The ideology of energy "independence," as expounded by the Bush administration, was no more than a "mask for our continuing dependence on imported energy," a state that in turn made dangerous foreign commitments inevitable.[44] Cussler's novel makes minimal concessions to this criticism by having its own populist president exhort voluntary and mandatory gas rationing but otherwise shows little concern for the disastrous inadequacies of the Bush policy that it promotes. The American energy policy presented in the novel, then, involves a set of inversions. The measures that served as a mask for America's deepening dependence on foreign oil figure as an essential contribution to national self-sufficiency. The United States becomes a victim of terrorist attacks on oil terminals *despite* its drive to achieve energy independence rather than an aggressor waging preemptive wars to secure means of satisfying its addiction to imported oil. These inversions suppress the entire history since 9/11, driving the novel toward a groundless political fantasy. Its restoration of American innocence can be read as an act of profound disavowal, indicating a deep anxiety over the ways in which the excess of the Bush administration's foreign policy after 9/11 affected the nation's political and moral status in the world.

The novel's anxiety is not simply of a political nature. It is also generic. If what characterizes the Dirk Pitt series is the hero's tireless defense of national interests and global peace against evil governments, organizations, and individuals, it is difficult to continue the Manichean politics of the series in an era of increased multipolarity, in both political and moral terms. Written at a time when American hegemony hurtled to a close in the smoke and fog of the Iraq War, therefore, *Treasure of Khan* took it upon itself to retell the story of oil and U.S. foreign entanglements. In this particular installment, Dirk Pitt and his NUMA colleagues are protecting America from not only foreign threats but the collapse of its self-perception as a civilizing, democratizing force as well. In restoring an idealized image of the United States, they are also defending the moral foundation of politicized adventure novels such as the ones that they themselves populate.

42. Klare, *Oil and Blood*, 15.
43. "President Orders Strategic Petroleum Reserve Filled."
44. Klare, *Blood and Oil*, 185–86.

As they proceed to fulfill their political and generic roles, the novel's heroes come to embody a limited version of liberal internationalism that harkens to the Wilsonian tradition. By helping Mongolia strengthen its democratic system, members of NUMA are practicing, in the most direct and literal way possible, the central Wilsonian principle of promoting liberal nationalism around the world. As terrorist disruptions of global oil supply are intertwined in the novel with conflicts between various territorial and nonterritorial empires, American interventions, as figured here, function to defend liberal nationalism against imperial forces. The novel taps into the Wilsonian tradition, arguably, to emphasize the idealist (as opposed to realpolitik) underpinnings of the history of American intervention in foreign countries and thus help to cast this history and, by extension, the premise of adventure novels like itself, as morally legitimate. Meanwhile, though the novel remains passionately attached to the comforting notion of American moral leadership in the world, it implies a pragmatic acknowledgment of the need to limit the level and scale of intervention. NUMA's involvement with restoring order and democracy in Mongolia is nothing but a fortunate accident, which started innocently with a survey project on Lake Baikal conducted in collaboration with Russian scientists. With the lives of the members of the abducted research team hanging in the balance, Dirk Pitt proceeds swiftly with his rescue plan without consulting any government officials other than NUMA's own technicians and scientists. He dismisses the idea of an expanded role for the government as inefficient at best ("would take days, if not weeks" to get off ground) and possibly risky (would cause an unnecessary "international incident").[45] Against the backdrop of the Iraq War and American military intervention throughout the post–Cold War years, Pitt's remarks read like an argument for small-scale, low-level global activism for democracy, conceivably an alternative mode of intervention, and for the continuing relevance of the adventure novel as a genre for imagining possible circumstances and means of such activism.

In staging a moderate form of liberal internationalism aimed at safeguarding liberal nationalism worldwide, *Treasure of Khan* converges, in part, with Francis Fukuyama's notion of "realistic Wilsonianism" in *America at the Crossroads*.[46] Distancing himself from the Bush administration's neoconservative foreign policy (which he sees as a perversion of neoconservatism), Fukuyama argues for maintaining American power in the post–Cold War "unipolar world" by crossing Wilsonian liberal idealism with political

45. Cussler, *Khan's Treasure*, 406, 433.
46. Francis Fukuyama, *America at the Crossroads*, 9.

realism.[47] To this end, Fukuyama argues against U.S. involvement in forced regime change through preemptive war on both moral and practical grounds. Though the United States should actively engage in supporting democracy around the world, it should do so in more prudent and internationally legitimated ways. If Fukuyama's well publicized defection from the hawkish unilateralism of the first Bush term is an attempt to "reconcile competing schools of U.S. foreign policy: neoconservatist, realist, liberal internationalist, and nationalist or Jacksonian," its eclectic quality resembles the ambiguous, oscillating politics of best-selling adventure novels like *Treasure of Khan*.[48] The novel presents NUMA as a participant in a semi-governmental version of Fukuyama's ideal of a measured, realist Wilsonian internationalism. As a highly autonomous government organization engaged in multilateral scientific collaboration, NUMA practices a kind of informal internationalism. At the same time, it works closely with the American government to coax other states (Mongolia in this case) into embracing or advancing a Western-style democratic system and allying themselves with the American interest.

If the novel's version of U.S. internationalism emphasizes the principles of liberal nationalism, its imagining of U.S. nationalism takes into consideration the ways in which the nation is embedded in world history. The novel not only emphasizes energy independence as a way of avoiding foreign policy with imperialist undertones but also goes out of its way to foreground transnational strands in American history, thereby presenting the United States as a multicultural nation that acknowledges and accepts its own heterogeneity. The novel's imagining of American pluralism can be seen in part in how it presents Hawaii. Hawaii first appears in the novel's opening vignette, which links the history of the landlocked Mongol empire to a web of sea adventures across the Pacific. During the Hakata Bay attack in 1281, the flagship of the Mongol fleet, captained by a fictional Mongol general Temur, was blown out to the sea and eventually drifted to Hawaii. The Mongol general then asked Mahu, an experienced Hawaii sailor, to help repair the canoe and bring him back to the Mongol empire, which had by then occupied Northern China. Mahu accompanied Temur to China and then sought to return to Hawaii on board a big Chinese junk, which, as the novel reveals later, sank in the Pacific. The defeat of the Mongol fleet by the storm certainly prefigures the ways in which contemporary empires find themselves at the mercy of natural forces, like earthquakes, especially when they are enhanced by technology. More important, Temur's adventures frame Hawaii as more than simply an

---

47. Ibid., 189. For an explanation of what "neoconservatism" means to Fukuyama, see Robert Jervis's review of *America at the Crossroads*.

48. Michael Allen's review of *America at the Crossroads*, 46.

American territory; instead, the islands figure in the novel as a station on the various travel and trade routes across the Pacific, a crucial component of what has now come to be known as the Asia Pacific.

At the same time, however, Hawaii also figures as a spatial symbol of the nation, to be protected forcefully by a strong federal government determined to uphold national security. Later in the novel, NUMA members Dirk and Summer (Dirk Pitt's son and daughter) discover traces of the ancient, sunken Chinese junk, along with some of the treasure it carried. This finding brings them into a confrontation with Borjin's minions, who are also hunting for the sunken ship. Summer, however, is unaware of the implications of this discovery; she is amazed that it "had caused a sensation" and had drawn media representatives to her "like vultures."[49] For NUMA, then, excavating sunken ships is a scientific, nonprofit endeavor far removed from Borjin's evil schemes. This contrast suggests that, while the transnational history of Hawaii needs to be excavated and studied, a goal that NUMA follows, this restorative effort is not intended to throw into question the U.S. annexation and exploitation of the islands. The novel's representation of Hawaii, in other words, serves to bolster the American claim to being a diverse, multicultural nation rather than, as it very well should, remind the reader of U.S. imperialism since the turn of the twentieth century. Hawaii's centrality to U.S. national security and its inseparability from the union are simply assumed in the novel. Realizing that Borjin's assistants have induced an artificial earthquake to blow apart the lava that seals the treasure from the sunken Chinese junk, a NUMA agent notifies the White House of the situation as a grave threat to national security. The vice president immediately orders a couple of F-15s stationed at a naval base in Oahu to the earthquake's epicenter. The novel's cavalier reference to Hawaii's naval bases invokes the history of American imperialist incursions into the Asia Pacific, which, as Chalmers Johnson puts it, constitute a 1989 parallel of the "expansionist agendas" openly espoused after 9/11.[50] Yet the vice president's military order is framed as a purely defensive act that symbolically fends off the tentacles of an evil power secretly aspiring to "[restore] the riches and glory of the Golden Clan" of Genghis Khan.[51] The novel's America is yet again idealized and insulated from the contradictions and tensions plaguing the America outside the text. It becomes an embodiment of a realist but robust form of liberalism that simultaneously stresses cultural pluralism in the domestic sphere and the

49. Cussler, *Treasure of Khan*, 368.
50. Chalmers Johnson, *Sorrows of Empire*, 2.
51. Cussler, *Khan's Treasure*, 278.

extension of this pluralism into foreign policy to promote nongovernmental scientific collaborations and morally legitimate interventions.

Clearly, this idealized United States is the novel's response to the post-9/11 disaffection with the imperialist nature of U.S. power, which had far exceeded the confines of the leftist academy. The novel expresses and disguises its anxiety over the decline of America's political and moral status in the world through a forceful reassertion of "quintessential" American virtues, including the tradition of Wilsonian internationalism and the ideal of national self-sufficiency (a rational, morally justifiable isolationism), which acquire an enhanced luster by being set against the apparently unjust practices espoused by the other political players in the novel. Ultimately, the novel's projection of a fantasized America does not so much reconcile the tensions between liberal (inter)nationalism and its imperialist underbelly as displace them onto other states, including the convenient target of China. The facile, or false, reconciliation staged in the novel provides the sense of moral closure that the reader expects from the adventure genre. The reader sees America and the world revolving around it threatened then redeemed. Although this chapter does not involve a study of Cussler's readership, the novel's popularity, to a certain extent, confirms the efficacy of its conciliatory impulse in generating textual pleasure.

Wolves on the Frontier

Clive Cussler is not a stranger to the Chinese audience either. Five of his Dirk Pitt novels have been translated into Chinese, including *Treasure of Khan,* the translation of which was published in 2008.[52] The Chinese translation, predictably, deletes the entire side plot of the Chinese government's secession of Inner Mongolia in exchange for oil.[53] Some of the more high-profile translations, such as that of Khaled Hosseini's *Kite Runner,* underwent even more stringent scrutiny. The novel's description of the Soviet-influenced communist regime in Kabul during the Cold War, for example, was removed for fear that it might trigger unwelcome reflections on some of the CCP's policies in China during the same period. At around the same time, however, a Chinese novel that invokes the historical Mongol empire and critiques the PRC's policy toward Inner Mongolia obtained surprising popularity across

52. The others are *Raise the Titanic* (1976), *Dragon* (1990), *Polar Shift* (2005), and *Inca Gold* (1991).

53. Yao hong et al., trans., *Kehan de baozang* [Khan's treasure].

the country, which was then translated into a kind of international value rarely bestowed upon modern and contemporary Chinese literature.[54] Jiang Rong's novel *Lang Tuteng*, published in 2004, draws on the experiences the author had during the eleven years, from 1967 to 1978, that he spent in Inner Mongolia. He had traveled there at the height of the Cultural Revolution, when a great number of urban youths were sent to rural and remote areas in China under Chairman Mao's instruction for them to be reeducated from the peasants.[55] The autobiographically based narrator details the Han students' fascination with traditional Mongol nomadic culture and critiques the Chinese government for causing irreversible ecological destruction in the area and forcing upon the ethnic Mongols an agrarian mode of production. *Lang Tuteng* became an instant cultural sensation upon its publication, giving rise in China to many impassioned readings. While praises of the novel do not necessarily focus on the same aspect, many of its criticisms make the same argument that the novel fuels Chinese nationalism.[56] The startling success of the novel in China convinced Penguin to purchase the rights of its English translation, later titled *The Wolf Totem*. Some readers in the West remark admiringly, as the *Times* reviewer Mishra does, on the novel's daring critique of the Chinese government's ethnic and environmental policies, without noting how it also echoes the discourses of ethnic amalgmation and nationalism in contemporary China.[57] On the opposite side of the spectrum of critical

54. Penguin paid an advance of $100,000 for the worldwide rights of the English version of the novel, setting a record for the highest amount ever paid for the translation rights of a novel. See Jürgen Kremb, "A Wolf in Sheep's Clothing: Beijing's Unwanted Best Seller." The Chinese publishing industry, in fact, sought to make a positive example out of the marketing of the novel.

55. Zuoya Cao points out, in *Out of the Crucible*, that "More than two million students were transferred to rural areas" during 1969, after Chairman Mao issued the instruction for the "educated youth" to go to the countryside (4). The rustification campaign, which eventually saw more than "sixteen million" urban youth sent to the countryside, started in the 1950s, reached its climax at the end of the 1960s, and ended in 1977, when the Cultural Revolution ended.

56. For a brief summary of these criticisms, see Xu Xinjian, "Dangdai zhongguo de minzu shenfen biaoshu" [Articulations of national identity in contemporary China], 109. For a specific critique of the novel for appealing to the mass market with parochial nationalism, see Li Jianjun, "Zhenzu haishi wandou" [Pearls or peas].

57. See Timothy Weston, "A Defense of Jiang Rong's *Wolf Totem*"; Jonathan Mirsky, "A Decade in the Grasslands." One might wonder why such a critique of the Chinese government was allowed to stay in print in China. It would seem more of an anomaly if one realizes that the author of the novel, whose real name is Lü Jiaming, became involved in the 1989 student movements and was imprisoned for the involvement. He published the novel under the pseudonym Jiang Rong, in part, to avoid government censorship. Jiang's avoidance of public exposure, however, only partially explains why the novel did not receive any censorship from the Chinese government. More important, as I point out, the novel is often construed in China to be for Chinese nationalism rather than against the Chinese government.

reactions outside of China, the German sinologist Wolfgang Kubin criticized the book as "fascist."[58] This extreme criticism of the novel's nationalist slant, however, stretches the meaning of fascism beyond recognition and obscures why the novel could have resonated with so many readers in different cultural and national contexts. Existing readings of the novel, from both within and outside China, are well justified, but they tend to focus on one of its particular aspects, failing to recognize that what defines the novel is precisely its formal and political oscillation—its simultaneous staging *and* reconciliation of the conflict between national unity and minority interests. Just like *Treasure of Khan*, *Lang Tuteng* illuminates the complex workings of conciliatory multiculturalism through a double narrative movement: It endorses a masculinized, or muscular, nationalism while at the same time separating it from imperialist expansion, which the novel explicitly critiques. In both novels, the double narrative movement rests upon a comparative framework that juxtaposes the United States and China. While they might seem to be two unrelated texts, the two novels are now available, through the work of translation, in the same language in both the United States and China. Their convergence on the book markets of the two countries can be seen as a somewhat fortuitous literalization of their more substantive connections.

Lang Tuteng's protagonist and narrator Chen Zhen, like the author Jiang Rong, is a Han Chinese student sent to Inner Mongolia during the Cultural Revolution. Chen works closely with local herdsmen to protect herds of sheep from the packs of wolves hovering around the grasslands. He quickly develops a strong fascination with wolves. The novel provides several extended scenes showing the complex interactions among sheep, dogs, humans, and wolves on the grasslands, which coexist in symbiotic yet antagonist relationships. Chen illustrates that the local Mongols treat wolves as instructors and protectors rather than enemies. They respect the ecological function that the wolves serve in curbing the population of rodents and sheep that might damage the grasslands, acquire battle skills by learning from wolves, and hunt them methodically but with restraint. As Bilge, a local sage, puts it, "the grasslands will be gone without the wolves."[59] Chen reflects extensively on the Mongols' reverence for the wolf and attributes it to an ancient form of totemism that constitutes an important part of their metaphysical outlook.

---

58. See Wolfgang Kubin's interview with broadcaster *Deutsche Welle*. It was translated into Chinese and published on the Chinese edition of the *Deutsche Welle* online as "89 nian qianhou, zhongguo zuojia ziji beipan le wenxue" [Chinese authors betrayed literature since 1989].

59. Jiang Rong, *Lang Tuteng* [The wolf totem], 77. I use my own translation of quotes from *Lang Tuteng* throughout, but I have also been influenced by Goldblatt's translation in preparing my own.

The worship of the "wolf totem," Chen believes, continues to shape the Mongols' attitudes toward wolves in important ways. The delicate ecosystem of the grasslands, however, is severely threatened when unreasonable quotas for wool, wolf skins, and army horses are imposed on the Mongol herdsmen. While Inner Mongolia remains nominally an autonomous region, many Han Chinese and nonlocal Mongols have moved in to take charge of economic matters in Inner Mongolia. The Inner Mongolia Production and Construction Corps, a paramilitary organization with economic as well as defense functions, is established in the second half of the narrative. The leaders of the corps, none of whom has much sympathy for the Mongol belief in human–nature harmony and reverence for the wolf, ordered that all wolves be killed and all grasslands be exploited to their maximum capacity. At the end of the novel, plans are in the works to promote settlements on the grasslands, thus completely replacing the traditional nomadic culture with one that combines agriculture and ranching. The novel is concluded by an epilogue that brings us to the end of the 1990s, when the narrator and his friends return to Inner Mongolia after a twenty-year absence. The transition to settlements indicated at the end of the main narrative has materialized, making the narrator lament that the logic of "one system fits all areas" continues to (mis)guide China's economic policy toward Inner Mongolia.[60] The process of decolletivization, moreover, continues to fuel overdevelopment, as many Mongol households now rent out their pastures to nonlocal herders who abuse them with chilling indifference. Chen fears, as he tours the grasslands for the first time since he left for a big city, that a final ecological collapse is looming, despite the "false prosperity" created by overdevelopment.[61]

The novel can be read as a recent variation on what has come to be known as "*xungen wenxue*" (roots-seeking literature). In the history of contemporary Chinese literature, roots-seeking literature designates a group of narratives and poems that appeared in the middle and late 1980s, many of them by writers and intellectuals who had been recently exposed to folk or ethnic cultures in remote areas in China during the Cultural Revolution. These works foreground the living customs, cultural forms, and ethical values of isolated communities in the hinterlands or far-flung provinces that had barely been affected by forces of modernization. Even though, as a literary movement, roots-seeking literature tapered off toward the end of the 1980s, its political and aesthetic concerns continue to inform more recent narratives. The word "roots" is misleading here. The literary investments in

60. Ibid., 357.
61. Ibid., 359.

folk and ethnic cultures did not signal an outpouring of nostalgia toward pristine, premodern cultures in China; they were instead an intellectual and aesthetic response to the influx of modern Western thought and art forms in the period immediately after the Cultural Revolution. Roots-seeking literature focuses on the countryside as a way of tapping into what the authors believe to be the substrata of Chinese culture and thereby exploring alternative ways of imagining modernity and China's relationship to it.[62] It is also important to point out that the rise of roots-seeking literature coincided with a revived interest in ethnic cultures at the beginning of China's economic reform.[63] Some of the writers associated with roots-seeking literature are themselves members of ethnic minorities devoted to excavating marginalized cultural traditions.[64] Moreover, roots-seeking literature can be seen as a distant precursor to Chinese-language writings in the United States since the 1980s, which also involve unfamiliar locales in which Chinese culture acquires new meanings. Indeed, many recent Chinese immigrants who came to the United States after the Cultural Revolution describe their experience as *"yang cha dui,"* which means, literally, a transnational analogue of Chinese students' experience of being sent to toil in remote areas during the Cultural Revolution.[65] All these permutations of roots-seeking literature address, explicitly or implicitly, China's integration into economic and cultural globalization, providing different models for thinking through the interactions between what is "traditionally" Chinese and what might compel it to change. *Lang Tuteng* offers a perfect site for examining the intersections of the various aspects of roots-seeking literature. Unlike many recent overseas Chinese-language writings that foreground the Western/U.S. bias against the Chinese, the novel turns its attention to the conflicts between Han Chinese (agrarian) culture and Mongol (pastoral-nomadic) culture. The West, however, is not absent from the narrative. On the contrary, it is a constant presence that dictates the way through which the Han–Mongol conflicts are revolved.

62. Chen Sihe, *Zhongguo dangdai wenxue shi* [History of modern and contemporary Chinese literature], 277–81; Mark Leenhouts, "Culture against Politics." Leenhouts describes roots-seeking literature as a movement against cultural "iconoclasm" in modern Chinese history and the politicization of art under Mao (543).

63. See Ralph Litzinger, *Other Chinas*. Litzinger argues that, after the end of the Cultural Revolution in 1976, intellectuals throughout China were asked to "seek truth from facts" as a way of advancing the country's effort to modernize itself (2). The study of "local cultures and histories" was seen as part of this intellectual project (Litzinger, 2).

64. Chen, *Zhongguo dangdai wenxueshi* [History of modern and contemporary Chinese literature], chapter 16.

65. For an instance in which this term is applied to Chinese students and workers who have come to the U.S. since the early 1980s, see Jiang Zengpei, ed., Zhongguo liuxuesheng wenxue daxi [An anthology of literature by Chinese students overseas], 4.

The Han–Mongol conflicts are emblematized in the novel by recurrent battles between the wolf and the sheep, representing nomadic culture and agrarian culture, respectively. In the novel, the military success of the Mongol empire is attributed to the Mongols' entanglements with wolves, which are portrayed in the novel as intelligent, disciplined, and organized hunters that offer important lessons to their human rivals. Having witnessed a pack of wolves coordinate an ambush on a herd of gazelles, Chen Zhen hazards that wolves acted as "supreme military instructors" to Genghis Khan and the tribal leaders of other northern nomadic peoples.[66] The passive and witless sheep, on the other hand, is used in the novel as a metaphor for the Han Chinese, who, according to the author, can be "selfish, numbed, and cowardly" even when their own people are being slaughtered.[67] The culture of the sheep, Han agrarian culture, however, has imposed its will upon Mongol nomadic culture in contemporary China. In a move that echoes Cussler's criticism of China's policies in Inner Mongolia, the novel holds the Chinese government responsible for overherding and destroying the grasslands. At several places, Jiang explicitly points out that the Inner Mongolia Production and Construction Corps's management of the grasslands aimed, in a wrongheaded way, to put an end to the "primitive nomadic culture" and introduce agriculture to maximize land utility.[68] Wolves, along with insects and mice, are seen as a "plague" to eliminate.[69] Han agrarian culture has overpowered the traditional order of life on the grasslands not because of its superiority in spirit or courage but because of its unscrupulous use of modern technology. Toward the end of the novel, the officers of the Production and Construction Corps decide to use guns and jeeps to wipe out the entire wolf population, reducing the human–wolf combat romanticized continuously throughout the novel to nothing but "light entertainment" for the hunters.[70] The figure of the gun is a common trope emblematizing the encroachment of Western modernity upon China since the mid-nineteenth century. The nineteenth-century British attempt to open China to international trade, after all, has been seen as a quintessential example of "gunboat diplomacy." Here, however, this trope is employed to dramatize Han incursions upon the autonomy of ethnic minorities within China.

The author's critique of Han Chinese's destruction of Mongol culture and the natural environment from which it sprang, however, takes on a tone

---

66. Jiang, *Lang Tuteng*, 19.
67. Ibid., 205.
68. Ibid., 163.
69. Ibid., 298.
70. Ibid., 318.

completely different from that of Cussler's criticism of the Chinese government's exploitation of Inner Mongolia and consequently leads to a very different conclusion. For Jiang, the biggest problem with the denigration of
Mongol culture is the impoverishment of Han-dominated Chinese culture
in general, which the author links to the decline of China's position in the
world after reaching its apex during the Tang Dynasty. As Jiang puts it, China
frequently fell to non-Han rulers (including the Mongols) after this period
precisely because of an "enfeebled" disposition rooted in its agrarian culture.[71] By contrast, as we have seen, Mongol nomadic culture, the culture of
the wolf, is exalted as a foundation for Genghis Khan's empire. Reflections
on the different elements of the Chinese "national character" and its implications for China's relationship to the world are characteristic of roots-seeking
literature. *Lang Tuteng,* however, invents a new, wildly popular formula for
such reflections. It not only offers a rarely told story featuring humans and
wolves involved in both heated battles and passionate love affairs; it also creates a meticulous balance between critiquing what the novel perceives as the
flaws of Han Chinese culture and highlighting its mutability, its potential for
change and transformation through encounters with other cultures in China.

Far from arguing for Mongol independence (as Cussler does), Jiang
advocates for resolving Han–Mongol conflicts by welding the "warrior spirit"
of the Mongols with the "peaceful, toiling inclinations" of the Han.[72] The
novel, in fact, argues emphatically that this form of cultural welding is integral to the history of the Han, though this point has often been neglected,
to the detriment of Chinese culture as a whole. Each chapter of *Lang Tuteng*
is preceded by excerpts from historical writings that document the various
ways in which the Mongols, among other peoples of inner Asia, identified
with or had mystical encounters with the wolf. A number of these epigraphs
imply or state explicitly that this human–wolf affinity implicates the Han
Chinese as well because they are intimately connected to the other peoples
around them through a history of miscegenation and cultural intermingling.
These epigraphs were omitted from the translation, perhaps to streamline
the English text. This omission can obscure the history of Han–Mongol
interactions the author seeks to construct. Toward the end of the novel, Jiang
cites renowned Chinese historian Fan Wenlan's *Zhongguo Tongshi* [Complete
history of China] (1978): "The tribal name of Emperor Yan is Jiang . . . The
Jiangs descend from a branch of the Qiang, who traveled to the middle land
from the west."[73] Emperor Yan is known as one of the two ancestors of the

71. Ibid., 186.
72. Ibid., 196.
73. Ibid., 343.

Han (the other is Emperor Huang). This excerpt, therefore, is used to high-light the mixed origin of the Han Chinese—their genealogical connection to the Qiang suggests that the agrarian Han and nomadic non-Han peoples were inseparable at their inception. Throughout the book, the narrator Chen alludes to historical periods, including the long reign of the Mongols and Manchus, during which Han culture was infused with heavy doses of non-Han traditions. This quote traces this history of cultural interpenetration to a point of originary heterogeneity.

Jiang's representation of the Han–Mongol cultural confluence functions to challenge the received notion of the cultural supremacy of the Han Chinese. Although the novel recycles the Han-centric cliché that the Mongols lack a literary tradition, which makes them culturally "backward," it challenges Han-centrism by arguing that the Han Chinese have been continuously transformed, on both cultural and genealogical levels, by other peoples around them.[74] (This epigraph also hints at the origin of the nom de plume the author adopts for the novel, which combines Emperor Yan's tribal name with "*Rong*," a term that the Han used historically to refer to the Qiang.) One can find parallels of Jiang's view in recent studies of the historical interactions between the Han and nomadic peoples that traditionally inhabited the Eurasian steppe. According to Thomas J. Barfield, the historical empires established by nomads in Mongolia can be seen as "shadow empires" that prospered by "extorting vast amounts of wealth from China through pillage, tribute payments, border trade, and international reexport of luxury goods—not by taxing steppe nomads."[75] The term "shadow empires," however, does not simply connate a parasitic relationship. What Barfield finds is a pattern of symbiosis and interdependence between the nomad empires and the native dynasties in China. The unification and prosperity of the native Chinese dynasties benefited the corresponding nomadic empires through trade and various peace arrangements, and leaders of imperial confederacies would lend military assistance to declining Chinese dynasties "to protect them from domestic rebellions."[76] The Han Chinese officially deemed the nomadic empires "tributaries" at various points, not because they were actually subordinate but only to "disguise embarrassing facts about its relationship with the steppe."[77]

Lang Tuteng's rewriting of the history of Han–Mongol relations is not simply to make a historical point. As the narrative goes back and forth

74. Ibid., 61.
75. Thomas J. Barfield, "The Shadow Empires," 10.
76. Ibid., 22.
77. Ibid., 23.

between observations of present-day Inner Mongolia (from the Cultural Revolution to the late 1990s) and meditations on the historical Mongol empire, the historical Han–Mongol intermixing that the author emphasizes is also projected onto the future. It is a model that the author promotes for rebuilding ethnic relations in contemporary China, a point made abundantly clear through a number of didactic monologues attributed to the protagonist Chen Zhen. While the author's critique of the government's policies in Inner Mongolia may be sharp, the remedy he proposes—the notion of ethnic intermixing—meshes quite well, ironically, with government rhetoric on ethnic minorities. As we have seen in the Introduction and chapter 1, the PRC's policy toward ethnic minorities emphasizes the idea of *ronghe*, or amalgamation, a term that has garnered different meanings since the founding of the country. Its connotations range from the notion that Han and different nationalities will eventually dissolve the distinctions in their levels of economic and social development under socialism to a form of cultural pluralism informed by Western liberalism. The idea of ethnic amalgamation has served to enable and consolidate the unity of the Chinese nation under the CCP leadership. Uradyn E. Bulag makes the same argument in his essay "Yearning for 'Friendship,'" where he surveys changes in the depictions of the role that Mongol communists played in the anti-Japanese war in Chinese historiography. The more contemporary, post–Cultural Revolution accounts all emphasize the "indestructible revolutionary friendship" between the Mongols and the Han Chinese in their purportedly shared struggles against the Japanese, conveniently erasing the historical Mongol antagonism toward what Bulag explicitly calls "settler colonization" on the part of the Han.[78] This focus on cross-ethnic "friendships" in the official policy has also given rise to much research in China on the mutual penetration of Han and non-Han cultures throughout Chinese history, intended to counter the more conventional thesis of sinicization or assimilation.[79] Jiang's vision for ethnic relations in historical and contemporary China, though critical of the ways in which the government distorted the principle of amalgamation into a kind of forced uniformity, sits very well with the overall thrust of the official ethnic policy, which, as I have argued, can be seen as a Chinese version of conciliatory multiculturalism that is indispensable to the project of state nationalism.

78. Uradyn Bulag, "The Yearning for 'Friendship,'" 20.
79. For a review of historical research that complicates the thesis of sinicization since the 1990s, see Qi Meiqin, "Guanyu shinianlai 'hanhua' yiji xiangguan wenti yanjiu de kaochao" [A review of research on "sinicization" and related issues], 103–13. As Qi points out, this research harks back to the revisionary theories that the pre-eminent Chinese historian Chen Yinque raised as early as the 1940s (108–9).

At times, the novel's endorsement of Chinese nationalism is quite explicit, taking on a didactic and strident tone. It appears, at such moments, that the call for Han–Mongol amalgamation aims to strengthen China against Western powers that, for the author, possess the same fierceness as the Mongols. At several places, the author ventures the theory, through the protagonist Chen, that the Germanic peoples who played an important role in the transformation of Rome in the medieval period were nomadic, just like the Mongols.[80] To compete with Western powers that descend from the Germanic people, therefore, China should learn from the wolves within. In one of the more didactic passages in the novel, Chen makes this point in unmistakable terms during a discussion with his friends. As he puts it,

> The worship of the wolf totem goes back further than Confucianism, and has remained naturally resilient through the generations. . . . If the Chinese can exorcize what is rotten in Confucianism and transplant a seed of the wolf totem into what is left, then the ethos of the wolf totem can merge with such Confucian precepts as pacifism and education. This way, the Chinese character can be reshaped and China made strong again.[81]

Based on this and similar sections of the novel, some critics have read into the novel an imperialist impulse that historically and conceptually overlaps with nationalism. One of the harshest critics describes the novel as "a mediocre, vulgarized interpretation of the Nietzschean notion of the Will to Power."[82] To the critic, the novel endorses "power" and "hegemony," thus generating a misleading impression about China's expansionist ambitions.[83]

The novel, however, does not present this trumpeted nationalism as a Chinese imitation of a coveted Western model. Its emphasis on the masculinization of "national character" is quite deliberately balanced against its call for cultural amalgamation and coexistence. What the novel projects is thus a vision of a harmonious world order that mirrors, on a larger scale, cultural pluralism within a nation. At a few points, Bilge explains to Chen local herdsmen's reluctance to upset natural balance by killing too many wolves. He calls the grasslands the "big life," a self-sufficient ecosystem that encompasses many "small lives" often engaged in life and death battles.[84]

---

80. Jiang, *Lang Tuteng*, 109, 195.

81. Ibid., 253.

82. He Tongbin, "Wenming yu yexing de jitai hejie" [A perverse reconciliation of civilization and wilderness], 91.

83. Ibid., 91.

84. Jiang, *Lang Tuteng*, 149

Natural ecological balance is invoked in the novel as a metaphor for the paradoxical relations among different ethnicities, races, and nations, which coexist in a shared environment, alternating between interdependence and mutual antagonism. In one of his monologues, Chen realizes that the ears of a wolf are stiff and unbendable, prompting him to reflect on the Chinese expression of "grabbing the ox by its ears," which carries the imperialist connotation of subjugating the weaker races and peoples.[85] Chen is quick to note that "modern nations" should not engage in "subjugating and oppressing" other peoples, though, if a country is not equipped with the ability to grab others by their "ears," it will only make itself vulnerable to being grabbed by others.[86] Clearly, the novel seeks to reconcile its vision of a muscular Chinese nationalism with both a pluralist ethnic policy and a democratic, nonaggressive model of foreign policy. Jiang is arguing that the open-ended and yet strong Chinese nationalism that the novel promotes is necessary not only for defending the Chinese national interest but also for shaping a more equitable world order that subverts Western hegemony.

The delicate balance that the novel maintains between its admiration for and critique of Western powers is emblematized in its invocations of the figure of Jack London, often mentioned merely in passing in various reviews of the novel. Chen had carried to Inner Mongolia two big cases of books, some of which were prohibited by the Chinese government during the Cultural Revolution. Jack London is the only fiction writer specifically named as someone that Chen and his friends love to read. Chen mentions the novel *The Sea-Wolf* in passing and the short story "Love of Life" at some length, identifying the latter as one of Lenin's favorite stories.[87] The allusion to London's naturalist celebration of a primordial drive for life in the story figures here as an analogue of what Chen sees in nomadic Mongols and, by extension, in the sturdy, warlike peoples all over the world. Chen employs evolutionary language in explaining the superiority of the wolves, "a species that had survived millions of years of selection in an unimaginably inhospitable environment" that naturally "weeds out the unfit."[88] This evolutionary language, which bleeds into Chen's exaltation of Western powers, is reminiscent of the racialist ideas articulated in many of London's writings. London's progressive, socialist leanings, as critics have pointed out, are inseparable from his racialist notions regarding the physical and moral superiority of the white race over the Asiatics, a group often reduced in his writings to a

85. Ibid., 296.
86. Ibid., 297.
87. Ibid., 171.
88. Ibid., 296, 331.

symbol of the dehumanizing power of monopoly capitalism.[89] It is arguable that Jiang is implying a kind of symmetry between London's understanding of class and racial struggles in the United States at the turn of the twentieth century and his own understanding of ethnic relations in China and the country's position vis-à-vis Western powers a century later.

The author, however, is not oblivious to the ways in which he might implicate his own work in London's racism. Instead, he deftly separates his own position on nation, race, and ethnicity from London's. Though Jiang does not elaborate specifically on the significance of *The Sea-Wolf,* he does share this particular London novel's ambivalence toward Nietzschean ethics, qualifying his endorsement of social Darwinism with an emphasis on interdependent coexistence. Most notably, Jiang consciously alludes to the notion of the "Yellow Peril," the title of an infamous essay London wrote in 1904 when he traveled to Manchuria as a war correspondent, to emphasize the disastrous effects of the ways in which the Han Chinese "subsumed" the Mongols under their agrarian lifestyle.[90] Arguably, Jiang reinterprets the thesis of the "Yellow Peril" as the imperialist domination that the Han Chinese have achieved over ethnic minorities on the country's frontiers, thus implicitly critiquing both London's view of the Chinese and other East Asians as a menace to the Western world and the Han Chinese's treatment of ethnic others. The novel's apparent endorsement of social Darwinism and racism has disturbed some readers, as we can see in Kubin's "fascism" accusation, but such reactions miss a much larger point. The novel, in fact, uses the "Yellow Peril" trope as a launching pad for a critique of processes of racialization in both American and Chinese histories and a plea for China to embrace a robust but restrained nationalism that will place it on equal footings, in both moral and material terms, with Western countries, while at the same time contributing to the construction of a new, harmonious world order. The extraordinary murkiness and elasticity of the novel's politics has certainly played a crucial role in securing its popularity in both China and the West. More important, we can argue that the novel's reflections on international relations—China's relationship with London's America and other Western powers—not only extend the symbiotic model that it prescribes for Han–Mongol relations but also, in fact, play a constitutive role in shaping this model. For Jiang, the construction of a new world order requires that China

89. For an extensive discussion of racism in London's writings, see Colleen Lye, *America's Asia,* chapters 1 and 2. London's short stories "An Unparalleled Invasion" and "Goliah," for example, feature the Chinese as dehumanized slaves who, through mass migration, infest and threaten to overtake the U.S. and even the entire Western world.

90. Jiang, *Lang Tuteng,* 226. The essay in question is Jack London's "The Yellow Peril."

embrace the ideal of ethnic intermingling, so as to strengthen its "national character" while averting the racialist and imperialist practices of Western nations.

The ideal world order projected in *Lang Tuteng,* just like the fantasized America in *Treasure of Khan,* speaks to our times. It serves implicitly to project an image of China as a promoter of world harmony rather than a newly anointed global power concerned only with advancing its own interests, grabbing for energy and resources in unscrupulous ways. The political affiliation of the novel's perspective on the ideal international order and China's position in it is more plainly on view if we compare it with the Chinese government's formulations of its own foreign policy. Since the early 1990s, the government has frequently affirmed and updated the Five Principles of Peaceful Coexistence, established in the 1950s as a foundation for China's foreign policy, to assure the world of the Chinese government's intention to act as a nonaggressive, peacemaking member of the international community. We catch a glimpse of this official rhetoric in Hu Jintao's speech at Yale on April 22, 2006, the last day of the Chinese president's three-day visit to the United States. In the speech, President Hu explains how the current Chinese government approaches development and modernization (what has come to be known as the party's "Scientific Development Concept"), and how it views the issues that concern all cultures, including human dignity, social harmony, and world peace. Sprinkled throughout the speech are various references to China's commitment to helping to foster diversity and harmony in the world:

> The Chinese civilization has always given prominence to good neighborliness. The Chinese nation cherishes peace. In foreign relations, the Chinese have always believed that "the strong should not oppress the weak and the rich should not bully the poor" and advocated that "all nations live side by side in perfect harmony."
>
> The Chinese held that "one should be as inclusive as the ocean, which is vast because it admits hundreds of rivers" and called for drawing upon the strength of others. Today, China holds high the banner of peace, development, and cooperation. It pursues an independent foreign policy of peace and commits itself firmly to peaceful development.
>
> . . .
>
> Cultural diversity is a basic feature of both human society and today's world and an important driving force for human progress. As history has shown, in the course of interactions between civilizations, not only do we need to remove natural barriers and overcome physical isolation; we also need to remove obstacles and obstructions of the mind and overcome vari-

ous prejudices and misunderstandings. Differences in ideology, social system, and development model should not stand in the way of exchanges among civilizations, still less should they become excuses for mutual confrontation. We should uphold the diversity of the world, enhance dialogue and interaction between civilizations, and draw on each other's strength instead of practicing mutual exclusion. When this is done, mankind will enjoy greater harmony and happiness and the world will become a more colorful place to live in.[91]

The first excerpt articulates, in almost euphemistic terms, two basic principles of China's foreign policy—state sovereignty ("the strong should not oppress the weak") and multilateral cooperation (all nations "in perfect harmony"). The language in which the speech elaborates on this policy is notably eclectic—one hears echoes of Confucian precepts as well as tenets of Western liberalism. Invoking and expanding on the notion of "*wenmin duoyangxing*" [cultural diversity], the ideal world order projected in Hu's speech figures as a globalized version of conciliatory multiculturalism, suggesting that material, ideological, and political differences between nations should simply be bracketed and contained. What starts with the liberal lingo of "cultural diversity," however, ends on the note of "harmony," a familiar gesture toward traditional Chinese values. Indeed, the president emphasizes a bit earlier in his speech that Chinese culture has traditionally "given prominence to social harmony, unity, and mutual assistance." The notion of "harmony" here, of course, is not of a homogeneous kind, as it is merged with that of diversity. The combination of the two deliberately invokes the Confucian ideal of "harmony without sameness." As William A. Callahan observes, the phrase, taken from a famous passage in *Analects,* where Confucius points out that "[t]he exemplary person harmonizes with others, but does not necessarily agree with them," has figured prominently in the Chinese leadership's explications of its idea of a peaceful world order since the beginning of the twenty-first century.[92]

Hu's emphasis on world "harmony" recasts on a broader level the government's goal to construct a "harmonious society" domestically, which was announced at the Sixth Plenum of the Sixteenth CCP Congress, held in the October of the same year. It also implicitly harks back to the concept of "peaceful rise," which emerged as a key principle of China's foreign policy in

91. The transcription of the original speech, given in Chinese, was translated into English and made available, along with the Chinese text, through various news outlets on the day of Hu's visit. My excerpt is taken from the official translation.

92. William A. Callahan, "Remembering the Future," 586, 588.

the beginning of the new millennium. The concept was initially conceived for the purpose of assuring the world that China would strive to rise to the status of a great power without waging war or causing a drastic change in the world order.[93] Although the rhetoric of peaceful rise gave way to "peace and development" in some key documents from 2004 onward, the ideas underlying the peaceful rise theory stayed in circulation, as we can see in the reference to "peaceful development" in Hu's Yale speech.[94]

Hu's reelection to a second term as president in 2007 did not fundamentally alter the tenor of China's foreign policy expressed in this 2006 speech. As Suisheng Zhao puts it, Hu's foreign policy agenda during his second term is to "find a balance between pursuing international influence and downplaying its aspirations to being a global power," which includes, more specifically, building strategic partnerships to facilitate the "likely emergence of a multipolar world of sovereign states."[95] This agenda, which has been described as a state-centric version of "multilateralism," borrows selectively, and superficially, from different intellectual and political traditions and implicitly contrasts itself with the widely criticized unilateralism in U.S. foreign policy during the George W. Bush years.[96] Returning to *Lang Tuteng*, we can see that the novel, in many ways, functions as a graphic explication of the government's vision of a pluralist world order, just as it echoes the official policy toward ethnic minorities. It calls for ethnic amalgamation while presenting this process as *always and already* inherent in Chinese history. It points to the history of Western/Mongol imperial conquests as a source of useful models for the empowerment of China in the contemporary moment,

93. The concept was first formulated by Communist Party official Zhen Bijian in 2003, at the Bo'ao Forum for Asia held in Beijing. See Robert L. Suettinger, "The Rise and Descent of 'Peaceful Rise,'" 3. According to Suettinger, Zhen had initially conceived the idea of "peaceful rise" as a response to two dominant U.S. views of China's future at the turn of this century, "either that it would emerge rapidly to threaten U.S. security, or that it might collapse as a failed state" (3).

94. Suettinger observes that it was decided in April 2004 that the leadership would not use the term "peaceful rise" in public (1). The reasons are unclear, but Suettinger speculates that it has much to do with the pressing possibility of Taiwan's declaration of independence (which might require a military response), the idea's lack of intellectual rigor, and a leadership contest within the government (6–8).

95. Zhao, Suisheng. "Chinese Foreign Policy in Hu's Second Term: Coping with Political Transition Abroad."

96. C. R. Hughes, "Nationalism and Multilateralism in Chinese Foreign Policy: Implications for Southeast Asia," 129. Hughes points out that, since 9/11, China has increased its efforts to increase cooperation with Southeast Asian countries, by participating in and forming regional economic organizations (such as the China-ASEAN FTA) and calling for the deployment of a "New Security Concept" that embraces a realist, state-centric concept of multilateralism. For Hughes, China uses its relationship with ASEAN to "develop a counterweight to US power," without making it appear to be an open challenge (130).

only to suggest that China transcends the existing models. In its own way, the novel registers the same conservative impulse that we can discern in Cussler's *Treasure of Khan,* an impulse that is unsettled at times but restored eventually. The social significance, and textual pleasure, of the two novels reside in their time-boundedness: The critical pressure they exert on the logic of the dominant model of multiculturalism in their respective nation is carefully contained.

It does not mean, of course, that such popular novels as *Treasure of Khan* and *Lang Tuteng* are uncomplicated. A set of generic conventions, as well as the possibilities of combining and reinventing these conventions, allow these novels to simultaneously create and resolve narrative tensions. Some of them, therefore, function as narrative corollaries of conciliatory multiculturalism, which binds a nation together through the containment and superficial reconciliation of ethno-racial conflicts. *Treasure of Khan* idealizes the U.S. nation in a way that simultaneously expresses and disavows anxiety over the imperialist excess of the U.S. government; *Lang Tuteng* launches a critique of the Chinese government, only to then call for a more muscular Chinese nationalism. Ultimately, the two novels credit contemporary America and China, respectively, with a morally legitimate form of nationalism, distinguishing them from what the novels consider to be premodern and modern empires. Integral to their politics is the comparative framework that they construct. The *other* country, be it China or the United States, is invoked to provide an implicit rationale for why "we" still need a strong nation and why it can be differentiated from the idea of empire. The formal logic of conciliatory multiculturalism, as it becomes manifest in the two authors discussed here, has serious limitations, but its complexity cannot be underestimated.

CHAPTER 3

Toward a Comparative Critique

Metaphor and Dissenting Nationalism in Alex Kuo

> There are only a few big states among all states in the world. All big states go through a period of growth, which includes the incorporation of territories, the integration of ethnicities, and the development of borderlands. . . . This process is most typically illustrated in the U.S. westward movement.
>
> —He Shunguo,
> "The Westward Movement and Modernization in U.S. History"

> Each day he grew more impatient as he tried to move the emphasis between metaphor and ambiguity, occasionally stumbling in his language of radical that added to, but took away more than it clarified.
>
> —Alex Kuo, *Panda Diaries*

IN *CHINESE OPERA,* Alex Kuo's first foray into fiction writing, a mixed-race American couple, Sonny Lin and Sissy George, visit the PRC in the days leading up to the 1989 Tiananmen Square protests. In a surprising twist of the plot toward the end of the novel, Sissy George, part Native American and part black, succeeds in helping a Chinese dissident intellectual, Professor Luo, flee the country using apparently little other than magic. According to a press dispatch about the miraculous escape, some Chinese witnesses recall that the alleged foreigner helping Luo escape was disguised as or perhaps really was a "tall Muslim from the north" of China, and the pair simply disappeared like "a mirage."[1] On one level, Sissy George being imagined as a Uyghur from Xinjiang can be construed to suggest

---

1. Alex Kuo, *Chinese Opera,* 116.

possible conceptual parallels between the experiences of racial minorities in the United States and those of certain ethnic groups in China. Such U.S.–China comparisons abound in *Chinese Opera*. Upon deciding to help Professor Luo, Sissy explicitly compares the Chinese government's suppression of the 1989 protests to Sand Creek and Wounded Knee.[2] She assures Luo that she can help him disappear because her people "have been doing this for many generations," thus invoking the memory of the Underground Railroad in antebellum America.[3] We quickly notice, however, that these comparisons are of a self-reflexive nature, often warning the reader not to take them at face value. The first example, after all, can also be read as a scene of misrecognition that indicates the tendency of the "Chinese witnesses" to conflate Uyghurs with foreigners or foreignness with whiteness (Sissy does not look white, so cannot be a real foreigner). While it certainly suggests that a loose analogy can be drawn between certain ethnic and racial groups from the two nations, this scene also points to the disturbing possibility that such analogies ground themselves in unexamined assumptions and stereotypes. Kuo's comparisons, in addition, are complexly structured, often operating in several dimensions at once. Though Sissy is paralleled with Uyghurs, she is also implicitly aligned with the dissident intellectual Luo, who might be seen as part of a non-ethno-racial minority in China. The same pattern is repeated in the other comparisons we have seen, where the histories of Native Americans and African Americans (Sand Creek, Wounded Knee, and the Underground Railroad) are linked metaphorically to the struggle for democracy and intellectual freedom in contemporary China. The self-reflexive, layered comparisons proliferating in Kuo's fiction and other related writings are the focus of this chapter, which analyzes the ways in which these comparisons enable a double critique of the United States and China, with a focus on ethno-racial injustices resulting from the process of national expansion. Kuo, I argue, challenges the logic of conciliatory multiculturalism on two counts. By foregrounding the various incompatibilities between nation-building projects and minority rights without prescribing an easy solution to them, he counters the notion that ethno-racial conflicts can be resolved without radical reconfigurations of how the nation is conceived. More important, Kuo proposes a new model for U.S.–China comparisons, which I describe as a form of "comparative critique," through intensive reflections on the entangled political implications of metaphor and its cognates. Chapter 1 discusses two authors who cover over and exonerate the imperialist excess of

2. Ibid., 108.
3. Ibid., 109.

one nation at the expense of the other. Kuo provides a sophisticated alternative to this unproductive but commonly adopted practice.

Born in Boston in 1939, Alex Kuo spent his childhood and adolescence in Chongqing, Shanghai, and British Hong Kong. He moved to the United States with his family in 1955 and has spent most of his adult life in the Pacific Northwest. He held numerous teaching and administrative positions between 1963 and 2007, including a chairmanship in the Department of English and Comparative American Cultures at Washington State University. Between 1989 and 1998, he taught in Beijing, Changchun, and Hong Kong, as lecturer, Senior Fulbright Fellow, and Lingnan Fellow, respectively. He embarked on a literary career in 1974 as a poet and has since published four collections of poetry.[4] His experiences in China and Hong Kong gave rise to a raft of stories and novels concerned with contemporary Chinese culture and individuals traveling or migrating between China and the United States. A large part of these writings remain unpublished. Not until 1998 did Asia 2000 Ltd., a Hong Kong-based small press (now defunct), publish Kuo's novel *Chinese Opera*, which was finished in 1989. The same press published his collection *Lipstick and Other Stories* (2001) after it had been rejected by 46 other publishers.[5] His *Panda Diaries* (2006) and *The White Jade and Other Stories* (2008) were both published by small presses, based on manuscripts composed in 1991–92 and 2003–4, respectively.[6] Although *Lipstick* won an American Book Award in 2002, Kuo's works have generated little discussion in Asian American literary studies.

The reasons for this neglect are many. When Alex Kuo was studying for his M.F.A at the Iowa Writers' Workshop, he crossed paths with Frank Chin and Lawson Inada, who, along with Shawn Wong and Jeffery Paul Chan, edited the first anthology of Asian American literature, *Aiiieeeee*, published in 1974. Although Kuo had published his first collection of poetry, *The Window Tree*, by 1971, his name did not appear in *Aiiieeeee* or its updated version, *The Big Aiiieeeee*, which came out in 1991. The circumstances for this omission were complicated, but the most important one involved the differences between the modernist poetics in *The Window Tree* and the anti-assimilationist aesthetics advocated by the editors of the two *Aiiieeeee* collections.[7]

4. Alex Kuo, *This Fierce Geography: Poems; Changing the River; New Letters from Hiroshima and Other Poems; The Window Tree.*

5. Interview with Alex Kuo, April 28, 2005.

6. Alex Kuo, *Panda Diaries; White Jade and Other Stories.*

7. Alex Kuo, in discussion with the author, April 28, 2005. Kuo also related that misunderstanding played a part in his exclusion as well. During the late 1960s, Kuo was writing for an anti-Vietnam War newspaper, so he took the pseudonym Spike Mulligan to protect his identity. Without knowing the context, Frank Chin saw Kuo's use of a white name as a form of racial betrayal.

The exclusion of Kuo from Asian American literature is unfortunate, especially because the issues of race, immigration, and U.S. imperialism figure prominently in both his poetry and fiction. Like his poetry, his fiction has drawn a very limited audience. Although he has quite recently appeared in a few anthologies of Asian American literature, his offbeat, experimental style does not fit in with the lyrical realistic narratives about immigration and return that tend to dominate the market for ethnic narratives.[8] Crafting his narratives as poetry, Kuo does not provide vivid, detailed accounts of national histories or ethnic experiences, as readers have come to expect from Chinese American and other Asian American writers, preferring instead spare, pared-down narratives sprinkled with ambiguous vignettes and interludes as well as with political and cultural references that are usually left unexplained. The lack of scholarly interest has further narrowed the already limited market for Kuo's works.

What is most notable about Kuo's fiction, most of which straddles the United States and China (among other places), is its deviation from the more familiar narratives about Chinese Americans' exploration of China, which emphasize the ambiguity of "homecoming," the futility of trying to recuperate the China permanently associated with the Chinese-born parents. One can compare Kuo's writings, for example, with two videos, Felicia Lowe's *China: Land of My Father* (1979) and Richard Fung's *The Way to My Father's Village* (1987), both of which feature a North American-born Chinese narrator seeking to reconstruct the parents' history in China. As Peter Feng argues, these visual texts accentuate the epistemological distance separating Chinese Americans from contemporary China, thereby "decentering the Middle Kingdom."[9] Kuo's fiction, by contrast, foregrounds China, in its various historical incarnations, as an object of intellectual inquiry and an integral part of American and Chinese American histories, without suggesting that Chinese Americans are racially or culturally Chinese. He is of course not alone in engaging in this transnational project. He shares a set of narrative and political concerns with fiction writers such as Kingston, Betty Bao Lord, and Lan Samantha Chang and journalists such as the late Iris Chang and Leslie Chang, whose recent book *Factory Girls* investigates the life of migrant workers in contemporary China.[10] Like these writers, Kuo gives pause to

8. See Guiyou Huang, ed., *Greenwood Encyclopedia of Asian American Literature*; Zhang Tong, ed., *An Anthology of Chinese American Literature*.

9. Peter Feng, "Decentering the Middle Kingdom," 104.

10. One can see parallels with the Chinese American narratives of return in Japanese and Korean American literature. See Patricia P. Chu, "Asian American Narratives of Return." Chu studies, among other themes, the ways in which *nisei* and *sansei* negotiate the tensions between different cultural identities while coming to terms with the various political issues in Japan,

any critical efforts to map out Chinese American writings around a fixed spatial or political center. Drawing attention to the mutual entanglements of American and Chinese histories, he calls for new critical practices that treat Chinese American writings as a switchboard through which different local histories intersect and gain new meanings.

Returning briefly to *Chinese Opera*, we can see that, although the novel tells a largely familiar story of a second-generation Chinese American returning to China for a temporary teaching position, it switches midway into a study of contemporary Chinese culture. The protagonist, Sonny Lin, arrives in China shortly before the Tiananmen Square protests, with a strong sense of his identity as a Chinese American, without the hyphen. He confesses to have only begun to learn Chinese, contesting that those who think he is a native-born Chinese "haven't looked close enough."[11] Sonny's insistence on distinguishing himself from native-born Chinese comes as a gentle reminder of the ever-existing danger of Asian Americans being excluded from civic life in the United States on grounds of their perceived "foreignness." His half-Native American, half-black partner Sissy George also chafes at the question from Professor Luo, whom she first meets on the flight to China, of whether she is an American, until she realizes that, coming from a Chinese professor, it is not a blatantly racist question. The typical "Chinese American" plot is disrupted, however, when Cao Feng, a Chinese journalist working for the Xinhua News Agency, meets Sonny at a postperformance reception at the U.S. Embassy in Beijing. The narrative, which has been filtered through Sonny up to this point, rechannels itself through the reporter Cao, who launches into a series of meditations on the issue of freedom in news reporting in China, which he compares to fiction making. Juxtaposing Sonny's and Cao Feng's perspectives, U.S.- and China-centered, respectively, *Chinese Opera* moves toward a binocular vision, which crystallizes in the various explicit comparisons mentioned in the beginning of this chapter. It offers a glimpse into Kuo's engagement with comparative cultural critique, which is more clearly demonstrated in some of his other writings.

What follows is devoted to tracing and unpacking this engagement. I examine the ways in which Kuo addresses ethno-racial politics and other issues in both the United States and China. Integral to Kuo's political investments is a formal one, namely, his re-employment of metaphor, which provides a conceptual basis for the comparative model that he constructs in his writings. I first discuss Kuo's 2006 novel *Panda Diaries*, which juxtaposes the

including its imperial and military history in the first half of the twentieth century.

11. Alex Kuo, *Chinese Opera*, 37.

Indian policies of the nineteenth-century United States and China's policy on modernizing ethnic areas during the Cultural Revolution. The novel, I argue, comments critically on the homogenization of national space and culture that occurred in the histories of both countries, thereby revealing the omissions and erasures at the heart of conciliatory multiculturalism. I underscore the singularity of Kuo's critical vision by showing how it differs from an emerging discourse in China that compares China's modernization of its western regions with the U.S. westward expansion. I then move backward to the author's 2001 short story collection *Lipstick* to offer a sense of the ways in which Kuo's literary project exceeds the U.S.–China binational framework.

The Two Wests

In one of his poems from the 1980s, "Andrew Jackson and the Red Guards," Kuo compares the fanaticism of the Red Guards in China, whose "cucumber legs" are "churning up power / As far as Tibet," with Jacksonian democracy implicated ironically in the removal of Indians.[12] This poem is emblematic of Kuo's literary projects in general, which often suggest a kind of imprecise congruence between the processes of national expansion and integration in the United States and China, both of which have involved a form of colonization. His *Panda Diaries,* in particular, weaves together the historical experiences of Native Americans and ethnic minorities in China. Kuo is not the only one drawing this parallel, but he approaches it differently from most others. The significance of Kuo's comparative vision can be illustrated more clearly when we place him alongside other cultural voices that engage in similar U.S.–China comparisons. Written largely in the early 1990s (though not published until more than a decade later), *Panda Diaries* foreshadowed the surge, since the turn of the twenty-first century, of academic writings in China that compare China's development of its western regions, home to many ethnic minorities, with the westward expansion of the United States.[13] In the early 2000s, the Chinese government launched the West China Development Program so as to close the developmental gap between the inland

12. Alex Kuo, *Changing the River,* 31.

13. Between 2000 and 2009, at least seven or eight book-length studies came out that study specific aspects of the history of the U.S. westward expansion with an eye on providing useful lessons for China's development of its own west. Hundreds of journal articles and academic theses, as well as a number of international conferences, were devoted to comparative studies of the two processes.

western provinces and the rest of China.[14] For many contemporary Chinese intellectuals, the history of American expansion (1803–98) from the purchase of Louisiana to the annexation of Hawaii provides a mixed model for China's development of its own west. Despite the temporal gap between the opening of the American West and the ongoing project of West China Development, these academics find it useful to discuss what may or may not be transferable from the American experience. The comparisons between the "two Wests" tend to cast the United States as a flawed but useful precedent that legitimizes China's own enterprise. Most of the scholars taking on this comparative project demonstrate an awareness of the implications of national expansion for the environment and the cultural integrity of ethnic minorities. However, they largely focus on what government policies and initiatives it might take to achieve the goal of environmental and cultural conservation in the process of developing China's west, making little effort to discover or advocate for minority perspectives on this issue. In contrast to Kuo's writings, the emerging intellectual discourse on the "two Wests" largely refrains from questioning the imperialist logic of national expansion.

He Chansheng, a professor in the Department of Geography at the University of Michigan, collaborated with Niu Shuwen and Cheng Shengkui, scholars based in China, on an article, pointing out in particular the practice of abusing natural resources during America's westward movement, including the destruction of forests in the Five Lakes region, the erosion of topsoil as a result of excessive mining, and the extinction of animal species (passenger pigeons, bison, and seals, among others).[15] They refer to the "Dust Bowl" phenomenon, which stemmed from this environmental deterioration and exacerbated the Great Depression, as a warning against irresponsible development in China.[16] Another article, penned by Shao Fen, professor of law at Yunnan University, echoes this view by pointing out that the U.S. government neglected environmental issues associated with the development of the West until the 1930s, when a series of environmental laws started to be instituted.[17]

Shao Fen also points out that, partially as a result of an awareness of historical precedents, like the U.S. example, the Chinese government started paying attention to environmental issues at the very beginning of the West

14. Ding Lu and William V. W. Neilson, ed., *China's West Region Development,* 1–24.

15. He Chansheng, Niu Shuwen, and Cheng Shenkui, "Meiguo xibu fazhan dui zhongguo xibu dakaifa de qishi" ["Lessons from development of the U.S. West to China's West Development Program"], 188–93.

16. Ibid., 191.

17. Shao Fen, "Meiguo xibu kaifa lifa jiyi jingyan jiaoxun" [Development of the West in the U.S. and its lessons].

China Development Project. The government integrated environmental protection into its basic policies in 1983 and ratified a number of international treaties on environmental protection, including the Declaration of the United Nations Conference on the Human Environment. A series of laws and regulations regarding natural resources and the environment were created during the 1980s as well. However, many years of irresponsible development in the west prior to the West China Development Project had already severely destroyed the region's ecosystem, leading to desertification and the loss of soil; and the new environmental policies were, for a long time, poorly implemented. It remains a serious question whether, despite the increased environmental awareness among the Chinese leadership, China can avoid the "destruction first, conservation afterwards" pitfall.[18] By being equally critical of the environmental record of both the United States and China, Shao is suggesting a point that has become a common understanding among many environmentalists, namely, that the two countries have a joint responsibility to conserve resources and improve the global environment. China should not use the historical model of the U.S. westward expansion as an excuse for pursuing a high rate of development at the expense of the environment, nor should the United States begrudge a commitment to joining global environmental efforts because developing countries like China and India are purportedly obdurate about their wasteful ways. Until recently, the two countries, the top two polluters in the world, had engaged in a kind of blame game over the environment. In a *New York Times* special column in August 2007, renowned China-hand Orville Schell described the situation as one in which "while the U.S. [hid] behind China, China [hid] behind the U.S.," both "sitting the game out."[19]

Closely related to the problem of the environment is the issue of protecting the lifeworlds of indigenous groups and ethnic minorities. He Changsheng and his collaborators mention in their article the killing of Indians and the destruction of their culture as the cost of the American westward expansion.[20] Shao Fen uses the example of Native Americans to argue against dismissing and destroying the cultural heritage of ethnic minorities living in

18. Ibid., 124.

19. Orville Schell, "Expert Roundtable." Many nonprofit organizations also devote themselves to building dialogue and concerted efforts on the environment between the two countries. Two examples: (1) U.S.–China Association for Environmental Education, which works closely with its sister organization in China, Global Village of Beijing; and (2) The China–U.S. Energy Efficiency Alliance, a nonprofit organization combating global climate change by promoting energy efficiency and clean energy in China. It pools financial and technical resources to help China design and implement large-scale energy-efficiency incentive programs.

20. He Chansheng, Niu Shuwen, and Cheng Shenkui, 191.

China's west. The minority population in western regions accounts for 87 percent of the country's entire minority population. Most of the minority members in these regions, as Shao points out, are "*shiju*," which translates roughly as "indigenous" (in the sense that they had established their habitats there long before the Han presence).[21]

Implicit in this argument is the centrality of the issue of ethnic minorities to China's development of its western regions. Indeed, the Chinese government's policy toward its western frontiers has long been shaped by its concerns with national security and the unity of the Han Chinese and various ethnic groups on the frontiers. Changes in the Chinese government's policy toward Tibet during the Mao era, for example, reflected its consideration of how best to minimize the resistance of Tibet's religious and aristocratic elites to the central Communist government.[22] As Robert Bedeski points out, the urgency of developing western regions in the new millennium follows largely from the sense that regional equality will be crucial not only for keeping up a high level of economic growth in China but also for maintaining the central government's authority over the many ethnic groups in the western regions in a post–Cold War world where the United States has become the "dominant power" in Central Asia.[23]

While minority interests occupy a prominent position in the ongoing intellectual discussion around the western region development, however, this concern remains largely subordinated to national interests, which are often equated with those of the ethnic majority, the Han Chinese. In urging

21. There are no rigorous definitions of "indigeneity." Current definitions emphasize that indigenous populations have "ancestral roots" deeply embedded in the lands they inhabit, thus differentiated from the "more powerful sectors of society living on the same lands or in close proximity." See S. James Anaya, *Indigenous People in International Law,* 3. It has been added that indigenous communities are also defined by their historical isolation from modernization and the modern process of state-formation. This is the rule-of-thumb distinction that Kymlicka draws between indigenous populations and stateless nations, both of which, for Kymlicka, fall under the category of national minorities. See Kymlicka, *Politics in the Vernacular,* 122. If one follows Anaya's definition, most ethnic groups in western China can be called "indigenous." If one applies Kymlicka's definition, which is narrower, then many of these groups are not strictly indigenous. As Colin Mackerras points out, while they have an ancestral claim to where they live, they had developed their own governments before being incorporated into imperial China and later republican and communist China (Mackerras, *China's Minorities,* 21–22). There are a number of exceptions, however. The Oroqens, the group specifically named in *Panda Diaries,* match the current definitions of "indigeneity." One of the smallest minority nationalities in China, they were hunters in the Xingan Mountains historically and did not develop a semi-agricultural lifestyle until after the founding of the PRC. Other examples include the Ewenki and the Hezhe in northeast China.

22. Goldstein, "Tibet and China in the Twentieth Century," 192–99.

23. Bedeski, "Western China," 43.

the Chinese state to assume a central role in conserving natural and cultural landscapes in western areas, some choose to emphasize the meaning that this project of conservation holds for the Han Chinese. In a sleight of hand dictated by the logic of Chinese nationalism, Shao believes that protecting important cultural sites in the west is about "preserving the roots of the Han Chinese," who first originated amidst ceaseless interactions among the various peoples of the region.[24] In offering a list of these sites, Shao mentions the burial site of Emperor Qin (the first Han Chinese emperor) and the Potala Palace of Tibet in one breath.

The privileging of the national (Han) interest entails the more severe blind spot of disregarding the potential incongruities between state conservation policies and the material and cultural needs of minority peoples. This point is manifest, for example, in an essay by Gu Jun and Yuan Li, professor of history and researcher in ethnology, respectively, on the history of environmental and cultural conservation in the American West as a model for comparable policies in China. The authors discuss in particular the idea of establishing U.S. national parks, traditionally credited to George Catlin's appeal for government-enforced measures to protect indigenous cultures and wildlife on the plains. They applaud the creation of the Yellowstone National Park in 1872, the establishment of National Park Service in 1916, and the appearance of many similar national parks between 1933 and World War II.[25] They neglect to point out, however, that Catlin's original proposal was actually not adopted by the planners of Yellowstone. The troubling legacy of Yellowstone has been addressed in scholarly writings. Stan Stevens points out that Catlin advocated the establishment of a park across a vast area of the Rocky Mountains "in effect to make most of the Great Plains a sanctuary where the scores of different Native American peoples could continue to live their traditional ways of life and the vast herds of buffalo, elk, and antelope could continue with their seasonal migration."[26] However, Native American tribes had been completely excluded from Yellowstone by the mid-1880s, due to the "government policies concerning the confinement of Native Americans on reservations" as well as "national park policies."[27] Stevens identifies the "Yellowstone model" as one in which strict nature protection is the main goal, to the exclusion of indigenous settlement and land use,

24. Shao, "Meiguo xibu kaifa lifa jiyi jingyan jiaoxun" [Development of the West in the U.S. and its lessons], 124.
25. Gu Jun and Yuan Li, "Meiguo wenhua ji ziran yichan baohu de lishi yu jingyan" [History of the protection of cultural and natural heritage], 168.
26. Stan Stevens, *Conservation through Cultural Survival*, 29–30.
27. Ibid., 29.

a model that was not questioned or revised until the second half of the twentieth century.[28] Much international effort has been made to promote conservation policies that establish governments and indigenous communities as co-owners and co-managers of protected areas.[29] The nature reserves policies in China, especially the western regions, have been subjected to critical scrutiny for their impact on local minority communities. It has been noted that the Chinese government has since the 1990s introduced a set of initiatives in nature conservation that consciously emphasize the economic needs of minority communities with a historical presence in the conserved areas, thus departing from the Yellowstone model from the very beginning.[30] The Chinese model, however, remains quite limited. The ecological values and knowledge of the indigenous and ethnic communities in western China have hardly been incorporated into the government's approaches to conservation and development.[31] While the government recognizes the economic needs and historical rights of indigenous communities, making allowances for limited use of agricultural and forest lands within protected areas, the local villagers are almost never involved in the management of these areas.[32] Intellectual discussions on the relationship between conservation and minority

28. Ibid., 28–32.

29. For a good literature review of international conventions and guidelines addressing indigenous rights in international conservation since the early 1980s, see Sanjay K Nepal, "Involving Indigenous Peoples in Protected Area Management," 749–51. Also see the various case studies from both developed and developing countries around the world in Stevens.

30. Clem Tisdell and Zhu Xiang, "Reconciling Economic Development, Nature Conservation and Local Communities"; Trevor Sofield and F. M. S. Li, "Processes in Formulating an Ecotourism Policy for Nature Reserves in Yunnan Province, China." Tisdell and Zhu point out that, as is the case with other developing countries, China's strategies for easing pressures on biodiversity conservation, which can be traced back to the of Agenda 21 in 1994, has placed a special focus on improving economic opportunities in the neighborhood of protected areas in a way that benefits local communities. Sofield and Li offer a study of the process of formulating an ecotourism strategy for five newly designated reserves in the Yunnan Province in China and find that it involves much negotiation of the "Western paradigms of environmental conservation, wilderness and sustainability, upon which ecotourism is based" (142). China's policy toward minority nationalities is cited as an important factor in the government's insistence that the ecotourism policy must benefit first and foremost the minority communities that inhabited the areas within the reserves in the past.

31. Xu Jianchu et al., "Integrating Sacred Knowledge for Conservation: Cultures and Landscapes in Southwest China." Using the southwestern province of Yunnan as an example, the authors call for a drive toward "pluralism" in conservation (Xu et al. 2005, under "Indigenous Knowledge and Pluralism in Conservation"). They acknowledge the efforts on the part of the various levels of government to heed customary wisdom, as in the case of moving away from the push to sedentary livestock management, but note that there needs to be more extensive interaction between indigenous specialists and environmental scientists, as well as between indigenous communities and local governments.

32. Sanjay K. Nepal, "Involving Indigenous Peoples in Protected Area Management," 759.

interests that are currently taking place in China, as we can see, do not push the limits of government policies on conservation. They in fact tend to mirror these limits, by neglecting the importance of employing minority perspectives and experiences in conservation policy making. Endorsing the Yellowstone legacy reflects a certain intellectual complacency that can preclude efforts to thoroughly critique and transform deeply flawed models of conservation and state–minority relations. This complacency, no doubt, results in a large part from the current intellectual climate in China, that is, the highly limited intellectual freedom available to Chinese intellectuals, but it also illustrates the unstable and ambiguous politics of cultural translation and cross-national comparisons.

The U.S.–China comparative discourse introduced here offers a hint at the ways in which China's intellectuals and policy makers scour American political and cultural history for what can provide a rationale as well as momentum for China's modernization, even as the United States perceives China as increasingly relevant to its own economic and security priorities. Though Chinese scholars and intellectuals have also shown interest in borrowing from development programs in other nations, they seem to find the U.S. case particularly pertinent.[33] As we see, the U.S. westward expansion figures in this comparative discourse as an instrument of legitimization, offering a largely effective model that the Chinese government can comfortably follow and improve on in pursuing its own development goals, without fundamentally reconsidering its approach to minority and environmental issues. Kuo's *Panda Diaries* engages in a similar comparison as the policy discussions just studied, but Kuo is far more critical of the histories of national expansion and integration in both countries. He is by no means sanguine that the state can preempt or correct the problems that this process entails for minority and indigenous populations. Instead of relying on the government to assume the responsibility to preserve local cultures and natural ecosystems, he presents the process of state-sponsored economic development and national expansion as an inevitable threat to both. *Panda Diaries,* I argue, can be read as a comparative critique of development projects that entail the elimination of certain species, habitats, and races from a modernized national space.

More important, Kuo complements the social scientific approaches often adopted in discussions of the nation as a colonizing force. *Panda Diaries* performs a critique of both the United States and China while offering sus-

---

33. See Gao Guoli, "Guowai qianfada diqu duiyu woguo xibu dakaifa de jidian qishi" [Lessons from under-developed areas in other countries], 32–36. Gao's article cites the development of Hokkaido in Japan and Southern Italy, along with that of the American West, as historical precedents from which China can learn.

tained reflections on the underlying metaphorical logic of comparative discourses. Metaphor, as Kuo suggests in extremely complex ways, provides a conceptual model for turning observations about the impasses of national modernization—its human and environmental costs—into a productive and transformative critique. The novel, in other words, presents metaphor as a productive hazard, a slippery but necessary conceptual tool for a comparative and transnational understanding of the making of homogenized national space.

A Panda Bear Is Not a Bear

In 1987, Native American (Anishinaabe) author Gerald Vizenor published *Griever: An American Monkey King in China,* a fictionalized memoir of his stint in Tianjing, China, as a foreign teacher.[34] In the opening chapter the author's persona dreams about encountering a bear shaman on the southern Silk Road, who shows him cave paintings in the desert featuring images of bear shamans. The bear shaman then asks the author to pick a birch scroll to take with him, holding him responsible for the secrets inscribed on the scroll. The subsequent narrative in the memoir is presented as the unfolding of what is prophesized in the scroll that the author receives in his dream. The author, in other words, merges with the bear shaman he sees in his dream and becomes a shaman with prophetic and healing powers. Throughout the novel, the narrator also dresses himself as or assumes some qualities of the Monkey King, a rebellious, powerful monkey in the classic Chinese fantasy *Journey to the West,* which figures as a Chinese analogue of the bear shaman in Native American myths. The bear and the monkey are among the many sacred and mundane animals that populate *Griever,* serving, along with the human beings connected to them, as mediums between everyday life and what lies beyond.

This essay is not about Vizenor but about the animal figures, especially the bear shaman, in *Griever* and the comparative vision it gestures toward are crucial for understanding the author that it does discuss. Alex Kuo's *Panda Diaries* also germinated from the author's experience in China as a foreign teacher in 1991 and 1992, not long after the publication of Vizenor's book. While it claims to be a novel, *Panda Diaries* can hardly be properly designated as such. It offers a few snippets from protagonist Ge's life in China, including growing up separated from his parents during the Cultural Revo-

34. Gerald Vizenor, *Griever,* 18.

lution and being demoted to the city of Changchun in northeast China after having presumably committed a political mistake as an intelligence officer in Beijing. The nonchronological narrative is further fragmented by various forms of authorial intrusion, including poetry, interpolated news stories, and critical reflections and commentaries on apparently unrelated historical events.

In the novel, Kuo weaves together the histories of small, endangered indigenous communities in both China and the United States, associating their precarious fate with the irresponsible killing of animals that have traditionally been endowed with mythical qualities in indigenous cultures, including wolves, horses, and deer. Kuo explicitly refers to the symbiotic relationship between Native Americans and bison as a parallel to the interdependence between the Oroqens in China and the animals that they worship and hunt. We can tease out at least two axes of comparison from Kuo's narrative. Vertically, animals and indigenous populations become metaphors for each other, occupying two interconnected worlds that are equally threatened by the process of modernization that nation-states propel. Horizontally, a metaphorical relationship is constructed between China's policy toward the Oroqens during the Cultural Revolution and the Indian policies of the nineteenth-century United States. In intertwining the vertical and horizontal metaphors, the novel reflects on the functions of metaphor as a rhetorical figure and conceptual model that grounds comparative narratives. While metaphor predicates itself on the structuring of a "source domain" and a "target domain," two discreet units bound up in a static, often hierarchized, relationship, it also implies the interdependence and interpenetration of the two domains that disrupt any given hierarchy imagined between them. Kuo demonstrates that, as the different functions of metaphor cannot be disentangled from each other, metaphor is best understood in terms of irresolvable ambiguity. Mediating between the disciplining and liberating power of metaphor, *Panda Diaries* suggests a nuanced form of cultural critique that brings together the experiences of indigenous peoples, as well as species, from disparate time–space configurations.

The novel also features an animal character, the Panda mailman, presented as Ge's best friend in the beginning of the narrative. The Panda mailman talks and behaves just like a human being, except for some dietary peculiarities. He looks different from human beings, and yet the characters in the novel are not often alarmed by his presence outside the confines of a zoo. In many senses, the Panda mailman, representing an endangered animal species in China, figures as an animal double for Ge, a contemporary Chinese intellectual who feels beleaguered, or endangered, in a China soon to be engulfed by the 1989 student protests. The Ge–Panda duo is related to the metaphorical pairing of indigenous people and their sacred animals. Kuo invokes the latter kind of pairing to comment on the simultaneous rise of species-based and race-based hierarchies, speciesism and racism, in the process of the modern nation's colonization of indigenous and minority space, and he uses the Panda–Ge duo to critique state-centric, paternalistic approaches toward ethno-cultural and environmental justice that purports to remedy the ills of national expansion. As the panda does not figure in any traditional myth, one might say that Kuo's novel creates a new urban myth modeled upon, in an inverted manner, the oral traditions of indigenous communities on both sides of the Pacific. In other words, the panda bear in Kuo's narrative can be read as an inverted, modern, Chinese parallel to the powerful bear in Native American myth. The panda's utter vulnerability and dependence on humans' loving care forms a sharp contrast with the bear's command of fear and respect from human beings. One cannot understand the figure of the panda bear in Kuo's novel, then, without comparing it to the animal figures in Native American myth and cultures, as seen in such works as Vizenor's *Griever*. It is only fitting that we use a comparative mode of reading to understand a text that organizes itself around a series of comparisons.

Kuo's narrative presents the panda as a singular exception to other animals that have crossed paths with human beings since the advent of modernity. In an earlier part of the novel, set in the Chinese city of Changchun, the Panda mailman and Ge drive to a California Noodle Company restaurant in the city, where Panda takes offense at the waitress who addressed him as "Animal Ambassador," demanding that the waitress respect his "difference" rather than use the label attached to all pandas. The scene at the noodle company is then followed by the author's reflections on the history of various genocides in the New World that involved humans and animal species simultaneously. Kuo relates the destruction of the plains Indians' bison commissary prior to the Battle of Little Big Horn "that was to change the colonial-native narrative forever" by depriving the Indians of their food source.[35] He then turns to a more general critique of the history of "wanton killing" in the "new, new world" that stemmed from European colonists' espousal of "the right to expansion and the right to kill everything in its way."[36] The Panda mailman, then, represents an animal species that mysteriously escapes the modern human impulse to kill animals and other humans at whim. Being constantly labeled as "Animal Ambassador," as Kuo suggests, constitutes a

35. Kuo, *Panda Diaries*, 30.
36. Ibid., 31, 32.

kind of character assassination—or, simply put, stereotyping—that, just as much as being physically annihilated, signifies a powerless position.

Kuo makes clear the metaphorical linkage between violence toward humans and violence toward animals in one of his explicitly intrusive passages: "Whose nightmare was it? Who had the ammunition, and who was the rifle pointed at? In the twinning of this metaphor, every half included another surrogate from the animal kingdom, always."[37]

On a specific level, Kuo is pointing out that the slaughtering of the American bison destroyed the livelihood of Native Americans, turning them into a historical analogue of the animals that they depended on. On a more general level, Kuo is arguing that the killing of animals naturalizes and logically facilitates the killing of people. In other words, the human practice of killing other human beings often arises from, or is motivated by, their experience of killing animals, whose characteristics are then mapped onto the human groups to be slaughtered. Zoltán Kövecses, a theorist of conceptual metaphor, argues that abstract ideas do not arise literally from experiences but always through the mechanism of metaphorical mapping whereby abstract experiences in general are constituted on the analogy of more physical ones.[38] Kuo echoes Kövecses's view of metaphor by showing that it can serve as a conceptual basis for the transformation of one form of killing into another. Right before the passage just quoted, Kuo attributes to the Texas legislature that created a fellowship program to reward hunters of the plains Indians' bison commissary a kind of "uncontrollable ambiguity" that "physically killed the body on both sides of the metaphor."[39] Kuo's remark on the "metaphorical twinning" of animals and humans suggests the historical entwining of speciesism (systematic discrimination based on species) and racism, the inseparability of environmental and ethnocultural injustices committed during the era of expansion in U.S. history.

As Cary Wolfe points out (via a quote from Derrida), speciesism makes

---

37. Ibid., 32.
38. Metaphor has been studied intensely in cognitive linguistic theory as a conceptual model constitutive of how humans think and speak. See Zoltán Kövecses, *Metaphor in Culture*. Elaborating on and refining the theory of conceptual metaphor that originated from Mark Johnson and George Lakoff, Zoltán explains that metaphor consists in a kind of cognitive mapping that parallels abstract ideas with embodied experiences. In many languages, for example, the various parts of a pressurized container are mapped onto various elements of anger, thus providing a structure for the latter abstract idea. As Kövecses puts it, "[t]hrough detailed mappings, the metaphor provides a coherent structure for the concepts [that anger compromises]" (Kövecses, 199). More important, Kövecses poses the question of whether metaphors motivate or simply express the abstract ideas that constitute the fabric of a specific cultural system. See chapter 9, in particular 216.
39. Kuo, *Panda Diaries*, 32.

possible a symbolic economy in which we engage in a "noncriminal putting to death" of not only animals but other humans as well "by marking them as animal."[40] Both speciesism and racism derived from the notion of the Great Chain of Being during the Enlightenment era, espoused by philosophers and writers as well as biologists and zoologists (Linnaeus and Buffon, for example). The implication of natural science in the rise of modern racism has been noted.[41] Kuo makes a similar point regarding natural scientists, quipping that their "specimen-gathering scientific rationality" is often "short-circuited by their anthropocentric will to kill."[42] But he goes further by placing the rise of both speciesism and racism against the background of European colonialism in the New World. John James Audubon, for example, believed in "hunting and poisoning passenger pigeons," which led to the eventual extinction of passenger pigeons on the U.S. continent.[43] The feat of putting an entire bird species to death echoes the slaughtering of bison herds and Indian populations, signaling that the expansion and homogenization of national space in the nineteenth-century United States were colonial processes with both a human and nonhuman cost.

As I mention earlier, the figure of the panda represents an intriguing complication to the extension of the twin phenomena of racism and speciesism into the contemporary era. Toward the end of the book, Ge starts to wonder whether the Panda mailman, the representative of the panda species in the novel, is a "message" he needs to heed and whether he should behave like some of the animal species that "have learned to make the adjustment between politics and environment."[44] Apparently, then, the panda comes to embody a kind of proximity to transcendent powers that resemble the status accorded to the mythical bear in the traditional cultures of Native Americans and other indigenous peoples. As David Rockwell argues, the bear is seen in these traditional cultures as a "furry person, a relative."[45] Tribal people model their lives upon the lives of bears, initiating their young into adulthood, for examples, in an elaborate ritual during which the initiated dress up and act

---

40. Cary Wolfe, *Animal Rites*, 43.

41. Kenan Malik, *Meaning of Race*, 87. Malik explains that, while the naturalists of the eighteenth century believed largely that a great gulf existed between humans and animals, nineteenth-century science was "drawn to the notion of human society constrained by natural laws" and saw "the origins of all human faculties in animal life" (87). Despite this difference, both outlooks enabled the construction of a naturalized hierarchy of life that entails both speciesism and racism.

42. Kuo, *Panda Diaries*, 31.

43. Ibid., 31.

44. Ibid., 96.

45. David Rockwell, *Give Voice to Bear*, 7.

like bears.[46] According to Lydia T. Black, bears are seen in many indigenous cultures in the circumpolar North, among many other places, as inhabiting an "in-between" world that mediates between the human world and the "domain of deities and spirits."[47] The boundaries between the animal domain and the human domain remain porous, the crossing of which are often conceptualized as "death, birth, and sexual congress."[48] This observation echoes Joseph Epes Brown's point that bears are considered in Native American cultures to have been created before human beings, closer to the Great Spirit in their anteriority.[49]

However, the panda in *Panda Diaries* can be read only as an *inverted* parallel to the bear shaman, representing a perverse extension of the premodern tradition of revering animals into our own times. Although the benevolence bestowed on the panda may seem to be a reversal of the human desire for territorial expansion that necessarily requires killing, it acts, at best, as a deceptive distraction from various forms of political and social violence. In fact, this benevolence is the flip side of speciesism, a manifestation of anthropocentrism, designating humans as benefactors of animals whose habitats are threatened by human practices in the first place.[50] *Panda Diaries* contains authorial comments and news inserts that satirize the ways in which pandas are cherished as national treasures in China and embraced all around the world. It opens with a Preface that tells the story of Ruth Hackness, the American fashion designer who, in 1936, brought back home wrapped in her arms the first live giant panda to be seen in the New World. The episode, for Kuo, inaugurated the ambassadorial role that the panda was to play ever since. As Kuo puts it,

> whenever a Nicolae Ceausescu is not losing his testicles in his own palace, or an Imelda Marcos is not counting her missing Parisian alligator shoes; or a Prince Charles is not traversing the remnants of the British commonwealth whining about the abuse of the English language; or the Palestinian and Israeli youths are not trying to kill each other with rubber bullets, stones, or more specific targeted killings; or another still-living Enola Gay airman or USS Arizona swabby is not saluting the flag; the world media

46. Ibid., 19–23.
47. Lydia T. Black, "Bear in Human Imagination and in Ritual," 344.
48. Ibid.
49. Joseph Epes Brown, *The Spiritual Legacy of the American Indian,* 38.
50. Anthropocentrism and speciesism do not mean the same thing, but are rather two sides of the same coin. Anthropocetrism assumes the animals are valuable only if they serve human interests, thus indirectly denigrating animals, while speciesism denotes negative attitudes toward animals based on their membership in a biological species other than *homo sapiens.*

focuses on the copulation effectiveness of these twenty-three zoo-bound pandas.[51]

Apparently capable of accomplishing the feat of uniting all countries on earth, the panda functions as a symbolic stand-in for what exceeds the symbolic, or human representational schemas, something that transcends the history of human strife. It provides human beings with a symbol of the sacredness of all creatures, an icon of the transcendent that, occasionally at least, elevates and cleanses the profane, anthropocentric world. In other words, the novel figures the panda as the center of a contemporary version of animal worship.

This worship, however, is clearly compromised by condescending benevolence, the belief that "only man can save the giant panda."[52] This point becomes clear in the coda of *Panda Diaries,* where a poem titled "Animal Grammar" offers a list of common English idioms that use animals as metaphors for qualities considered to be subhuman. The panda is the only animal in "Animal Grammar" that is not part of everyday English idioms involving animals. It, instead, appears as part of "Panda-monium," a silly instance of wordplay. The absence of the word "panda" in common English expressions can be seen as a linguistic corollary of the exoticized, exalted place that the panda occupies in Western culture, but the idle wordplay reveals the ironic tension between the panda's semi-sacred status in the contemporary Western and world imagination and its easy slide into an object of ridicule. Kuo is suggesting that the logic of contemporary forms of animal worship, as one sees in the rush to save and love giant pandas, is haunted by the irreversible loss of a premodern world where humans and animals worked in close proximity with each other as interdependent parties, if not equal partners. The social position the panda occupies in our times is a far cry from the position accorded to the mythical bear in traditional tribal cultures. As Richard Tapper explains, the modern urban–industrial society is characterized by the marginalization of animals, which impinge on human lives only as pets or zoo animals or symbolically as animal toys and characters in children's literature.[53] This marginalization reflects the decreased reliance on animals in the relations of production prevalent in urban–industrial societies, which has led conceptually to the anthropocentric belief that humans should reign over animals and their environments.

More important, in *Panda Diaries,* the anthropocentric approach to animal rights and nature conservation is closely associated with the policies and

51. Kuo, *Panda Diaries,* 2.
52. Ibid., 35.
53. Richard Tapper, "Animality, Humanity, Morality, Society," in *What Is an Animal?* 56–57.

political attitudes affecting ethno-racial minorities in the United States and China. As the Panda mailman is paired up with the disaffected Chinese intellectual Ge, one might read Panda as an animal counterpart of the figure of the Chinese dissident, be it Wei Jingsheng, Harry Wu, or the Dalai Lama, that is often embraced and championed in the West. We can thus project the doubleness—exalted and yet vulnerable—ascribed to pandas onto the Chinese dissidents. In the beginning of *Panda Diaries,* the Panda mailman visits Ge at his apartment and reminisces about his visit to the National Zoo in Washington, DC. While many visitors were busy taking photos of the pandas inside the cage, they ignored Panda because he was "not where he was supposed to be."[54] The pandas, in other words, are turned into a media spectacle rather than integrated into the fabric of everyday American life. This situation can be read as an implicit critique of the kind of role that Chinese dissidents play in American culture. Like the pandas in the cage, they are often staged in the U.S. media as adorable novelties, objects of paternalistic love and pity, or an endangered species in need of Western protection. The protective impulse they elicit, however, does not quite extend to the raced and ethnicized bodies outside the limits of the staged spectacles. Arguably, Kuo is making a point about the contradiction between America's claim to a liberal empire, a benign world power advocating for the rights of racial, ethnic, and other minorities at home and around the world, and the persistence of political and economic inequalities in the country. Kuo's critique, of course, is not confined to the United States. It also concerns itself with the state-centered approach toward the rights of minority and indigenous populations practiced in contemporary China.

Early on in *Panda Diaries,* we see a scene from the Cultural Revolution, when a twelve-year-old Ge is forced to live with the Oroqens after his parents were sent to a separate place for political re-education. The scene shows that, during the Cultural Revolution, the Oroqens' habitat was irrevocably reduced by the government policy of assimilating them into an agricultural mode of production, coupled with the dwindling of reindeer herds as a result of environmental degradation.[55] At one point, the author intrudes upon the

---

54. Kuo, *Panda Diaries,* 25.

55. English-language sources on the history of the Oroqens are far and few in between, most of which focus on the grammar of the disappearing Oroqen language. However, see Lindsay Whaley, "The Growing Shadow of the Oroqen Language and Culture." Wayley provides a brief history of the Oroqens' transformation from a community of hunter–gatherers in the 1950s to the predominantly farming, fast shrinking ethnic group in the twenty-first century. Wayley attributes this transformation largely to the modernization policies implemented in Mao's China, which pushed them into "communal living with other minorities and the Han majority," but he also points out the role played by the earlier history of the Oroqens, who unfortunately set up

narrative and offers two conflicting accounts of the current population of the Oroqens. One version sets the number at 500, and the other, apparently culled from a government document, offers the figure 10,000 and credits the government for the great social progress achieved among the Oroqens.[56] It is likely that Kuo invokes this official figure to suggest, aside from baseless exaggeration on the part of the government, the fact that a large number of Han Chinese have married the Oroqens since the end of Mao's era to gain the preferential treatment benefits that come with minority status. The larger figure clearly serves to bolster the claim that the official ethnic policy preserves ethnic cultures, when in fact increased intermarriage has further dissipated the already endangered Oroqen culture.[57]

Kuo's comments on the fate of the Oroqens complement his critique of the pattern of the "metaphorical twinning" of humans and animals in the nineteenth-century United States by showing how it is mirrored in post-1949 China. They also offer a useful rebuttal to the view, expressed by the Chinese scholars discussed earlier, that state initiatives can eliminate any possible negative implications of China's current effort to develop its minority areas, especially those in the west. One can argue, to extrapolate from Kuo's argument against the government's policy toward the Oroqens both during the Cultural Revolution and in more recent years, that this misguided view is not too far from U.S. exceptionalism, which celebrates the westward expansion as a Puritan errand into the wilderness that, as Amy Kaplan puts it, proved "antithetical to the historical experience of imperialism," rather than an encroachment on the world of indigenous peoples.[58]

In his article "Globalization, Indigenism, and the Politics of Place," Arif Dirlik reminds us that at the center of contemporary struggles against the simultaneously homogenizing and fragmentary forces of globalization is the effort to reclaim singular, and yet not isolated, places from these forces, often organized under the term "indigenism." It is important, Dirlik argues, to differentiate between the "indigenism" that simply reacts against the global and the "indigenism" that derives its meaning from "substantial autonomous claims" to "an almost absolute attachment to place understood concretely,"

---

their hunting grounds at a place that has become "a corridor for a succession of military powers" (13).

56. Kuo, *Panda Diaries*, 69–70.

57. Wayley discusses the issue of Han–Oroqen intermarriage in his article, explaining that, in the post-Mao era, the government offered the Oroqens "special dispensations," including exempting them from the "one child policy," thus providing a strong incentive for Han–Oroqen intermarriage (14).

58. Amy Kaplan, "'Left Alone with America': The Absence of Empire in the Study of American Culture," 4.

in all its biosocial complexity.[59] The former sense of "indigenism" often takes the form of a nation-state, which in itself is "a colonial force that erases the local and the place-based in the name of its own universalistic claims."[60] The second sense of "indigenism," by contrast, "appears in its full critical significance against the colonialism not only of the global but also of the national."[61] More important, Dirlik interprets the place-consciousness that underlies the second sense of "indigenism" not as "localized parochialism" but as an ability to recognize the "interactions between the global and the local that cut across the boundaries of the nation, projecting the local into transnational spaces."[62] Not unlike Dirlik, Kuo works toward a comparative, transnational approach to the tensions between colonial and indigenous, anticolonial attitudes toward place. The history of Native Americans has hardly been understood in relation to that of ethnic minorities in China. Kuo's novel is part of an emerging cultural discourse that both constitutes and reflects upon these connections. Its juxtaposition and comparison of the two histories subject both the U.S. and China—their governments and political cultures at large—to critical scrutiny. Against cultural relativism and (Western-centric) moral universalism at once, Kuo argues that the West needs a stronger dose of self-criticism in decrying minority rights violations in the non-West and that developing countries cannot be exonerated from charges of such violations simply because they have been victimized by Western colonialism and imperialism. Reading Kuo does not show us what it is like to establish "actual" contact between Native Americans and indigenous or minority groups in China, and yet he helps lay an important conceptual basis for such contact. Kuo not only bridges disparate histories imaginatively by figuring them as metaphors for each other but also reflects consciously on the conflicting political implications of metaphorical logic. We have caught a few glimpses of Kuo's comments on and reemployment of metaphor, but this dynamic deserves a closer look.

Metaphorical Diffusion

In the second of Coetzee's Tanner lectures at Princeton, later published as *The Lives of Animals,* novelist Elizabeth Costello suggests in her impassioned speech on animal abuse that Swift's satire "A Modest Proposal" has perhaps

59. Arif Dirlik, "Globalization, Indigenism, and the Politics of Place," 16.
60. Ibid., 20.
61. Ibid., 20.
62. Ibid., 19.

been misread all along.[63] The mock proposal that Irish families save themselves from poverty by raising babies for the dinner table of their English masters may be more than an oblique comment on the ways in which the English rule in Ireland was causing starvation and, in a sense, already killing Irish babies. How is it, Costello asks, that we never read Swift's essay as a critique of the practice of killing and eating piglets? Costello certainly does not represent a reliable perspective in Coetzee's lectures, delivered in fictional form, but this particular question is insightful and relevant to my discussion of Kuo's *Panda Diaries*. It is indeed unimaginable for readers of Swift, wherever they are, to read Irish babies as a metaphor for piglets. One implication of Costello's question is that the two parts that constitute a metaphorical expression are often not equal. Since such an expression customarily illustrates the meaning of an abstract concept by mapping it onto a concrete object or embodied experience, it is a conceptual mechanism contingent upon and constitutive of the construction of a set of hierarchical orders in which objects and experiences are ranked according to their perceived level of sophistication. While humans can be compared to animals, that is to say, they cannot be a vehicle for animals. This truism both reflects and reinforces the hierarchical relationship constructed between animals and humans under the reign of speciesism and anthropocentrism. This is also part of the point that Kuo makes in his critique of the various instances of "metaphorical twinning" under colonialism, which compare members of the human species, ethnicized and racialized groups in many cases, to particular animals (plains Indians–bison, the Oroqens–reindeer), thus reducing these groups to subhumans fit for mass slaughter. This logic is highlighted in "Animal Grammar," which consists of a litany of familiar metaphorical expressions, such as "dumb as an ox," "crazy like a loon," and "to leech," among others. These expressions compare a person to an animal to the effect of denigrating both. Echoing Kuo's critique of "metaphorical twinning" within the body of his narrative, "Animal Grammar" demonstrates, on a broader level, the ways in which metaphorical language registers and facilitates colonial violence that affects both animals and humans. Metaphor has long been theorized as a figure of identity, organicity, or consummate union, and as such, it has become a bête noire in poststructural criticisms, as seen, for example, in De Man's privileging of allegories and Homi Bhabha's elevation of metonymy over metaphor.[64] The

---

63. J. M. Coetzee, *The Lives of Animals*, 55–56.

64. De Man critiques the Romantic privileging of metaphor in his early and mid-career writings. "Reading (Proust)," 57–58; "Anthropomorphism and Trope in the Lyric," whereas De Man deconstructs the Romantic conception of metaphor as an expression of essential connections. Homi Bhabha differentiates between metaphor and metonymy as two conceptual models

other side of the coin, metaphor's power to create and preserve hierarchical orders, has strangely eluded critical attention. Kuo, shows us a different face of metaphor, suggesting that, as a figure of comparison or cognitive mapping, it both flattens and hardens differences. These two sides of metaphor can be seen as a figurative corollary of the interplay of incorporation and exclusion that defines nation-building projects. As *Panda Diaries* suggests, both the United States and China have stretched themselves across a diverse range of terrains and cultures, imposing, with more or less coercive force, a homogenizing vision of development upon certain species and communities, which are at the same time separated from the majority nation on grounds of their purported inferiority or backwardness. The process of national expansion in both countries, in other words, is captured formally in the structure of metaphor.

By bringing together U.S. and Chinese histories as imprecise parallels of each other, moreover, Kuo shows that there is yet another side to metaphor. While metaphorical logic undergirds nation-building projects, it can also enable the emergence of comparative perspectives on these projects by allowing us to draw connections between and among them. *Panda Diaries* explores many such connections. Even as the plight of the Oroqens and that of Native Americans are brought into a metaphorical relationship with each other, they are also linked, metaphorically, to other ecological, political, and cultural injustices on both sides of the Pacific, including the silencing of dissident intellectuals in contemporary China. The continuous proliferation and layering of metaphors, a pattern that one might describe as metaphorical diffusion, suggests that Native Americans do not exactly constitute a North American equivalent of the Oroqens or exist in a dyad with the latter, just as animals and humans do not constitute a closed circuit, even though they can be productively compared. By allowing his metaphors to be destabilized by other metaphors, Kuo does not engage so much in cognitive mapping as in cognitive demapping. The juxtaposition of the United States and China in *Panda Diaries* gestures toward a new comparative framework without by any means seeking to map out a stable structure for it. Tapping into the deterritorializing power of metaphor, Kuo recalls Jahan Ramazani's theorization of the figure. For Ramazani, metaphor can operate as a "rhetorical site of resemblance and 'double vision'" and a "linguistic and conceptual 'contact

---

underlying two conflicting kinds of collectivities, the former grounding bounded unities like nation-states and the latter helping to shape interstitial, hybrid, postnational cultural formations that instantiates what Bhabha terms the "Third Space." See Bhabha, *The Location of Culture*, 155, 227.

zone' and 'third space.'"[65] It has been employed in the work of Indian dia-sporic poet A. K. Ramanujan, for instance, to "[mediate] postcoloniality," that is, illustrate rhetorically the spatial movement and the process of cultural hybridization that constitute the postcolonial condition.[66] It is not a stretch to say that writing under the postcolonial condition, or in the diapora, as Kuo shows, generates a special connection with metaphor.

Kuo's complex approach to metaphor is clearly captured in a key passage in *Panda Diaries*. In the midst of the narrative about Ge's experience with the Oroqens, we find a stand-alone lyrical interlude functioning as a miniatur-ized version of the novel as a whole. This passage illustrates, while comment-ing explicitly on, the pattern of metaphorical diffusion that suffuses the novel as a whole. It starts, appropriately, with a metaphor: "This is a tent in a dream forward where he lives, and it does not have a door. In its place, choose an empty space, whether square, rectangle or circle, or any shape of his imagin-ing, and he will have lived in it. His eulogy is a history of doors and passages, of light to dark, or dark to light, or those journeys in between. But there is no door to this tent."[67] The tent can be seen as a spatial metaphor for Chinese history, which can be accessed only through the workings of imagination. The nebulous "he" in this paragraph can refer to both an imagined historical subject and the one doing the imagining, thus formally mimicking the for-mation of a coherent national identity based on individual acts of identifica-tion. Indeed, "his eulogy," an apparently clichéd narrative of the vicissitudes of Chinese history and the inexhaustible resilience of the Chinese people ("doors and passages," "light to dark, or dark to light"), is simultaneously a eulogy about "him" and created by "him." The image of the tent, then, signi-fies a self-contained historical narrative that aims to circumscribe national consciousness with a fixed set of tropes. It presents the nation as an enclosed space standing apart from the world outside. There is "no door" to this tent; one finds a way in by mentally inhabiting it. National membership, in this case, is contingent upon accepting a particular narrative of Chinese history and weaving oneself into it.

The singular "he" in the first paragraph of the interlude gives way, how-ever, to a collective "we" in the third paragraph. For a moment, "we" also walk through the space inside the tent, watching various events unfolding within it, including what seems to be the Tiananmen Square protests, during which "a young history student" hurls a rock at an army tank. But "we" soon realize that being completely captivated by a given narrative of the nation entails a

65. Jahan Ramazani, *The Hybrid Muse*, 77, 101.
66. Ibid., 77.
67. Kuo, *Panda Diaries*, 14, 15.

kind of epistemological blindness. In the beginning of the fourth paragraph, then, "we" reflect on this blindness and then abruptly leave the tent for a different site: "But we are too far off ourselves, as reliable as the metaphors seem to be. So let's step aside and check our omissions and exaggerations. There, the sun is rising unstoppable, nothing turning it back there. There are walls here, too, some covered with revolutionary words, THE BIRD STILL LIVES in several colors. The only sound rising from the thronging crowd is an inept gasp anticipating irreversible dreams. We must move cautiously here, renew our identities, cross our hearts, if we are to avoid the stray lunatic endangering every species."[68]

"We" have realized that figuring Chinese history as an enclosed, doorless tent is a case of abusive use of metaphor. It isolates the nation, through "omissions and exaggerations," from its messy entanglements with other spaces, thus delimiting conceptions of national identity. With this realization, "we" venture into an altogether different world as a way of uncovering these entanglements. "Stepping aside" from the imaginary tent of China, "we" now speak from a different but no more innocent place simply referred to as "here," as opposed to "there," where "the sun is rising unstoppable." The place denoted as "here" can certainly be read as the United States, the destination of many Chinese immigrants since the nineteenth century as well as Chinese political dissidents who escaped their home country after the suppression of the 1989 protests, while "there" can be seen as a reference to the ascending China, which has taken over the mantel of the "rising sun" from Japan. Forced to "move cautiously," "renew our identities," and "cross our hearts," "we" are now subjected, in this new land, to genocidal impulses "endangering" every species that does not fit in, a predicament that foreshadows the novel's later references to the "metaphorical twinning" of animals and humans that facilitates the killing of certain members of both categories. "We" now redefine our collective identity by engaging in struggles against exclusionary conceptions of legal and cultural citizenship in the United States. The aim of these struggles, the author suggests, is not assimilation, but instead the expansion of conventional coordinates of American culture. The grammar-conscious, strangely unidiomatic phrase "The Bird Still Lives" in this paragraph might be read as a Chinese American variation on the more idiomatic version "Bird Lives." Invoking the famous graffiti commemorating the death of jazz musician Charlie Parker, Kuo is arguably drawing an imprecise analogy between Chinese immigrants in the United States and African Americans or, in another metaphorical twist, between Chinese immigrants and social and artistic out-

68. Ibid., 15.

casts in general. "The Bird Still Lives" suggests, on a grammatical level, the ways in which Chinese Americans pluralize American culture while being transformed in the very same process.

We can see now that even though this interlude begins with a disavowal of metaphor, it goes on to suggest a metaphorical, parallel relationship between Chinese and U.S. histories and the traces of genocidal lunacy embedded in both. Rather than construct spatial metaphors to territorialize history, Kuo uses the logic of metaphor to illuminate historical passages between presumably self-contained national spaces. Traversing "here" and "there," "we" reveal the inextricable connections between the two spaces and challenge the myth of coherent national identity. I should qualify my previous reading—namely, mapping "here" and "there" onto the United States and China in this particular order—by pointing out that such an exact correspondence does not exist. The point of this interlude is to blur the distinctions between "here" and "there," not to consolidate their internal unity. In the same vein, the pronoun "we" does not just refer to a clearly defined identity—Chinese Americans, for example—but gestures more broadly to new collective identities formed on the basis of physical or conceptual movement between and among different national spaces and cultures.

Metaphors proliferate swiftly in the rest of the interlude. "We" briefly mention other locations, such as Bogota, where "history is declaring its own martial law," before returning to the tent that started it all.[69] Kuo, clearly, not only is drawing connections between ethno-racial and other injustices in the United States and China but also is gesturing toward a global perspective on political violence in general. He demonstrates that metaphorical diffusion is an indispensable discursive tactic for presenting the history of a nation in terms of how it spills out of state borders, in the form of both the border-crossing movement of its citizens and its entanglements with other national histories. It is also, at the same time, crucial for highlighting the linkages between and among different political symptoms of modernity, including anthropocentrism, racism, and colonialism. In other words, Kuo shows us a way of mitigating the conceptual violence of metaphor and reappropriating it for a multiply comparative mode of cultural critique.

Even though the pattern of metaphorical diffusion in *Panda Diaries* suggests a conceptual basis for productively comparative critique, it of course does not solve all the paradoxes entailed in comparative modes of thinking. We can in fact argue that the proliferation of metaphors in the text generates the kind of problem that Paul Breslin identifies in Derek Walcott's epic

69. Ibid., 15.

poem *Omeros*. As Breslin points out, in *Omeros*, especially the last chapters of book IV and book V, the poet's persona "extends his wanderings to North America and Europe, seeking to make every event rhyme with a Caribbean counterpart."[70] Although the poem's rage for parallelisms is reversed toward the end of the poem, where the Walcott persona "begins to criticize his own obsession with Homeric parallels," it nevertheless tangles these particular chapters in "serpentine coils of dubious analogy."[71] Unlike Walcott, Kuo does not reflect consciously on the excessive diffusion of metaphors into form-less associations, preferring to leave the dilemma to critics, but neither does he indulge in it. Indeed, in *Panda Diaries*, Kuo quickly wraps up the lyrical interlude just analyzed and moves on to a snapshot of Ge's life among the Oroqens.

Counting and Seriality

The organizing principle of metaphorical diffusion can also be seen in the collection of short stories *Lipstick* and Kuo's earlier poetry. *Lipstick* can be read as a more associative version of *Panda Diaries;* both were indeed com-posed around the same time and both came to print more than ten years after they were written. If the central concern of *Panda Diaries* is metaphor, *Lip-stick* focuses on the idea of "counting" as a political act predicted upon con-ceptual metaphor. To count, first and foremost, means to construct a series based on certain perceived commonalities or historical connections among purported members of this series.

Going back to *Panda Diaries* for the moment, the trope of counting also emerges there but in a muted way. Late in the narrative, we learn that Ge used to be a top national security official in Beijing and was asked to "com-pile an accurate and reliable body count of the fatalities" resultant from the Tiananmen "riot."[72] His reluctance to offer an official estimate led to his exile to the remote city of Changchun, which made him realize that "there is no room for the story-teller to escape."[73] Counting is storytelling and he could not bring himself to sacrifice its principles for careerism. This scene shows the logical linkage between giving a *count* and giving an *account,* or telling a story. Trying to estimate how many were killed during the suppression of the Tiananmen Square protests involves not only the task of counting bodies but also that of determining which bodies deserve being included in the count.

70. Paul Breslin, *Nobody's Nation*, 262.
71. Ibid., 262, 72.
72. Kuo, *Panda Diaries*, 72.
73. Ibid., 73.

It is a political act instrumental for establishing the contour and structure of a given historical narrative. The question of counting raised in this particular section reverberates throughout *Panda Diaries,* which recounts U.S. and Chinese histories in relation to each other, as part of an expansive series of stories about the violence entailed in the modernization and homogenization of national space. On a smaller scale, the stories in *Lipstick* also juxtapose or translate between different national histories, suggesting ways in which they can be examined as a loosely connected series.

In a story titled "Definitions," Kuo places the Chinese government's suppression of the 1989 protests in the context of many other forms of state-sponsored violence characteristic of the twentieth century. The protagonist Shen, a news anchor in China who has been warned to follow the "definitive dogma on disappearance" in reporting on those killed and arrested during the Tiananmen Square protests,[74] picks up a few archived newspapers that had spilled from file cabinets and finds stories of a number of seemingly-disjointed events:

> *Dateline Buenos Aires, August 7, 1977. Disappeared today, Pepe, Marianna and Angela Mendoza, father, wife and daughter, 27, 24 and infant, witnesses said, whisked away in a green Ford Falcon while they were walking along Avenida Florida in broad daylight. No known political activism or membership. . . .* Shanghai 1937, then Selma 1966, Warsaw 1945, and on and on, the room full of it, until he got to Hiroshima and Nagasaki 1945.[75]

In this story, the protagonist is literally counting: the Junta that came to power in Argentina in 1973 and waged a "Dirty War" afterward; the Japanese occupation of Shanghai in 1937; the slaughtering of civil rights marchers in Selma, Alabama, in 1965; the Nazi's leveling of Warsaw at the end of World War II; and, finally, the U.S. bombing of Hiroshima and Nagasaki to wrap up the same war. Dazed from all this data, Shen walks into the lobby and finds the entire building and the streets outside deserted. He realizes that, to everyone else, he has become one of the "disappeared," and can now tell their stories "in the first person."[76] The "disappeared" is a term that first emerged in studies of Cold War Latin American history, referring to victims of state-organized abductions, torture, and murder.[77] The abstraction of the "disappeared" into a transnational and transhistorical identity category in Kuo's story is reminiscent of Benedict Anderson's theorization of the emergence of collective

---

74. Kuo, *Lipstick,* 57.
75. Ibid., 59; italics in original.
76. Ibid., 59.
77. Diana Taylor, *Disappearing Acts,* x, 98.

identities in the modern world. In his article "Nationalism, Identity, and the World-in-Motion," Anderson continues his argument in *Imagined Communities*, making a distinction between collective, including national, identities engendered by cultural forms like newspapers and such tools of governance as the census. By erasing the boundaries between local and nonlocal through the use of a standardized vocabulary, newspapers allowed what can be called "quotidian universals," such concepts as "nationalists," "agitators," and "leaders," to "[seep] through and across all print languages," thus giving rise to collective identities without uniformity or clearly demarcated boundaries.[78] Newspapers enabled the rise of what Anderson calls "serial thinking," that is, the construction of identities with internal coherence that are nevertheless radically open and performative.[79] The unbound serial identities can be differentiated, though not in an absolute sense, from the essentialized, bound identities that census categories prescribe. The nature of a collective identity, to extrapolate from Anderson, is contingent not upon who is included but upon the style of inclusion. "Definitions" dramatizes an instance of Anderson's idea of "serial thinking," which gives rise to the mental construction, if not the actual emergence, of a new kind of collective identity. The category of the "disappeared" that Shen invents in the story, not unlike that of the "stateless" or "illegal aliens," is a paradox, as it is founded upon a shared state of being deprived of recognizable social identities. It constitutes an unbound identity that counters the state's power to tie individuals to or tear them away from fixed identities.

"Serial thinking" figures prominently throughout *Lipstick*, giving the stories a subtle continuity. Another story, titled "Keepers," offers an extended dream scene that stages an imagined meeting of the "disappeared," as defined in the story "Definitions." Xiao Baba, the protagonist, dreams about dipping into a picture of a high mountain lake and swimming across it to the "topological legends of the opposite shore," which takes the shape of a "citrus country."[80] The orchard is under the care of an unnamed couple, "runaways from the Guatemalan highlands" (implicitly referring to a history of indigenous movements and civil insurrections in that region), who share food and drinks with Xiao and a "recent defector," a Tiananmen Square mainlander.[81] Tapping into Xiao's consciousness, the third-person narrator describes both the caretaker couple and the mainlander as "dissenting nationalist[s]" from

78. Benedict Anderson, "Nationalism, Identity, and the World-in-Motion," 121.
79. Ibid., 121.
80. Kuo, *Lipstick*, 84.
81. Ibid. For more details about the history of civil strife and indigenous movements in Guatemala, see Jennifer Shirmer, "Appropriating the Indigenous, Creating Complicity."

an "origin of hyphens," who are now "weav[ing] their stories unhurriedly."[82] As the various dissidents gather, the "opposite shore" becomes, to Xiao, an "expanding universe of colors."[83] When Xiao stands up to leave, he feels that he has become completely interchangeable with the dissidents whom he met: "he [knows] he [is] them, there by the side of the shelter, and they [are] him, in this orchard, here now swimming strong, back across the lake."[84] The merging of different individual identities in this scene is a familiar move for Kuo, which, like the use of "we" in the *Panda Diaries* passage that starts with the image of a doorless tent, sutures artificial boundaries through "serial thinking." The dissidents in this imaginary orchard are "dissenting nationalist[s]" not just because of the particular causes they had devoted themselves to, which certainly involve rebellion against state policies, but also because they embody a nonconventional way of imagining collective, including national, identities, encapsulated in Xiao Baba's vision of "an expansive universe of colors" that does not break apart or collapse into a unitary, carefully bound series. Through the perspective of Xiao Baba, Kuo is suggesting a form of pluralist nationalism that resists the homogenizing and hierarchizing impulses of many historical and ongoing nation-building projects. The legendary "opposite shore" in the story spatializes the political power that coalitions of "dissenting nationalists" can generate while implying the degree to which these coalitions engage literally in struggles over space and habitats. We can see that Kuo's comparative critique of state violence and reimagining of the nation are intimately connected with each other, both underlined by his reflections on seriality. At the end of the story, as Xiao swims back across the lake, he knows that the image of the legendary shore will become "memory that would keep and not shift and change" and "hope looking for a random child to give itself to," like "that one waiting at the West Bank, rock already in hand."[85] Dreams matter to our empirical reality, in other words, just as metaphor is something we live by.

Trading Places

As this chapter started with a scene of misrecognition that accidentally bridges a set of ethnic and national divisions, it is apt to close it with a story that dramatizes a conscious effort to build connections across these divisions.

82. Kuo, *Lipstick*, 84.
83. Ibid., 83.
84. Ibid., 84.
85. Ibid., 84–85.

The open-ended model of pluralist nationalism that Kuo suggests is by no means easy to realize, but the author would not allow us to give up on it. In the story "Smoke," also collected in *Lipstick,* Kuo transplants, while rewriting, Native American (Creek) poet Joy Harjo's poem "The Woman Hanging from the Thirteenth Floor Window." Harjo's poem depicts the thoughts going through the mind of a Creek woman hanging from a building in eastside Chicago while she considers whether to commit suicide. Kuo's story, on the other hand, centers on a woman hanging from the thirteenth-floor window of the Bank of China building in Beijing, a new hub of an ever-expanding circuit of global finance. The thirteenth floor, which literally does not exist in some buildings, signals the ways in which both the Creek woman in Harjo's poem and the unnamed woman in Kuo's story are excluded from inhabitable social space and therefore have to claim one for themselves from the wilderness of invisibility. More interesting, the story presents the image of the hanging woman from the perspective of a Chinese official Shen, head of the Ministry of Therapy, a recently established branch of government. Having received psychiatric training in the United States, Shen is now charged with the task of maintaining the mental health of the citizens of a modernizing nation. Shen urges the woman to speak about what drove her to suicidal despair and to turn her despair into active social protest, and the woman responds by asking, "If I do, will you trade places with me?"[86] This simple question launches an ethical challenge that sends the U.S.-trained Minister of Therapy into silence. While Shen reflects upon the difficulties of entering the consciousness of another, the narrative itself offers an affirmative answer to the challenge. By translating Harjo's poem into a story about contemporary urban China, Kuo is exploring the possibility of stepping into the form, or imaginary space, created by Harjo. Much of Kuo's lifelong work, indeed, is devoted to the idea of trading places as a process of creating new connections and generating new metaphors; it is what turns the nonplace of the thirteenth floor into an interface of many possible worlds.

86. Ibid., 63.

CHAPTER 4

A New Politics of Faith

Zhang Chengzhi's *Xinling Shi* and
Rabih Alameddine's *Koolaids: The Art of War*

> Deep pluralism . . . reinstates the link between practice and belief
> that had been artificially severed by secularism; and it also over-
> turns the impossible counsel to bracket your faith when you par-
> ticipate in politics.
>
> —William Connolly, *Pluralism*

> Radicals might discover [in the Jewish and Christian Scriptures]
> some valuable insights into human emancipation, in an era when
> the political left stands in dire need of good ideas.
>
> —Terry Eagleton, *Reason, Faith, and Revolution:*
> *Reflections on the God Debate*

IN HIS 1993 essay "Helpless Thought," Hui Muslim writer Zhang
Chengzhi revisits his anger at the assertion of America military
power during the first Gulf War, which he sees as a step toward
consolidating the unipolar world order that prevailed in the decade
following the collapse of the Soviet Union. What angered Zhang
most, however, was the ways in which Chinese news broadcasters
ventriloquized the "Anglo-Saxon" tone on the war.[1] In another essay,
written ten years later but included in the same collection, Zhang
reiterates his distaste for the Chinese media's embrace of "Anglo-
Saxon orthodoxy," this time in condemning Islamic "terrorists."[2]
Although the Hui Muslims, one of the nine Muslim groups in China,
are linguistically and culturally different from the Uyghur Muslims,

---

1. Zhang Chengzhi, "Wuyuan de sixiang" [Helpless thought], 39.
2. Zhang Chengzhi, "Gou de diaoxiang" [A statue of a dog], 23.

the group that the Chinese government has linked to Islamist terrorist organizations in Central Asia, they have also been frequently accused of harboring an Islam-inspired propensity toward antistate violence.[3] As one of the most important Hui Muslim writers active today, Zhang has since the early 1990s written extensively about the question of Muslim militancy in relation to specific historical and geopolitical contexts as a way of rebuffing the equation, in both the West and China, of Muslim struggles with terrorism.[4] Since the early 2000s, the Chinese government's campaigns against Uyghur unrest in Xinjiang and Uyghur independence organizations overseas have been thoroughly infused with antiterror rhetoric. Like Tibet, Xinjiang has come to embody a perpetual state of emergency that requires special government control techniques, which in this case range from the successive tides of "strike hard" campaigns in the 1990s to the newly launched "Tianshan Project" aiming to clamp down on the distribution of pro-independence material in Xinjiang and four other Northwest provinces.[5] Such measures, if we extend Zhang's point about China's adoption of antiterror rhetoric as an infelicitous instance of translation, mirror the U.S. government's curtailment of civil liberties after 9/11 that dislocated the American people from the "normal political order," "the nation as a shared way of life."[6] This is certainly not an exact parallel, but what we can say, at the very least, is that the two governments' responses to Islamic militancy in the post–Cold War era, before and after 9/11 in particular, reveal the structural limits of the two nations' multiculturalisms.

This chapter brings together two narratives that, as Kuo does in *Panda Diaries,* address these limits obliquely by turning to the (distant and recent) past. One of them is Zhang Chengzhi's fictionalized history *Xinling Shi* [A history of the soul], a 1991 work that has not yet been translated into English. The other is Arab American author Rabih Alameddine's first novel *Koolaids: The Art of War,* published in the United States in 1998. *Xinling Shi* reconstructs the history of the Jahriya, a suborder of Sufism, in eighteenth- and nineteenth-century China, with a focus on the popular insurrections in northwest and southwest regions that the Jahriya spearheaded during the period in reaction to, among other things, the imperial government's sup-

---

3. Jonathan Lipman points out, in *Familiar Strangers,* that all the Chinese judgments of the Hui Muslims that he recounts in his book "have included a proclivity for antisocial behavior" (Lipman, 118).

4. He has written, for example, in support of the Palestinian resistance movement and in commemoration of the life of Malcome X. See "Toushi de sushuo" [A story of stone throwing]; "Zhenzheng de ren shi X" [X embodies true humanity].

5. Pan Ying, "Xibei wushenqu qian xieyi lianshou daji 'sangu shili'" [Five northwest provinces signed agreement to clamp down on "Three Forces"].

6. Donald Pease, "The Global Homeland State," 6–7.

pression of their spiritual belief. *Koolaids* is a collage of voices that constitute a fragmentary narrative of the complex causes and consequences of the prolonged Lebanese Civil War as well as the struggles of the religious, racial, and sexual others in 1980s and 1990s America. By reconstructing histories of ethno-religious or racio-religious wars, Zhang and Alameddine draw attention to what conciliatory multiculturalism writes out of national consciousness. Ethno-religious harmony, they seem to say, is not to be achieved in the present or the future if these histories of violence are allowed to be forgotten and repeated.

In unearthing histories of ethno-religious conflicts, these narratives take on momentous questions central to contemporary discussions of multiculturalism. How would an awareness of these histories challenge or reshape China's ethnic policy or U.S. liberal multiculturalism? What positions do ethno-religious minorities and religious values occupy in multicultural projects? Stanley Fish has famously argued that even the strongest version of liberal multiculturalism, what he calls the "politics of difference," cannot help delimiting itself because "sooner or later the culture whose core you are tolerating will reveal itself to be intolerant at the same core."[7] The example he uses to illustrate what he means by "intolerant" is, predictably, the *fatwa* against Rushdie. Is it true that religious faith, especially the Islamic faith, engenders a form of intolerance incompatible with multicultural values? Can there be alternative perspectives on how religion relates to various multiculturalisms? The two narratives studied here offer extremely nuanced commentaries on all of the questions just posed. Before I say more about them, however, I would like to go on a theoretical detour, since the relationship between religion and politics has become an intensely discussed topic since 9/11, especially as it pertains to the position of Muslims and Islam in modern secular nations. It is a discussion in which both Zhang and Alameddine intervene.

One of the key works on this topic is Gil Anidjar's *The Jew, the Arab,* which builds on the Schmittian concept of political theology to offer an intellectual genealogy, since the medieval period, that casts the Arab and the Jew as two separated and yet conjoined figures of the enemy vis-à-vis the Christian West. Arabs are largely considered to be the military, political, and external enemy and Jews the theological, internal enemy, though this distinction often proves unstable. Underlying, and mirroring, this complicated history is the simultaneous bifurcation and conflation of the political and the theological in Western history. An early sign of the separation of the two spheres can be seen in Augustine, for example, whose "[j]ust-war theory was developed in almost complete isolation from the [Christian] command-

7. Stanley Fish, "Boutique Multiculturalism," 382–83.

ment to love one's enemy."[8] The modern conception of the state, as Anidjar points out, à la Schmitt, also depended on the "separation of theology from politics."[9] Simultaneous with this separation, however, was "a structural translation of theology into politics," or, in other words, the shaping of a homology between concepts of modern state theory such as sovereignty and metaphysical concepts.[10] The mutual penetration of the political and the theological, however, is masked by their institutional separation, with the consequence that Arabs and Jews have come to be imagined in the Christian West as distinct from or antagonist toward each other despite their historical connections, as captured in the term "Semite." Talal Asad offers a converging and complementary argument regarding politics and religion in *Formations of the Secular*. Asad also insists on the inseparability of religion and secular politics, but points out that the entwining the two involves more than "structural analogies between premodern theological concepts and those deployed in secular constitutional discourse," which came about as a result of the process of translation that Schmitt identified.[11] More important, for Asad, the rise of the modern concept of secular politics presupposed and required a specific notion of religion. Modern secular states (including, but not excluded to, those rooted in Western Christendom) did not, as conventional arguments for secularism as a normative ideal would have it, protect civil freedoms "from the tyranny of religious discourse," for the very concepts of civil freedoms and religious tyranny are modern inventions.[12] The secular state created itself by constructing a *"specific political realm—* representative democracy, citizenship, law and order, civil liberties" that purportedly "transcend[ed] particular and differentiating practices of the self . . . articulated through class, gender, and religion."[13] Religious authority, in the meantime, was recast as sectarian, irrational, and tyrannical, precluded from competing for the loyalty of citizens or engaging in public talk on nonreligious issues. The ascendance of secular nationalism was, in other words, predicated on the belief that religious organizations and institutions, and Islamic ones in particular, are incongruous with the properly political, even when they engage in procedural politics.[14] This point is echoed in William Connolly's *Why I am Not a Secularist,* where the author theorizes

---

8. Gil Anidjar, *The Jew, The Arab,* 24.
9. Ibid. 106.
10. Ibid.
11. Ibid. 191, 255.
12. Talal Asad, *Formations of the Secular,* 255.
13. Ibid., 5, emphasis in the original.
14. The examples Asad uses here include "the call by Muslim movements to reform the social body through the authority of popular majorities in the national parliament . . . as in Algeria in 1992 and in Turkey in 1997" (*Formations of the Secular,* 199).

secular nationalism and political liberalism as two concurrent and symbi-otic processes (at least in the West) that need to be reconfigured simulta-neously.[15] Going back to Anidjar, we can say that Arab Muslims have not just become the primary political enemy of the Christian West; they have become antithetical to modern definitions of politics. The process in which Arab Muslims became the enemy, moreover, should also be seen as a process of racialization. In the case of Muslims, religion and race should be seen, to quote Anidjar again, as *"contemporary,* indeed, coextensive and, moreover, co-concealing categories."[16]

The particular point I wish to make through this theoretical excursion is that studying the experiences of racio-religious and ethno-religious minori-ties such as Arab Muslims in modern, secular nation-states is crucial for critiquing various versions of conciliatory multiculturalism at the core of the self-representations of these nation-states. Extrapolating from scholars like Anidja and Asad, one can argue that, as an integral aspect of modern, secu-lar nationalism, multicultural policies establish their own legitimacy on the basis of their supposed distinctions from "intolerant" religious and cultural values, even as these distinctions mask the deep continuity between politi-cal and religious spheres. Conciliatory multiculturalism's claim to tolerance obscures the mechanisms of exclusion inherent in it. Stanley Fish is right that liberal multiculturalism as it is practiced in the contemporary United States is naturally incongruous with certain cultural or religious values, but it is not because these values are intolerant in themselves. They must be defined as intolerant under liberal multiculturalism. Rather than recycle secularist biases by dichotomizing liberal tolerance and religious bigotry, therefore, we should instead challenge the limits of U.S. multiculturalism by reconsidering the relations of religion to secular politics. The Chinese ethnic policy needs to be questioned in a similar way. It carries important parallels with U.S. liberal multiculturalism as a secularized instrument of nation-building that is nevertheless inflected by ideas "translated" from traditional value systems with metaphysical dimensions (Confucianism, most obviously), if not reli-gion. Not unlike U.S. liberal multiculturalism, it has shown an inability to accommodate the radical ethno-religious difference embodied in militant elements of Muslim communities. As Zhang Chengzhi reminds us, the trope of Islamic terrorism has traveled across state and ideological borders with alarming ease. It is therefore important to examine the experiences and cul-

15. Connolly objects in particular to the belief that nation-states provide "the best hope for democracy," arguing instead that the idea of national unity is what in many cases restricts, rather than facilitates, pluralistic democracy (89).

16. Gil Anidjar, *Semites: Race, Religion, and Literature,* 28.

tural production of Muslim communities in the two countries comparatively. My study of the two narratives in this chapter does so by focusing on what they suggest about the structural limits of Chinese and U.S. multicultural-isms and possible tactics for reconfiguring their formal logic.

Both *Xinling Shi* and *Koolaids* came out and received critical claim in the decade immediately before 9/11, a decade when Muslim communities were subjected to increasing surveillance and pressure in both countries. They foreshadowed academic discussions around the resurgence of religion in the post-9/11 era, proposing their own visions of genuinely inclusive forms of multiculturalism that fully accommodate radical ethno-religious differences. Both authors rework religious concepts—the Jahriya's exaltation of spiritual freedom and the Christian doctrine of universal love—as promising supple-ments to secular conceptions of multiculturalism. In what follows, I first situate the two narratives in historical contexts, that is, the development of Hui Muslim and Arab American identities and literary articulations. Then, through a reading of the two texts, I argue that they help us imagine ways of extending the limits of Chinese and U.S. multiculturalisms, respectively, by breaking down the conceptual opposition between religion and secular politics. To further illustrate the significance of the authors' interventions, I situate their ideas in the context of intellectual discussions on the politics of religion in their respective context. The juxtaposition of the two writers in this chapter does not mean to suggest an exact symmetry. If the previous chapter on Alex Kuo teaches us anything, it is that a cross-national compari-son can never be blind to its own excesses and reductions. My comparison here, therefore, does not seek to offer general remarks on overlaps between Hui Muslim and Arab American experiences. It does argue, however, that both groups have produced important reflections on ethno-religious and racio-religious differences that cannot be metabolized by conciliatory mul-ticulturalism. Zhang and Alammedine offer particularly illuminating speci-mens of these reflections, consciously rebelling, in their own ways, against the violence engendered from the workings of the "coextensive, co-conceal-ing" categories of race/ethnicity and religion by, paradoxically, revealing the extent of this violence. By retracing paths of war, they help answer the ques-tion of how contemporary nations might minimize its scourge.

Muslims in China and the U.S.

Unknown to many, Islam has been propagated in China for over 1,300 years. In his groundbreaking work *Muslim Chinese: Ethnic Nationalism in the*

People's Republic, Gru Gladney delineates four tides of Islam in Chinese history.[17] The first tide, spanning between the seventh and the fourteenth centuries, was the constitution of Muslim communities along China's southeast coast and in the northwest, where descendants of the Arab, Persian, Central Asian, and Mongolian Muslim merchants, militia, and officials settled. The second wave began in the late seventeenth century, as Sufism spread to China and Sufi communities formed around descendants of saintly leaders. The third tide rose at the end of the Qing Dynasty, when increased contact between Muslims in China and the Middle East spurred several reform movements that projected conflicting visions on how Islamic ideas should mesh with Chinese culture.[18] The fourth tide, which continues today, started as China opened itself to the West in the early 1980s, upon the end of the Cultural Revolution. Partially encouraged by the Chinese state, Muslims in China began to travel abroad for pilgrimages and religious studies more frequently and became increasingly vocal in voicing their cultural concerns.[19]

As Jonathan Lipman, author of *Familiar Strangers,* points out, Muslims in China were all referred to as Hui during the Ming and Qing Dynasty, and this designation continued to be used during republican China.[20] After the founding of the PRC, however, the government identified ten Muslim minority nationalities, using the category of Hui to designate Muslims "who do not have a language of their own but speak the dialects of the peoples among whom they live," as opposed to the nine Turkish-Altaic and Indo-European Muslim language groups."[21] The Hui are thus different from the other Muslim groups, not only because they were affected by all four tides of Islam in China but also because they are not distinguished from the majority Han by language or locality. However, although the Hui were granted the status of a minority nationality largely on the basis of their religious belief, they

17. Dru C. Gladney, *Muslim Chinese,* 36–64.

18. The Ikwan Muslim Brotherhood, for example, advocated a "purified, 'non-Chinese' Islam," while Xi Dao Tang, a small, completely "native" Islamic movement promoted the study of the "Chinese Confucian-Islamic classics" (Gladney, *Muslim Chinese,* 55, 57). There are contradictions internal to these movements as well: the Ikwan, or Yihewani in its sinicized version, for example, supported Muslim unity as well as Chinese national consciousness (Gladney, *Muslim Chinese,* 55).

19. A Muslim protest in Beijing in May 1989, for example, was organized to condemn the publication of a book entitled *Sexual Customs,* which the Muslims believed denigrated Islam. See Gladney, *Muslim Chinese,* 2.

20. Historically, Hui was a shortened version of *Huihui,* which came originally from *Huihe* (Lipman, *Familiar Strangers,* xxiii). Since the 1950s, Hui refers to "a Muslim or descendent of Muslims who lives in China but does not belong to one of the nine linguistically or territorially defined Muslim *minzu* (nationalities)" (Lipman, xxiii).

21. Gladney, *Muslim Chinese,* 19. The other nine are Uighur, Kazak, Dongxiang, Kirghiz, Salar, Tadjik, Uzbek, Baoan, and Tatar.

are not a purely religious category. A Hui person can maintain her minority status without believing in Islam, since the Hui identity passes down, as Gladney points out, "through migration, intermarriage, and adoption."[22] In *Xinling Shi,* which excavates and rewrites the history of the Jahriya in imperial China, Zhang Chengzhi accepts the PRC definition of the Hui, referring consistently to the Jahriya as part of *Huimin* (the Hui people). I follow the author in using the term "Hui" to refer to Chinese-speaking Muslims in both historical and contemporary China.

Compared with the other Muslim minorities in China, the Hui Muslims have a particularly ambiguous relationship with Chinese culture. Gladney limns the two extreme views on this relationship, the view that the Hui are virtually indistinguishable from the Han majority, essentially assimilated except for "certain religious beliefs and archaic customs," and the opposite view that they constitute an "isolated religious enclave" that historically fomented reform movements and armed rebellions against secular Chinese authorities.[23] The events of 9/11 brought the question of Islam to the fore in China, though, as many have pointed out, due to a surge in Uyghur separatist activities in Xinjiang, attention to religiously fueled "terrorism" mounted in China throughout the 1990s.[24] These developments have affected the Uyghurs more than the other Muslim minorities in China, but the tensions between Islam and secular Chinese culture have become an urgent issue for all Muslims in the country. Zhang Chengzhi's *Xinling Shi* is one of the few literary works in China that tackle this issue directly. The timeline of the narrative overlaps largely with what Gladney identifies as the second tide of Islamic influence in China, when the spread of Sufism crystallized the conflicts between Islam and the secular authorities of imperial China. On the

22. Ibid., 59. Gladney explains that Hui Muslims encompass a "spectrum of ethnoreligious expression" (*Muslim Chinese,* 113). For some Hui communities in northwest China, Islam is the most salient aspect of Hui identity. For others (in the southeast, for example), Hui identity is based almost entirely on genealogical descent from foreign Arab ancestors. In between are Hui Muslims for whom identity is a "mixture of ethnic ancestry and religious commitment" (Gladney, *Muslim Chinese,* 113).

23. Ibid., 22–24.

24. See Gladney, "Islam in China," 455–61. Gladney explains several factors that make the Xinjiang Uyghur Autonomous Region central to China's national interests. First of all, the government is concerned with the separatist movement in Xinjiang and the advocacy for it overseas and on the Internet. The large Akto insurrection in April 1990 (the first major uprising in Xinjiang) was suppressed and Amnesty International claims that there have been frequent roundups of "terrorists" since then. Alleged incursions of Talibans into China through Xinjiang prior to 9/11 swamped the area with Chinese security forces, a development only to be intensified afterwards. Gladney also analyzes the economic factor (China's increased trade with Central Asian and Arab countries for oil) and the political factor (the credibility of China's cultural pluralism and its international image) that make Xinjiang an important issue.

one hand, Zhang presents the Jahriya during the eighteenth and nineteenth century as fearless protagonists of spectacular dramas of antistate rebellions, no less than the earliest group of jihadists in Chinese history. On the other, however, he advocates for their incorporation into mainstream Chinese history by staging their struggles as a precursor to the peasant and nationalist revolutions in later eras that were to put an end to imperial China and launch China onto a path toward modernization. For Zhang, then, the Jahriya should be accorded a crucial position in Chinese history although they have never fully assimilated into secular Chinese culture. By making this apparently paradoxical argument, as I elaborate later, Zhang is renegotiating the structure and boundaries of Chinese national identity, the meanings, that is, of its "center" and "margins." The Jahriya's antistate struggles figure in Zhang's narrative as a crucible in which contradictory views of the relationship between Islam and secular Chinese culture clash and weld with each other, gesturing in the end toward a new, fluid understanding of Chinese history and identity that does away with a fixed center. *Xinling Shi*, therefore, is both a fictionalized, personalized history and a parable of a new model of pluralism for contemporary China.

Xinling Shi should also be situated in the history of contemporary Hui Muslim literature. In her article "Hui Writers: A Hundred-Year Précis," Hui Muslim scholar Ma Lirong argues that a conscious exploration of the Hui experience in literary forms began around the mid-1950s, when the PRC government started the Ethnic Classification Project.[25] Yang Jiguo makes a similar point in an earlier essay "Characteristics of Contemporary Hui Literature," emphasizing the enabling role that government initiatives played in the rapid growth of Hui literature since the end of the Cultural Revolution.[26] He praises the government for spurring Hui and other minority writers into expressing ethnic self-consciousness through efforts to collect and compile Hui writings, organize symposiums and discussions on this topic, and launch journals devoted to Hui literature.[27] Overall, Ma's and Yang's historical surveys rehash the official narratives of the PRC's ethnic policy and its historical origin. For Ma, especially, the rise of Hui Muslim literature bears out a uniquely Chinese history of cultural pluralism, which began with a homegrown ideal of cultural "amalgamation" articulated during the anti-Japanese war in the 1930s as a means of uniting different ethnic groups in China against a com-

---

25. Ma Lirong, "Jin bainian huizu zuojia gailun" [Hui writers: A hundred year précis], 96.
26. Yang, Jiguo, "Dangdai huizu wenxue de chuangzuo tezheng" [Characteristics of contemporary Hui literature].
27. Ibid., 73.

mon enemy.[28] This ideal has, since the 1980s, found reinforcement in the government's renewed emphasis on cultural pluralism on both the national and international levels, allowing Hui Muslims to foreground their ethno-religious heritage in the context of the Chinese nation-state as well as global Islam, thus offering a further impetus to Hui Muslim literature.[29] Since the 1980s, this literature has continued to grow in many regions of the country, reaching as wide a distribution as the Hui people themselves, some of whom live in ethnic enclaves (including but not limited to the Ningxia Hui Autono-mous Region) while others are dispersed among the Han majority. What is more interesting in Ma's account is her description of Hui–Han relations as they are registered in Hui literature. Not unlike Zhang, Ma casts the relations in ambiguous and paradoxical terms—the Hui are simultaneously inside and outside secular Chinese culture. As she sees it, the aesthetic and political val-ues of Hui Muslim literature reside in its focus on both the spiritual and the secular, both religious devotion and integration into surrounding Han and non-Han cultures through trade and other secular activities.[30] It is not clear, however, what sociopolitical conditions underlie this dual relationship and what tensions, conflicts, and cultural changes can arise from it. Ma lays great emphasis on Hui writers' devotion to the ideal of *qingjie,* which translates literally as "pure and clean," connoting, as Gladney explains, "Islamic moral purity and the authenticity of ethnic ancestry, lifestyle, and heritage."[31] Much, however, remains to be said about the ways in which literary representations of this ideal can disrupt or help reorganize the secular sphere within which they circulate. *Xinling Shi* is one of the most important texts in contemporary China that explore the political implications of the ideal of *qingjie.* Its con-struction of Jahriya history accentuates the conflicts between the spiritual and the secular, while at the same time demonstrating that these two spheres are inseparable and mutually susceptible.

Like the Hui Muslims, Arab Americans can be seen as an ethno-religious, or more precisely racio-religious, category. It is only in the 1990s that "Arab Americans" emerged as "an organized ethnic designation" at the intersec-

28. Ma, "Jin bainian huizu zuojia gailun" [Hui writers: A hundred year précis], 100. The one who put forth this idea is Hui leftist translator and writer Ma Zongrong. An advocate of Chinese national unity during the Anti-Japanese War (1937–45), Ma Zongrong cofounded the Chinese Hui Culture Institute under the auspices of the Chinese Hui Patriotic Association in 1939. The mission of the institute included "amalgamating ethnic cultures in China into one" (Ma, 95).

29. Ibid., 96.

30. Ibid., 97. The ideal of *qingjie* extends into the portrayal of secular life in Hui literature, as one sees in the depictions of love for one's parents and romantic love in a number of novels by Hui authors.

31. Gladney, "Islam in China," 13. In China Islam is sometimes referred to as *qingzhen jiao*—the Doctrine of Purity and Truth.

tion of Arab immigration in the United States, U.S. relations with the Middle East, and wars and political conflicts in the region.[32] Michael Suleiman documents that there have been two major waves of Arab immigration to North America. The first lasted from the 1870s to World War II, consisting largely of Christian immigrants from the greater Syria region, and the second went from World War II to the present, including immigrants (of various religious affiliations) from Israel and all twenty-two Arab nations.[33] Emigration from Syria began to assume large proportions in the 1890s, but the number declined sharply in the post–World War I years, largely as a result of changes in U.S. immigration laws.[34] These early immigrants experienced discrimination based on their association with their Turkish/Muslim overlords and were occasionally classified in a legal sense as Asiatics and denied U.S. citizenship. Consequently, these Syrian immigrants actively identified themselves as Arabs to stake a claim to a Semitic identity and, by extension, whiteness.[35] Evelyn Shakir's survey of the history of Arab American fiction provides an illuminating detail about the racial status of early Arab immigrants from Syria. As Robert Woods observes in *The City Wilderness* (1898), "[N]ext to the Chinese, who can never be in any real sense Americans, the Syrians [i.e., Lebanese and Syrians] are the most foreign of all our foreigners, and out of the nationalities would be distinguished for nothing whatever excepting as curiosities."[36] While "Arab" compared slightly more favorably with "Asiatic" at the turn of the twentieth century and became officially white in the following decades, the term took on new meanings in the post–World War II era. The influx of Muslim Arab immigrants after the 1948 Palestinian exodus changed the religious and political composition of Arab America. As Nouri Gana points out, Arab immigrants met increasing challenges because of their "faith and political agendas," and consequently, their claim to whiteness became attenuated.[37] Steven Salaita also argues that Arab American

---

32. Steven Salaita, *Arab American Literary Fictions, Cultures, and Politics,* 26.

33. Michael W. Suleiman, "Early Arab-Americans," 1.

34. Samir Khalaf, "The Background and Causes of Lebanese/Syrian Immigration to the United States before World War I," 18.

35. Suleiman documents that Syrians "had come in large numbers and were admitted into the U.S. and granted U.S. citizenship since the 1880s" (44). But in 1914 a certain George Dow was denied his petition to become a U.S. citizen by Judge Henry A. M. Smith, district judge in Charleston, SC, on the grounds that Dow was a "Syrian of Asiatic birth" (Suleiman, 44). In reaction to the judge's decision, Kalil A. Bishara wrote in the English section of his *Origin of the Modern Syrian* that Syrians were Arabs and thus were the "purest type of the Semitic race" and had a "better claim upon the White Race than that of any modern nation of Europe" (Suleiman, 44). The case of George Dow was eventually reversed.

36. Evelyn Shakir, "Arab American Literature," 5.

37. Nouri Gana, "Introduction," 1574.

racialization became a "de facto reality" in the post–World War II United States, especially during and after the 1990s.[38]

With increased racialization comes an enhanced racial consciousness among Arab Americans. Suleiman finds that, by the 1967 Arab–Israeli War, third-generation Arab immigrants "had started to awaken to their own identity and see their identity as 'Arab,' not just Syrian."[39] Simultaneous with and constitutive of the rise of an Arab American political consciousness was a correlated cultural consciousness on the verge of a "critical breakthrough," as Salaita puts it, as evident in the publication of a number of Arab American literary anthologies and the rise to fame of a group of Arab American writers.[40] An impressive number of Arab American authors have dealt with the Israeli–Palestine conflict in their works, for example.[41] Besides the Israeli–Palestine conflict, the Lebanese Civil War, the Palestinian diaspora in the Middle East and in the United States, and anti-Arabic racism since the early 1990s (Joseph Geha's *Through and Through,* for example) are also frequent topics in recent Arab American literature. Alameddine's *Koolaids* is a notable example of these writings, focusing simultaneously on the local, regional, and international politics shaping the prolonged Lebanese Civil War and cultural politics in the 1980s United States. The novel illustrates the ways in which religious doctrines inflect the political culture of both Lebanon and the United States, ironically erasing their purported distinctions. In a way reminiscent of Zhang, Alameddine is careful not to cast theologico-political divisions as a force destined to break nations apart. Instead, he proposes reworking religious doctrines as a way of reactivating the ideal of a genuinely pluralistic universalism that can help broaden our conceptions of the modern nation.

A Metaphysical Challenge

Zhang Chengzhi's *Xinling Shi* is a fictionalized history of the Jahriya sect, a suborder of the Naqshabandi Sufis, in eighteenth- and nineteenth-century China (during the Qing Dynasty). It has been described as a kind of "apocryphal history" that acquired a "biblical status" among Jahriya followers in China.[42] In the Preface, the author provides an account of his immersion in the world of the Jahriya in Western China since 1984. Eight extended trips to

38. Steven Salaita, *Anti-Arab Racism in the USA,* 23.
39. Suleiman, 10.
40. Ibid., 76.
41. Salaita, *Arab American Literary Fictions,* 52.
42. Jian Xu, "Radical Ethnicity and Apocryphal History," 527.

western parts of China inspired in him the resolve to write a book that Jahriya followers "would protect with their lives."[43] He was subsequently embraced by many members of the Jahriya, who showed him a number of secretly circulated religious histories, written in Persian or Arabic and translated into Chinese for him, along with "nearly a hundred and sixty family genealogies and other manuscripts."[44] The narrative of *Xinling Shi* starts with the introduction of Sufi revivalism into China in the eighteenth century through the work of Naqshabandi Ma Mingxin, among others. It offers a narrative of the long-lasting conflicts, since the 1760s, within the Sufi communities in northwest China, especially between the rival Sufi suborders of the Jahriya and the Khafiya. The increasing internecine fighting culminated in 1781, when legal disputes and street violence between the competing orders brought the imperial army to Xunhua (a region in northwest China) for an intervention. The Khafiya sect allied with the Qing court and received the positive appellation the "Old Teaching," while the Jahriya, which sought to represent the spirit of Islamic renewal and remained more militant toward state authorities, was given the pejorative epithet of the "New Teaching."[45] The imperial army engaged Jahriya followers in merciless battles in 1781 and 1784, succeeding nearly in obliterating the entire sect. The Jahriya, however, managed to survive. Zhang's narrative then jumps to a century later, when violent confrontations between the Hui and the Qing army erupted in northwest regions. The Jahriya played a crucial role in the major battles during the ten-year war (1862–73), especially in the last stage of the conflicts. In the meantime, a Hui-led multiethnic rebellion, the Panthay Rebellion (1855–73), occurred in Yunnan in southwest China, offering another stage for the inspired valor of the Jahriya.[46] Scholarly studies of the Hui Muslim role in the waves of violence in eighteenth- and nineteenth-century China have tended to argue against reducing them to "Muslim rebellions" and emphasize instead numerous other contributing factors.[47] This critical move is certainly effective in

43. Zhang Chengzhi, *Xinling Shi* [*History of the soul*], 7.

44. Ibid., 8.

45. Ibid., 91. What sects the "New Teaching" and the "Old Teaching" actually referred to historically are not fully settled. For a fuller discussion, see Raphael Israeli, *Islam in China,* chapter 8. What is certain, as Israeli points out, is that the "New Teaching" was identified with the Naqshbandi Jahriya during Ma Mingxin's lifetime (142).

46. "Panthay Rebellion" is the most common term given to the rebellion in the English language. The word "panthay" might come from "*pa-ti,*" the Burmese term for Muslim. The rebellion is virtually unknown in China.

47. For example, Lipman argues that the eighteenth-century wars between the Jahris and the Qing army should not be described as "ethnic conflicts" or "Muslim rebellions;" rather, the Jahri insurrections in northwest China that lasted a century and a half were due to a combination of "the complex of national policy decisions regarding the New Teaching, provincial maladministration, local religious and political rivalries, military officials overzealous in their

refuting racialist and secularist stereotypes of Islam as violent and irrational, but it is not the only alternative to rehashing common assumptions. Zhang Chengzhi takes an opposite route. He moves the question of religion to the center of his narrative, maximizing the role of the Jahriya faith in his account of the violent conflicts in Hui areas during the Qing era. I argue that his approach supplements the ongoing discussion of the formation of ethnic and racial identities in the Qing era by highlighting the factor of religion. More important, he intervenes productively in the official discourse on multiculturalism in contemporary China, which relies on muting references to ethnic and religious conflicts in the past and present of the nation. An authoritative account of the Hui-led rebellion in Yunnan, for example, casts them as "a form of class struggle" and as "part of the struggle of all China against the Qing."[48] Zhang's history of the Jahriya, in other words, exerts pressure on dominant narratives of the relationship between ethno-racial and religious differences in both imperial and contemporary China.

Historical scholarship on the late Qing, when Zhang's history of the Jahriya is set, offers convincing rationales for employing the concepts of race and ethnicity to describe group identities during that period. It has been argued that indigenous Chinese equivalents of modern Western notions of racial and ethnic identity were at work during this period. Frank Dikötter believes that the ideology of descent is deeply rooted in Qing history. He describes the Qing era as "marked by a consolidation of the cult of patrilineal descent," as manifest in the various lineage feuds throughout the empire and in the turn towards "a rigid taxonomy of distinct descent lines" during the period of the Qianlong emperor.[49] Similarly, Pamela Crossley argues that, while the Western notion of race was not imported into China until the late-nineteenth century, the Qing court had produced its own version of racial ideology during the eighteenth century.[50] To stave off the dissipation of Manchu culture, the Qing court moved increasingly toward a "racial conceptionalization" of the Manchus, based on bloodlines and genealogy.[51] Elaborating on Crossley's point, Mark Elliott contends that, from the very beginning of their rule in China, the Manchus created a political universalism by blending

---

obedience to unenforceable orders, and currents from the Muslim west" (Lipman, *Familiar Strangers*, 114). Also see David G. Atwill, *The Chinese Sultanate*. Atwill also points out that the conventional understanding of the Penthay rebellion in the southwest is "deceptive" because it "overemphasizes ethnic and religious divisions" (9), underestimating the involvement of other non-Han people in the region.

48. Israeli, *Islam in China*, 191.
49. Dikötter, "Racial Discourse in China," 14–15.
50. Crossley, "Thinking about Ethnicity in Early Modern China," 11.
51. Crossley, "The Qianlong Retrospect on the Chinese-Martial (*hanjun*) Banners," 85.

generally accepted norms of virtue and culture of the Han elite, namely, neo-Confucianism, with political institutions, most important, the Eight Banners system (a banner is a military–civilian organization led by a banner nobility) that separated the Manchus from Han society, a separation that Elliott refers to as "Ethnic Sovereignty."[52] This mixture allowed the Qing Dynasty to become a heterogeneous empire "composed of multiple hierarchies of lordships based on different types of authority."[53] The institutionalization of "Ethnic Sovereignty" was instrumental in preventing the "fusion" of the Manchus with the Han elite class, thus allowing the Manchus to maintain a separate identity from and power over the Han majority up until the end of the Qing in 1911.[54]

While these histories all demonstrate the formation of the notions of race and ethnicity during the Qing era, they focus largely on the Han–Manchu dynamic. The Hui, however, were on neither side of this opposition, possessed of neither cultural influence nor political power. The Qing court and its officials, in many cases, protected the interests of Han immigrants and residents, especially in Yunnan, at the expense of the native Hui people.[55] The history of Hui Muslims, then, complicates existing academic discourses around race and ethnicity in late Qing, showing that the era witnessed multiple ethno-racial rivalries that cannot all be subsumed under the divide between the Manchus, the ruling minority, and the Han, the ethnic majority. A point more crucial to reading Zhang's *Xinling Shi*, however, is that existing historical studies of ethnicity and race during this era hardly touch on the issue of religion. The antistate struggles of Hui Muslims, as Zhang points out, also had a great deal to do with the state's decision to interfere with the conflicts between two rivaling sects of Sufism, the Jahriya and the Khafiya, dubbed by the Qing court as the "New Teaching" and the "Old Teaching," respectively. These struggles, in other words, entail an element inexplicable within a simple paradigm of race and ethnicity.

By folding religion back into discussions of ethnic and racial formation during the Qing era, *Xinling Shi* frames the violent history that it describes as a confrontation between the Confucian conception of universal imperial power and the Jahriya notion of an alternative moral universe presided over by a spiritual power. It figures Confucianism as a form of political theology—though distinct from religion, it carries important religious undertones. In so doing, the narrative holds under critical lens a central foundation of the

---

52. Mark Elliott, *The Manchu Way*, 4.
53. Ibid.
54. Ibid., 7.
55. See Atwill, 80–83, 94–97.

Qing's political system and, by extension, the political system of contemporary China.

Northwest China, in Zhang's description, is an unruly region where "secular political economy" and orthodox Confucian teachings never took root.[56] Having had to survive the condition of extreme poverty and isolation, various peoples living in the northwest were uniquely primed for conversion to Sufism. They were quickly swept up by the intoxicating belief in a higher spiritual power that would help them make sense of the endlessly grinding pain of earthly life. With Ma Mingxin's missionary work, the Jahriya flourished in parts of northwest China, providing an "invisible, iron-clad refuge" for the souls of those toiling at the bottom of the Qing society.[57] Zhang's account of the origin of the Jahriya in Confucian China goes beyond a class analysis, as he locates its base in those who were completely excluded from "secular political economy." There is something radically different about the Jahriya. In Zhang's account of the war in 1781, the Jahriya became the "most potent enemy" of the state because they displayed a level of resistance that the Qing rulers had never seen before.[58] Aside from the corruption of local officials, which, for Zhang, manifested the "false prosperity" of the eighteenth-century Qing, what also drove Qing rulers into a ruthless attempt to obliterate the Jahriya was the believers' astounding strength, resilience, and willingness to sacrifice for their cause, which struck the emperor as dangerously irreconcilable with a secular understanding of his imperial subjects.[59] The emperor was deeply disturbed when several unexpected storms gave an advantage to the Jahriya warriors during their first major battle with the Qing troops, sensing the presence of a divine power that did not bow to his sovereignty. As Zhang puts it, the emperor had in fact been "defeated psychologically" before the battle ended in his favor, and he developed the ominous vision that the dirt-poor people of the northwest had become a "strange rival" that must be annihilated.[60] Ironically, in attributing changes on the battlefield to a divine power, the emperor comes to mirror his enemy. He reveals a perspective on political power that is not fundamentally different from that of the Jahriya. Like the Jahriya, the emperor believes that the legitimacy of secular rule is founded on the will of transcendent forces, and the strange resilience of the Jahriya warriors testifies to the existence of such a force operating against him. The threat that the Jahriya posed to the Qing court, as Zhang suggests

56. Zhang, *Xinling Shi*, 21.
57. Ibid., 37.
58. Ibid., 145.
59. Ibid., 51.
60. Ibid., 64.

through the emperor's reaction, was not only military and political but also metaphysical. It goes right to the heart of the issue of legitimacy.

Zhang's depiction of the metaphysical panic caused by Jahriya resistance gestures toward an argument about the imbrication of the theological and the political in Chinese history. Neo-Confucianism (the fourth stage of the Confucian tradition formed during the twelfth century), adopted by Qing rulers as their own political and moral orthodox, is known for its concern with maintaining a stable, hierarchical social order, with a moral ruler at its pinnacle, but it also, in the words of John Berthrong, "probed the transcendent dimensions of what it means to understand the Will of Heaven."[61] The moral ruler is considered to be the "Son of Heaven" who knows and carries out the Will or Mandate of Heaven, understood as the "primordial creativity of the cosmos that provides a model" for human virtues.[62] The Will or Mandate of Heaven is one of a set of concepts that constitute the metaphysical foundation of neo-Confucianism, making it comparable, to a certain degree, with such monotheistic religions as Christianity.[63] Another connection between Confucianism and Christianity, indicated more implicitly in Zhang, is their shared universalism. As many have pointed out, Confucianists were largely uninterested in converting those from other cultures, believing that Confucian principles are of "universal value" and its cultural superiority could be recognized without instruction or pressure.[64] Confucianism's nonaggressive attitude toward other cultures is arguably analogous to the Christian commandment to love one's enemy, which, as Anidjar points out in *The Jew, The Arab*, in fact disables thinking or loving "the enemy as the enemy," for, in its perfected form, the universal Christian love "abolishes . . . the divisions" that

61. John H. Berthrong, *All under Heaven*, 73.

62. Ibid.

63. Ibid. Though many would argue that Confucianism is not a religion, it also concerns itself with metaphysical dimensions of reality, a characteristic most pronounced in neo-Confucianism, the fourth stage of the Confucian tradition formed during the twelfth century and appropriated by the Qing court as the orthodoxy. Drawing from Buddhist and Daoist thought, neo-Confucianism builds on a metasystem hinged upon the ideas of *li* (principle), *ming* (Mandate of Heaven), and *taiji* (the Supreme Ultimate). See Berthrong, 88–101.

64. James Townsend, 2. As Townsend points out, this view of Confucianism has often been referred to as the thesis of culturalism. The thesis contains two parts: (1) Confucianism has unrivaled superiority over other cultural systems and (2) legitimate rule rests on adherence to Confucian norms. In "Thinking about Ethnicity in Early Modern China," Pamela Crossley summarized this thesis as the belief that (1) "Chinese culture was somehow autochthonous" and (2) "through nothing much more subtle than the sheer charisma of Chinese culture, peoples were attracted to China and its society from elsewhere and, no great obstacle withstanding, were consumed in the flames of *hanhua*" (2). For Crossley, this view distorts the much more contentious and fluid dynamic between Han and the many peoples bordering them throughout history.

created the enemy in the first place.[65] Confucian universalism, too, lacks a mechanism of actively engaging the other on the other's terms. Even as it disavows violence, Confucian universalism justifies the subjugation of theologico-political enemies, including the Jahriya, in a way that is reminiscent of the historical failure of Christianity's doctrine of universal love to enable an ethos of generosity or forbearance toward such enemies.

Furthermore, Zhang suggests that the Qing state's fears of Jahriya mysticism and its consequent suppression of the faith through military force facilitated the cultivation of close bonds among Jahriya followers that became analogous to the bonds constituting ethnic and racial identities. In making this point, Zhang recovers, or at least hypothesizes, a history of the ethnicization of Jahriya followers that is distinct from the more explored process through which the ruling Manchus shaped their own ethnic identity. Throughout Zhang's narrative, the Jahriya followers' eagerness to sacrifice for their faith and the emergence of a genealogically based Jahriya identity are linked through blood imagery, which signals both religious sacrifices and the passing down of religious tradition through successive biological generations. This semantic conflation suggests that religious affiliation became entwined with ethnic affiliation in the case of the Jahriya. Zhang explains that the Jahriya ideal of sacrificing one's life for the sanctity of Islam—religious martyrdom in other words—enveloped and comforted the believers like "hot and thick" blood.[66] In the middle of his narrative, Zhang provides a genealogical tree of the third-generation sheikh of the Jahriya in China, with annotations of when each of his ancestors and descendants suffered—exiled or killed—at the hands of Qing officials. The collective sacrifices that these individuals made for the Jahriya are overlaid upon their genealogical linkages. Indeed, Zhang points out explicitly that his construction of these "bloodlines" brings together biological and spiritual lineages.[67] As mentioned earlier, Hui identity is at least partially based on descent and lineage, in both imperial China and the PRC.[68] Zhang, however, departs from "narrow understandings of bloodlines" or biological lineage, suggesting that the collective Jahriya identity was forged in shared faith and sacrifices, which created ties akin to, and even stronger than, bonds of kinship.[69] The Jahriya, as rendered in *Xinling Shi,* emerged as an oppositional, antihegemonic iden-

65. Anidjar, *The Jew, The Arab,* 27.

66. Zhang, *Xinling Shi,* 76.

67. Ibid., 212.

68. Lipman also argues that Hui identity in China, at least since the Ming Dynasty, has been based more on lineage than on religious observance, thus on "a definition of 'Huiness' appropriate to the *minzu* (ethnicity/nationality) paradigm" (*Familiar Strangers,* 40).

69. Zhang, *Xinling Shi,* 94.

tity, never easily classifiable, from mutually constitutive religious and political conflicts. Their pursuit of "spiritual fulfillment, absolute justice, and freedom of the soul" constituted an ardent "indictment" of "a dark era" in Chinese history.[70]

As I pointed out previously, some have called *Xinling Shi* an "apocryphal" or fictionalized history, and I largely adopt this generic designation. It is indeed a history that has obtained a "biblical status" by rejecting dominant definitions of historical truth. The style as well as substance of *Xinling Shi* speaks of a politics of resistance and opposition. Over the course of his narrative, the author gradually collapses the distance between himself and his subjects. He confesses to having felt disappointed by the pedantic, tendentious style that characterizes historical studies from both the Qing era and the post-1949 period, thus spurring himself into a quest for an alternative approach to historiography. He found an example in the style of Jahriya chroniclers, who often do not bother with "moralization" or "meticulous descriptions of facts."[71] Their documentation of the Jahriya's wars with the Qing army in Gansu, for example, is summary, bare-boned, stripped of any explicit expressions of aversion to death and sacrifice. The narrator's immersion in this style guides him toward rejecting his "formal historical training" and writing a new kind of history that, instead of seeking to provide accurate detail, would approach the inner experience of the believer by surrendering itself to a form of mysticism.[72] *Xinling Shi,* then, is not only a story about the historical emergence of the Jahriya identity but also a narrative of a personal transformation, the author's journey toward a religious, epistemological, and ethical conversion.

However, if these aspects of the narrative bear out a separatist impulse, setting the Jahriya apart from secular Chinese culture, this impulse is checked with a countercurrent of integration. As the author puts it in apostrophe in the Preface, "I have not forgotten about you, my Han, Mongol readers and all the others, whom I do not see!"[73] The book, then, is also intended to be read as an allegory of the possibilities of political opposition under hegemonic power, which turns the anomalous case of the Jahriya into an analogue of peasant rebellions and nationalist revolutions in Chinese history since the late Qing. Lest the readers interpret the book as an articulation of a narrowly ethno-religious affiliation, Zhang makes a point of explicitly proposing the practice of subordinating ethnic and national origins to "the ideal of

70. Ibid., 42.
71. Ibid., 169.
72. Ibid.
73. Ibid., 9.

humanism," which, as I discuss a bit later, he places at the core of the Jahriya's struggles for spiritual freedom.[74] He reincorporates the Jahriya into secular Chinese culture by proclaiming that its members share with other Chinese a passionate love of the homeland, except that they display a more fierce resolve to defend theirs.[75] The Hui rebellions in northwest and southwest China during the Qing era, thus, are portrayed in *Xinling Shi* as a history that brought to relief the revolutionary spirit latent in all Chinese, which expressed itself in "people's insurrections" throughout eighteenth- and nineteenth-century China, culminating in the Taiping Uprising, led by Hong Xiuquan, a Christian convert.[76] In Zhang's narrative, "the Jahriya moved farther and farther away from [Islamic] fundamentalism" and increasingly transformed into "something entirely new, a Chinese belief system."[77] In his own way, Zhang constructs a history of the Jahriya's simultaneous assimilation into and exclusion from secular Chinese culture, a history filled with violent confrontations as well as nonviolent forms of adaptation.

Humanist Jihadism

Zhang uses the word "*shenzhan*" (a literal Chinese translation of jihad, the Holy War) throughout *Xinling Shi* to describe religion-inspired collective insurrections aimed at hegemonic political power, as exemplified by Hui rebellions during the Qing era. He insists that jihad is legitimate only when it aims to protect the "faith of the soul" from "intolerable" religious oppression.[78] This view recalls, but also differs from, Talal Asad's point that Muslim scholars do not support militant Islamism because the legal preconditions of jihad must include "both the presence of a genuine threat to Islam and the likelihood of success in opposing it."[79] As there has never been a "centralized theological authority" in the Islamic world, Zhang's interpretation of jihad does not function as either an affirmation or a revision of an orthodox view.[80] In any case, Islam in China, as Israeli Raphael puts it, is a "Chinese-Muslim innovation" with numerous sects that nobody can tabulate.[81] Zhang's idea of jihad, insofar as it becomes a metaphor for antihegemonic, collective strug-

74. Ibid., 77.
75. Ibid., 23.
76. Ibid., 160.
77. Ibid., 206.
78. Ibid., 58.
79. Talal Asad, *On Suicide Bombing*, 11.
80. Ibid.
81. Israeli, 142.

gles, necessarily implies a comment on the socialist revolution that brought the Communists to power in 1949 and the successive leftist movements that followed. Framing jihad as a form of opposition to extreme oppression can be read as Zhang's way of projecting an ideal form of the socialist revolution that does not lead to the suppression of individual freedom. It is not surprising, then, that Zhang makes a point of parsing his understanding of jihad as a form of humanism. Writing about the death of one of the Jahriya leaders, the author exalts him as a monument to the survival of "humanism," the triumph of "human faith" over what seeks to annihilate it.[82] The Jahriya's jihad must be understood, the author suggests, not just as a religiously motivated political act but as a political act in a broader sense (especially since part of his point is that the political is inevitably theological). The ideal of spiritual freedom that they fought for constitutes a condition and metonym for the more generalized ideal of human freedom, the genuine autonomy of thought and action. Defending this ideal requires the formation of oppositional collectivities that take on dominant power in both peaceful and military means, the latter only if there are extreme circumstances. In writing about the Jahriya, therefore, the author is envisioning the possibilities of continuing the tradition of the Chinese socialist revolution while replacing the homogeneous collectivism embodied in the idea of a proletarian dictatorship, which in a way echoes that of an obedient people under a benign Confucian ruler, with a pluralist model of multiple, competing collectivisms. What he means by a kind of humanist jihad at once challenges the foundation of China's secular modernity and allows for the reintegration of Chinese identity on a renewed, necessarily hybridized basis. Zhang is doing no less than propose a new vision of Chinese national identity grounded in the confrontations and mutual adaptation between competing notions of equality and freedom drawn from different theologico-political traditions. At one point in *Xinling Shi*, the author expresses the ambiguity of his vision of Chinese national identity by casting it as a paradoxical formal ideal: He wants to write in a "Chinese language" that is not completely tied to Chinese "characters."[83]

Many critics, however, have not fully appreciated the complexity of Zhang's oppositional politics. His perceived investment in the notion of popular uprisings made *Xinling Shi* a political liability before it was published.[84]

82. Zhang, *Xinling Shi*, 286.

83. Ibid., 276.

84. It has been documented that Zhang was not able to find a literary journal to publish his manuscript before it finally came out as in book form in 1991. See Liu Fusheng, "Linglei de zongjiao xiezuo: Zhang Chengzhi zongjiao xiezuo de yiyi" [Religion in literature: Meaning of Zhang Chengzhi's writings], 64.

Some critics, however, have endorsed the book based on the assumption that the Jahriya's struggles described in it are simply intended as an allegory of socialist and leftist movements. One critic, indeed, argues that *Xinling Shi* locates the possibility of social transformation in the collective energy of the oppressed, thus continuing the tradition of leftist writings in twentieth-century China. For the critic, the book constitutes a Chinese example of Herbert Marcuse's notion of "transforming mimesis," giving visibility to the revolutionary potential inherent in Jahriya subjectivity.[85] This is of course not an incorrect interpretation. Zhang has certainly not been reticent about his adulations for Mao for uniting the Chinese against Western incursions or his objections to the continuing dominance of Western, especially U.S., power. In his epilogue to *Xinling Shi*, an extended free verse poem, the author's persona addresses Mao directly, "I love you more than any party member does."[86] The author has also stated in unmistakable terms his opposition to ethnic separatism, an issue intensified in areas such as Tibet and Xinjiang after the collapse of the Soviet Union.[87] Nevertheless, even though *Xinling Shi* can be read allegorically, it should also be appreciated for its ethno-religious specificity. Purely allegorical readings inevitably leave out the linkage that the author draws between religious faith and humanism, failing to point out how Zhang's vision of national identity differs from the official rhetoric of *minzu tuanjie* [ethnic unity] in contemporary China.

The juxtaposition of religious faith and humanism in *Xinling Shi* is not an isolated incident. Zhang reiterates their connection in his more recent essays.[88] This move, moreover, resonates with a series of discussions of "the humanistic spirit" that took place among Chinese intellectuals and writers in the middle of the 1990s. In these discussions, as in Zhang's work, religion is often identified as a crucial condition for fostering humanism in China. Participants in the discussions largely associate the ideal of humanism with the flourishing of independent, political engaged intellectual work, whereas Zhang predicates humanism upon the forging of antihegemonic collective identities. However, their conceptions of humanism overlap with Zhang's

85. Zhang Hong, "Zhuti renting, geming yishi yu renmin meixue—lun zhang chengzhi zai xin shiqi de wenxue shijian" [Identification, revolutionary consciousness, and people's aesthetics: Zheng Chengzhi's literary writings since the reform era], 81.

86. Zhang, *Xinling Shi*, 307.

87. Zhang Chengzhi, "Sanfen meiyou yinzai shushing de yanyan" [Three prefaces that did not come to print], In *Qingjie de Jiingshen* [The clean spirit], 161.

88. The author states that he hopes young people in the future will stand up to power and systems but always remember the importance of "the human soul, humanism, respect for humans" and show special concern for the "lowest social stratum, the poor, and justice" (Zhang Chengzhi, "Sanfen meiyou yinzai shushang de xuanyan," 156).

around an emphasis on the sovereignty of the individual mind and on seeking sustenance for this ideal in religious belief.

Between March and July of 1994, the prestigious Chinese intellectual journal *Dushu* [Reading] published the transcripts of five roundtable discussions focusing on the question of how to develop humanism in contemporary Chinese society, all with the title "Renwen jingshen xunsilu" [Reflections on the humanistic spirit].[89] As the transcripts show, the Shanghai-based intellectuals trace the absence of a strong humanist tradition in China to a history of political pragmatism among Chinese intellectuals since the turn of the twentieth century, which places the political task of preserving national independence over and above the quest for moral and spiritual values that may transform the individual mind.[90] This pragmatism, which also stemmed from Confucianism's conception of intellectuals as architects of state governance,[91] has taken on new, more troubling guises since the 1980s, with the increasing commercialization of Chinese society.[92] To provide an antidote to the pragmatic, narrowly political orientation of the Chinese intelligentsia, participants of the roundtable discussions invoke a countertradition. It is pointed out that, while Western Humanism constructed itself over and against institutionalized religion, Chinese reformers at the end of the nineteenth century believed that religion (new forms of Confucianism and Buddhism in particular) had a major role to play in cultivating a general respect in society for the notion of human dignity.[93] This countertradition resurfaced in the work of individual Chinese intellectuals throughout the twentieth century, but it remains feeble and obscured by official intellectual histories. Ultimately, two bifurcating positions derive from this argument. Some discussants argue for detaching intellectual labor from state ideology (including the emphasis on state sovereignty) and reorienting it toward the "perfection and liberation" of man.[94] Others call on intellectuals to devote themselves to disseminating particular moral and spiritual values as a way of helping to generate critical consciousness in China's incomplete civil society.[95] Anticipating and underscoring the

---

89. This discussion on the topic of the humanistic spirit has been studied by scholars but not in relation to Zhang Chengzhi. See Gloria Davies, *Worrying about China,* 87–105.

90. Gao Ruiquan et al., "Renwen jingshen: Part II," 78.

91. Zhang Rulun et al., "Renwen jingshen: Part I," 5.

92. Gao Ruiquan et al., "Renwen jingshen: Part II," 80.

93. Xu Jilin et al., "Renwen jingshen: Part II," 76.

94. Gao Ruiquan et al., "Renwen jingshen: Part II," 79; also see Xu Jilin, "Renwen Jingshen, Part III," 54. For a critique of this aspect of the movement, see Liu Kang, "Is There an Alternative to (Capitalist) Globalization?" Liu compares the discussion of humanism to the projects of "cultural conservatives" in the U.S., including E. D. Hirsch and Allan Bloom, criticizing it for "denying from the outset the validity of any political engaged criticism" (214).

95. Wu Xuan et al., "Renwen jingshen: Part IV," 72–74.

latter of these two positions, Zhang critiqued conceptions of national identity in contemporary China through an exploration of the history and values of the Jahriya. Indeed, Zhang is explicitly applauded during one of the roundtable discussions as an ideal model of a freethinking, politically active intellectual.[96]

What we can conclude from this reading of Zhang Chengzhi and the related intellectual discourse on humanism is that religion figures importantly in the project of rethinking the meaning of political opposition in contemporary China. *Xinling Shi* has played an important role in this ongoing project, mediating between ethno-religious separatism and state-centered nationalism that emphasizes government control over cultural and religious matters. Ethno-religious wars, for Zhang, are not to be celebrated or suppressed from history; read a certain way, they suggest the importance of forging a robust pluralism that not only tolerates radical ethno-religious communities but also incorporates them into the process of negotiating the terms of national identity. The next section discusses Rabih Alameddine's *Koolaids: The Art of War,* a text equally fascinated with violent conflicts. By juxtaposing a word associated with an insider status in religious, political, or cultural groups with the title of a sixth-century treatise on war by Sun Tzu, Alameddine suggests an intimate connection between the inside–outside distinction and state-sponsored violence. Alameddine, like Zhang, concerns himself with the ways in which the atrocities of war force us to reflect on the possibilities of bridging the underlying religious and political divisions.

A Politics of Love

Koolaids: The Art of War is Lebanese American writer Rabih Alameddine's first novel. It is a collage of first- and third-person narrations revolving around the impact of sectarian violence during the Lebanese Civil War, which lasted from 1975 to the early 1990s, and the lived experience of Lebanese in the United States, some of whom are gay men living in New York City coping with the height of the AIDS epidemic. The novel offers glimpses into a number of interlinked patterns of life that together constitute a panoramic study of the religious conflicts and power politics that turned Lebanon into an "unstated" state and the racialization of Arab Americans in the two decades leading up to 9/11.[97] Some of the myriad voices in the novel are attributed to

96. Ibid., 73.
97. Salah D. Hassan, "Unstated." As Hassan puts it, "Despite its de jure existence, Lebanon has always existed de facto as an unstated state, a state without sovereignty and always in the

specific characters, including Lebanese painter Mohammad (the character closest to the author, who is also a painter, in a biographical sense), fellow Lebanese Samir, Samir's mother who lives through part of the civil war, and gay partners and friends of Mohammad and Samir in New York. One of the voices, which sometimes narrates dream sequences and feverish fantasies, is harder to identify, though it is attributed to Mohammad toward the end of the novel. This free-floating, largely unidentified voice often engages in satirizing the theological wrangling between Christianity and Islam, critiquing the universalistic claims of both and the politics they inform. Through this voice and the juxtaposition of many others with it, the novel presents both the war-torn Lebanon and the contemporary United States as sites of sectarian violence, their distinctions ironically erased by the shared ways in which they embrace the logic of war, the imperative of the friend–enemy distinction. Violence and war, in other words, have a way of leveling the differences between self and other, creating what might be described as a space of negative universalism, where all parties involved are reduced to mutually mirroring factions of a broken whole. The novel not only dissects this undesirable universalism but also seeks, toward the end, to remake it as well.

The novel traces the Lebanese Civil War, in part, to rivaling essentialist conceptions of Lebanese national identity. Early on in the narrative, an unnamed narrator points out the "European complex" that the Lebanese have long harbored, which has also shaped their relationship with the United States.[98] The narrator cites a mass-circulated e-mail message that calls on all "fellow Maronites" to "throw away the Arab shackles" and restore Lebanon as the "homeland of Christians."[99] The gist of this militant message resonates with a quote that David Gilmour attributes to Maronite Émile Eddé, president of Lebanon under the French Mandate from 1936 to 1941, who called Lebanon a "Christian refuge, an outpost of European civilization in the backward East."[100] On the other side of this obsession with everything European, as Alameddine puts it, is the resurgence of "Arabism," or "Islamic Fundamentalism," that resorts to guerilla warfare and suicide tactics.[101] Besides critiquing the politicization of religious differences in Lebanon, Alameddine also sheds light on the complex local and international power dynamics surrounding the prolonged civil war. The various narrators in the novel offer snapshots, mostly out of chronological order, of the course of the war, including the

---

process of dissolution" (1622).

98. Rabih Alameddine, *Koolaids*, 28.
99. Ibid., 59.
100. David Gilmour, *Lebanon*, 27.
101. Alameddine, *Koolaids*, 28.

massacre of Palestine refugees in Ain El Rummanneh, which set off the war, military interventions on the part of Syria and Israel, both with their own political proxies and supporters in Lebanon, and the impotent peace efforts of the United States. The Israelis and Syrians continued to jockey for power in Lebanon after the official end of the civil war in 1991, creating scenarios that, as Alameddine puts it, only Kafka would have been able to imagine.[102]

The Kafkaesque undertones of the civil war have much to do with its ironic effect of creating a zone of indifferentiation. As various religious groups engage in sectarian and internecine violence, they quickly lose any coherent identity that can separate them from their enemies. Citing the old Lebanese proverb "My brother and I against my cousin, my cousin and I against the stranger. Just let me hate somebody," Alameddine emphasizes that theologico-political rivals often come to imitate and resemble each other, becoming virtually undifferentiated in their moral stances and military tactics.[103] The author provides a mocking account of a few highlights during the civil war to show the affinity among various warring factions. While Hizballah evolved from the Shiite militia that originally fought the PLO, they later on used the war tactics "learned . . . from the PLO" against the Israelis.[104] Israel, Hizballah, and Syria in turn mirrored one another in employing the "*Ya Robbi Tegi Fi Aino*" tactic, which had originally been used by Egypt in the 1967 Israeli–Arab War. "*Ya Robbi Tegi Fi Aino*" is the Egyptian for "Oh God, I hope this gets him in the eye," referring in the book to haphazard, aimless attacks that, deliberately or not, target civilians as well as military camps.[105] The various forms of mirroring are referred to in *Koolaids* as the "Middle East version of *The Art of War*," an ironic allusion to Sun Tze's ubiquitous classic on war strategy that has aestheticized the concept of war for many of its Western readers.[106] The literalized war, as Alameddine suggests, is far less elegant; it erases all patterns of distinction that make tactical or moral victories possible.

A kind of mutual mirroring, Alameddine suggests, also aptly describes the relationship between Lebanon and the West, purportedly divided along the Christian–Muslim line. One stand-alone passage in the first half of the book, filtered through the unidentified, sardonic voice recurrent throughout the novel, blends the central ideas of the New Testament and those of the Qur'an, offering no comments on their clear incongruence. The passage opens by grafting the name Mohammad onto the beginning of the Gospel of

102. Ibid., 237.
103. Ibid., 138.
104. Ibid., 97.
105. Ibid.
106. Ibid.

John, "In the beginning was the Word, and the Word was with God, and the Word was Mohammad."[107] This statement mixes together the Christian belief that God's will expresses itself in the fundamental order of the world (the Word, logos) and the Muslim belief in Mohammad as the last of the prophets or messengers of God, gleefully blasphemous toward both. The passage goes on to juxtapose two contrasting doctrines from the two religions:

> For God so loved the world that He gave His one and only Son, that whoever believes in Him shall not perish, but have eternal life . . . Whoever believes in Him is not condemned, but whosoever does not believe stands condemned already because he has not believed in the name of God's one and only Son. For Mohammad, peace be upon Him, said God was neither a son nor a father . . . Say not "Trinity": desist: it will be better for you: for Allah is one Allah.[108]

Here, a statement of the Christian doctrine of the Holy Trinity is rudely juxtaposed with one that indicates the Muslim objection to it. Even though both sentences start with "For," neither flows logically from the preceding one. This juxtaposition, therefore, does not simply point out a central theological difference; its perplexing, illogical style can be read as a mocking imitation of the assertive, prophetic tone in which both Christian and Muslim doctrines are conveyed. The sentence in the middle ostensibly recasts the Christian commandment of faith, which works to exclude nonbelievers from God's love, and yet it can simultaneously be construed as a reference to the equally rigid distinction between believers and nonbelievers in Islam. The passage, among others in *Koolaids,* simultaneously mocks Christianity and Islam while showing how their doctrines mirror each other in style and substance. The author's theological critique is coupled with political commentaries about the ways in which both the West and Lebanon's Arab neighbors carelessly squandered the lives of Lebanese during the civil war and in its aftermath: Assad "kidnaps and tortures thousands of Lebanese," just like the U.S. ally Israel, while American State Secretary Warren Christopher condones the former and "kisses [Israel's] ass."[109] All the intervening parties here share the guilt of normalizing wanton killing and making it no longer "newsworthy."[110] Alamaddine's critique of the U.S. role in the war extends the well-rehearsed argument that U.S. foreign policy in the Middle East follows from and per-

107. Ibid., 76.
108. Ibid.
109. Ibid., 153.
110. Ibid.

petuates the politicization of Christian–Muslim conflicts that can be traced back to Medieval Europe.[111]

Koolaids furthers its critique of American politics and culture by invoking a long history of prejudices against Arabs within the United States. Samir's mother, whose diary entries are dispersed throughout the book, laments that Americans "make fun of" Arabs all the time, as if they were "all crazy, maybe even degenerate."[112] A federal building in Oklahoma is blown up, and Arab-looking images of possible suspects are spread "all over the news."[113] These details prefigure the intensification of the profiling and racialization of Arab Americans after 9/11. As Salaita points out, anti-Islam orientalism and right-wing Christian values have played a significant role in the rise of "imperative patriotism" in the post-9/11 period, an ideology that equates the national interest with the defeat of what had come to be known as Islamism.[114] Religion and politics are so thoroughly enmeshed in the contemporary American public sphere that "anti-Arab racism" and "Islamaphobia" have become inseparable, referring in general to the "same thing," even though they are by no means identical terms.[115] Implied in Sailata's critique is the point that proliferating public expressions of Christian religiosity in American domestic and foreign policy and the racialization of Arabs and Muslims threaten to turn the United States into a "theocracy," a mirror image of what it identifies as the enemy.[116] Not unlike Salaita, Alameddine draws attention to the parallel ways in which religion figures in the political culture of both the United States and Lebanon, generating a relationship of near symmetry.

The same symmetry, Alameddine suggests, can be seen in the religiously sanctioned discrimination against homosexuals in both cultures, an issue

111. In *Contending Visions of the Middle East,* Zachary Lockman underscores the slippery line between Muslim (a religious category) and Arab (a political category) in Western perceptions. "Yet it can be argued that Islam occupied a unique (though never simple) place in the imaginations of western Europeans from at least the eleventh or twelfth century onward—that it was Europe's 'other' in a unique sense. The Jews were close at hand; and though they were sometimes regarded as an ideological problem as a result of their steadfast refusal to accept that Jesus was the messiah and the son of God, they never constituted a political or military threat to the hegemony of Christianity in Europe" (Lockman, 36). During the Cold War, the U.S. assumed the mantle of European colonial powers to become the guarantor of stability in the Middle East. As Lockman explains, "Despite talk of pressing friendly regimes to accommodate political and social change, however, US policymakers gave priority to maintaining the paramount position of the US in the region, keeping the Soviet Union out and protecting local clients" (Lockman, 118). The 1950s saw the cooling of U.S.–Egyptian relations, the U.S. military interventions in Lebanon in 1957, as well as the CIA-sponsored military coup in Iran in 1953 that overthrew the government and installed the shah (Iran's king) as absolute ruler.

112. Alameddine, 54.

113. Ibid., 196.

114. Salaita, *Anti-Arab Racism in the USA,* 82.

115. Ibid., 11.

116. Ibid. 168.

that intersects with both the daily indignities of racism and the sudden trauma of war. At one point, the free-floating, unidentified narrative voice ridicules the story of Lot in the Genesis, calling attention to its implication that a father offering his daughters to "horny buggers" is more acceptable than "men fucking men."[117] *Koolaids* also alludes to the Muslim version of the same story, incorporating excerpts from the Qur'an (Surahs 26, 27) about how Allah destroys Sodom and Gomorrah after Angels instruct Lut and his family to leave.[118] If the civil war dissolves the differences among the various theologico-political factions in Lebanon, the war against sodomy has the same leveling effect on Christianity and Islam. Muhammad is alienated from his family in Lebanon because of his gay identity even as he struggles with the predicament of being an Arab gay man in the United States. He finds himself in a war zone wherever he turns. He and his gay lovers and friends battle the havoc of AIDS and cultural isolation with the kind of grit and forbearance that characterize victims of all wars. One of the passages in the novel, filtered again through the unidentified voice, draws an explicit analogy between the Lebanese Civil War and the war on "sodomy" and AIDS. It points out that, after the American troops' unsuccessful intervention in 1984, President Reagan "avoided discussing Lebanon" the same way he avoided mentioning AIDS.[119] In the meantime, the "doctors, pharmacists, and various medical personnel" that gained from the AIDS epidemic are compared to a contingent of "war profiteers."[120]

We can see that just as Zhang Chengzhi critiques the Confucian tradition in China by unearthing the history of its suppression of the Jahriya, Alameddine focuses on the mass casualties resultant from the Lebanese Civil War and the AIDS epidemic in the contemporary United States as a way of critiquing Christian extremism along with its Islamic counterpart. This critique is also crystallized in the dream scene that opens the novel and recurs throughout the text in slightly different forms. The scene restages the biblical passage about the Four Horsemen of the Apocalypse, commonly interpreted to represent conquest, war, plague, and death.[121] The rider of the White Horse, who has generated different interpretations among Christians, figures in this dream scene as Christ, who has come to save true believers from the Great Tribulation. The horseman refuses to take the initially unidentified dreamer (who is revealed at the end of the novel to be Mohammad), for he is a "non-

---

117. Alameddine, *Koolaids,* 64.
118. Ibid., 177.
119. Ibid., 235.
120. Ibid., 167.
121. Ibid., 1, 53, 98, 166.

Christian homosexual," "a fucking fag, a heathen."[122] "I didn't die for this dingbat's sins," the horseman growls.[123] This passage mimics the Dispensational view that the Book of Revelation represents events that will happen in the future and that Christ will return invisibly before the seven-year Tribulation to take Christians bodily up to Heaven.[124] By dramatizing this interpretation of the Apocalypse from the perspective of one of those doomed to be "left behind," this recurring scene suggests that, to those excluded from the Rapture, the savior and the force presiding over the Tribulation are one and the same.[125] Christ and Antichrist, in other words, are partners in sowing violence and suffering on earth. This scene is emblematic of the novel's critique of right-wing interpretations of Christian scriptures (the story of Sodom and Gomorrah, for example), which, as the author suggests, have a powerful influence on public policy in the contemporary United States, turning Christian moral laws into political weapons against various social groups, Muslims and homosexuals in particular.

However, Alameddine is not simply calling for cleansing political culture and public policy of vestiges of religious dogmas. By underscoring the permeation of religiosity in American politics even prior to 9/11, he effectively dismantles the standard secularist assertion that modern conceptions of political space represent a triumph over religious sectarianism. Instead, he suggests the possibility of transforming religious teachings into ethical principles with a genuinely universalistic agenda that may help reduce, rather than engender, sectarian conflicts. Toward the end of the narrative, the author implies that there is an important distinction between adhering to the letter of religious teachings and adhering to their spirit. Furthermore, he suggests that this distinction can in fact be seen as an integral part of Christianity, namely, what Saint Paul refers to as the distinction between the law of works and the law of faith. It is not a coincidence that toward the end of the novel the unidentified narrative voice recounts a funeral service that starts with an opening prayer and a reading from Paul's Letter to the Romans. The Romans excerpt offers assurance, to Jews and Gentiles alike, of salvation through Christ's sacrifice: "[t]hrough baptism into His death we were buried with Him, so that, just as Christ was raised from the dead by

---

122. Ibid., 1.
123. Ibid.
124. This is a futurist, pre-Tribulationist (the Rapture happens before the Tribulation and all true Christians will be saved from the suffering) interpretation of the Book of Revelation. Dispensational Christians, a group that dominates the religious right in the U.S., mostly hold this view.
125. A reference to Jerry Jenkins and Tim LaHaye's *Left Behind* novels, the first of which appeared in 1995. The series has popularized the Dispensational view of the Book of Revelation.

the glory of the Father, we too might live a new life" (Rom 6.4).[126] Both Jews and Gentiles are folded into Paul's view of salvation, which is founded on faith in Christ's blood rather than mere adherence to God's commandments. Conceivably, Alameddine is arguing, through Paul, that faith in the universal address of God's love, *agape,* manifest through the sacrifice of his only Son, can be reappropriated as a basis for a new kind of human subject defined by a relation of love to oneself and to others ("love your neighbor as yourself"). The Romans excerpt, then, leads logically to a fragment from the Gospel of Matthews, where Jesus makes it clear that "as often as" we neglect the needs of "those least ones," we neglect to do it to Jesus.[127] The labor of human love, like God's love, is defined by its universal address, such that neglecting any one individual is neglecting God. Here, Alameddine is driving at a point reminiscent of Alain Badiou's provocative argument about Paul. Badiou reads Paul as a "new militant figure" who teaches us that the act of declaring faith in God constitutes a revolutionary "event," "a rupture, an overturning" of the subjection of humans to legal commandments, the law of works.[128] The faith-event is neither material nor subjective, because it represents a union of the two, a "thought-practice," in other words, that inaugurates the labor of "tire-lessly addressing itself to all the others" and thereby effectuating collective liberation.[129] For Badiou, then, practicing the Christian teaching of universal love contains the promise of a new kind of revolution, a post-Marxist form of militancy. As he puts it, the "materiality" of the labor of universal love is "the militant dimension" of faith.[130] The value of Badiou's interpretation of Paul is the reinvigoration of religious and political universalism: Human subjectivity is defined here not in terms of what it excludes or submits to but in terms of its power to actualize universal love and break from exclusionary regimes of power. To a certain extent, Alameddine seems to agree with Badiou's reading of Paul and the Christian faith. He writes that the universalistic impulses of Christianity jibe with the ambitions of the best of art, which also projects the possibility for individuals to transcend their limitations by participating in a generalized idea of humanity. Just a few pages after the excerpt from Paul's letter, the unidentified narrator cites Borges's "Tlön, Uqbar, Orbis Tertius," which features an imaginary region Tlon, where "all men who repeat one line of Shakespeare *are* William Shakespeare."[131]

At the same time, Alameddine wonders aloud whether the doctrine of

126. Alameddine, *Koolaids,* 204.
127. Ibid., 206.
128. Alain Badiou, *Saint Paul: The Foundation of Universalism,* 2.
129. Ibid., 92.
130. Ibid.
131. Alameddine, *Koolaids,* 212, emphasis in the original.

universal love does not hide something much less savory. Even though Paul, in Badiou's reading, announces a new law of faith, a "nonliteral" law, that ruptures the law of works, it is clear that the two kinds of law remain thoroughly intertwined in Paul and Christianity in general.[132] The segment of the Romans excerpted in *Koolaids* runs on a bit longer. Immediately after proclaiming the possibility of salvation for everyone, Paul turns his attention to the body as a locus of sin that has no place in God's universal love. As humans partake in Christ's resurrection, their "sinful [bodies]" will have been left behind, crucified with Christ.[133] The "sinful [bodies]" do not just point to the absolute limits of the Christian universalism signified by the doctrines of faith and love. They constitute its very condition, as salvation has no meaning other than the transcendence of the bondage of the body. For some, indeed, the Romans can be read as a "theory . . . of the enemy," structured around tropes of warfare ("let us lay aside the works of darkness, but let us put on the weapons of light").[134] War, of course, is also Alameddine's main theme. The mass casualties of the Lebanese Civil War and the AIDS epidemic in the contemporary United States bear witness to the deadly consequences of the entwining of theological and political exclusions. Just as harrowing as literal death, perhaps, is the death of a spiritual and emotional kind. In the novel, Mohammad is pressured to leave Lebanon and join his uncle in Los Angeles in 1975. His relationship with his father, as well as the fatherland, is consistently strained. His decision to attend an art school angers his father but not nearly as much as his confession to being gay, a confession that leads to his complete exile from his family. Mohammad's gay friends in New York experience similar pain. One of them receives a letter from his stepfather urging him to "confess [his] sins" so that God will open His arms to him.[135] In scenes like this, religious faith, whether Christian and Islamic, signifies an absolute form of subjectivation—one's voluntary submission to the law—rather than the beginning of a new life underlined by universal love. Death, indeed, is a far more universal experience than salvation. As the novel puts it at one point, "[i]n the commemoration of death, I unearthed myself."[136]

The novel's allusions to parts of the New Testament, then, can be read as an emblem of the narrative's oscillation between a sardonic dissection of the lethal consequences of theologico-religious wars and an earnest search for ways of putting an end to the endless cycles of death, which, as the author

132. Badiou, 87.
133. Rom 6.6, quoted in Alameddine, *Koolaids*, 204.
134. Anidjar, *The Jew, The Arab*, 6.
135. Alameddine, *Koolaids*, 111.
136. Ibid., 21.

puts it, always "begin all over again" as if nothing happened before.[137] The ideal of universal love, based on the most appealing part of Christianity, does not completely wither away under the crushing weight of senseless death. Ultimately, it figures as a possible enabler of an elusively radical set of social relations. Mohammad's quest for physical and spiritual healing encapsulates this trajectory. On the one hand, a cynical version of him questions how death can ever be redeemed. In one of his monologues, he expresses doubt that "there is conclusive proof an afterlife exists" or that consciousness is made of more than matter.[138] In conjunction with these expressions of spiritual skepticism, the novel also quotes, and implicitly critiques, several literary voices that romanticize death by turning it into a spiritual experience. Hermann Hesse's view of death as one of the great transformers of life and Louis Ferdinand-Celine's complaint that antibiotics took half of the tragedy out of medicine, for example, come across, in the midst of all the human misery described in the novel, as cruelly insensitive.[139] Mohammad also pokes fun at the New Age spirituality for offering facile antidotes to death. At two different points in the novel, he writes mockingly of his turn to a Hindu guru for a spiritual cure for AIDS, which leaves him with nothing but a renewed "sense of humor" inspired by the apparent absurdity of the pursuit.[140] The novel cheers this bitter sarcasm on by sprinkling the narrative with comical, imaginary exchanges that lampoon spiritual quests. In one of these passages, a dialogue takes place among Arjuna, his charioteer Krsna, Eleanor Roosevelt, Krishnamurti, Julio Cortázar, and Tom Cruise, where contempt is hurled at such religious gurus as Krishnamurti for telling vague parables about the meaning of life.[141] Eventually, however, the novel does offer an alternative to the cynical, nonredemptive conception of death, as Mohammad's life and quest come to an end. In the final iteration of the dream scene involving the Four Horsemen of the Apocalypse, which is also the last section of the entire novel, the rider of the white horse at last extends acceptance to Mohammad, comforting him with the words "I love you, Mohammad" before he takes his last breath.[142] In this scene, the redemptive power of the Christian notion of universal love makes room for what the law forcefully excludes, the "sinful body" of a Lebanese, non-Christian, gay man in this case, rather than relegate it to the hopeless realm of eternal death. Through the ending of the novel, Alameddine detaches the notion of universal love from its Christian roots,

137. Ibid., 30, 55.
138. Ibid., 120.
139. Ibid., 15, 22.
140. Ibid., 74, 157.
141. Ibid., 38.
142. Ibid., 245.

thus expanding its claim to true universality. It becomes, arguably, an ethical principle that may help engender an unbounded form of pluralism. This final moment of closure does not privilege Christianity over Islam or other religious traditions, but instead signals the possibility of transforming these traditions from within based on an unflinching study of the ways in which they collude in casting the seeds of death. This deliberately utopian ending is foreshadowed in the novel's projection, at one point, of an idyllic Lebanon before the civil war, a nation at the center of the Arab world where various cultural and religious crosscurrents in the East and West intermingled freely. It is a place where people felt comfortable considering themselves to be "both nationals and foreigners."[143] Just like the novel's ending, this passage imagines a genuinely nonexclusive form of pluralism that might serve to suture together the fragments of modern nation-states (Lebanon, the United States) and dilute the symbolic power of their internal and external borders. Taken as a whole, *Koolaids*'s critiques various kinds of sectarianism, the "koolaid syndrome" one might say, while gesturing toward the possibility of a new form of political theology that is genuinely universalistic *and* pluralist. Its relations to Zhang Chengzhi's *Xinling Shi* are clear at this point. Paralleling what Alameddine does with Christian theology, Zhang recasts the tenets of the Jahriya to articulate a new model of pluralist universalism that challenges the limits of both Confucianism and official multiculturalism in contemporary China.

It is conceivable that Alameddine's effort to hold the Christian faith up to its own ideal is a way of forcing his audience, most of them Americans, to reflect on the belief system most familiar to them. The author is certainly not alone in exploring the ways in which religion is indispensable for discussions of multiculturalism, and progressive politics in general, in the contemporary United States, where religion remains a robust component of public discourses, a phenomenon that has come to be seen as a challenge (one of many in fact) to standard narratives of the rise of secular modernity.[144] On the one hand, a civil religion, a nondenominational Christianity continues to be regarded as a treasured ingredient of good Americanism and civic national identity; on the other, since the colonial period, struggles for religious diversity have effected legal and cultural changes that favor equal protection and recognition of religious rights, ensuring the flourishing of "an

143. Ibid., 149.
144. See Jose Casanova, "Religion, the New Millennium, and Globalization." Quoting Steven Warner, Casanova argues for the existence of an "emerging American paradigm" (426). As Casanova argues, increasing social differentiation in the U.S. is coupled with "an open, free, competitive, and pluralistic religious market, and high levels of individual religiosity" (426). Also see Charles Taylor, *A Secular Age*, 528.

open, free, competitive, and pluralistic religious market" as well as "high levels of individual religiosity."[145] It has recently been argued that the post–World War II rise of liberal multiculturalism owes a debt to the legal efforts of non-Protestant religious groups, especially Jewish and Catholic groups, to fight "sectarian attempt(s) to insert Protestantism into public education," a process that helped solidify the belief that the state should actively help level the playing ground for different religious organizations as they strive to maintain and grow their influence.[146] In a similar vein, Chris Beneke has argued that the earliest origins of American pluralism lay in the explosion of religious differences during the mid-eighteenth century, which drastically broadened the "range of acceptable opinions" in print while fostering the integration of colonial politics and the opening of American colleges— a cultural constellation that Beneke compares to the accommodation of ethno-racial differences in post–World War II multiculturalism.[147] Beyond this specific connection between religion and multiculturalism, as R. Marie Griffith and Melani McAlister point out, there is a long "history of both religious activism and political religiosity in the United States," including phenomena "ranging from the religious beliefs of the 'founding fathers' to the international origins of religious pacifism to the socioreligious meanings of the 'home birth' movement."[148] A movement for "religious politics" started occurring in the 1980s, when a new generation of religious intellectuals "worked to raise awareness, legitimize religious concerns in policy-making, and increase funding for faith-based organizations in general."[149] Since the 2000 presidential election, the rise of the Christian Right and what Steven Salaita has called a "theocracy" in the United States underscore the many ways in which religion entails, incites, and fuels political struggles, but it should not obfuscate the more productive roles it can play in politics, which often require crossing "political and denomination lines."[150] These roles take many forms: the writings of the evangelical left "on poverty, racial injustice, and global inequality, as well as spiritual renewal," the founding of *Tikkun* magazine that supports a "loving criticism" of Israeli policies toward the Palestinians, and various faith-based organizations advocating religious and other social liberties.[151] Although Alameddine's novel does not sketch out institutional means of integrating religion productively into debates around

145. Casanova, 426.
146. Kevin Schultz, "'Favoritism Cannot Be Tolerated,'" 585.
147. See Chris Beneke, *Beyond Toleration*, 88.
148. R. Marie Griffith and Melani McAlister, "Introduction," 539.
149. Ibid., 550.
150. Ibid.
151. Ibid., 548.

public policy and political culture, his rewriting of the Christian doctrine of universal love supplements the academic discussions cited previously. Like Zhang, he suggests that a thoroughly pluralist universalism needs to address and draw upon religious teachings.

The historical narratives offered by Zhang and Alameddine address the challenge that Muslim difference poses to the multicultural order in the United States and China in the post–Cold War era. Revisiting ethno-religious wars without papering over their massive toll or lingering legacies leads the authors to intriguingly similar arguments. If there are ethno-religious differences that conciliatory multiculturalism cannot accommodate, the answer is not that religion should be confined firmly to the private sphere. After all, the "secular" political sphere, as it is manifest in contemporary America and China, is inseparable from the religious—the continual dominance of Christian and Confucian values in their respective political sphere is but one example. As secularism is founded on the artificial dichotomization of the religious and the political, insisting on the complete secularization of political culture can only cover over, or even entrench, existing ethno-religious divisions. In other words, it can only further undermine the project of multiculturalism. Instead of pursuing a strictly secularist version of multiculturalism, the two authors studied here provide us with a provocative alternative, by emphasizing the importance of recognizing and employing the power of religion. They propose genuinely universalistic understandings of religious doctrines (Christian as well as Islamic) as an alternative ethical foundation for social relations and in so doing point to an expanded model of multiculturalism that draws from political theories *and* religious thought while creatively reworking both to mediate their mutual antagonism. Under this model of multiculturalism, ethno-religious minorities are not simply beneficiaries of the majority nation-state but full participants in political discussions of how to restructure the ways in which a nation as a whole approaches social differences. Put another way, ethno-religious conflicts should not be seen as polarizing forces to be contained by multiculturalism. Rather, they should be conceived as integral to the continuous negotiations over the key terms of multiculturalism in a given national context. Reading Zhang and Alameddine in conjunction with each other, then, turns an infelicitous instance of translation—the global dissemination of the idea of "Islamic terrorism"—into an opportunity for a productive dialogue on ways of pushing the frontiers of contemporary multiculturalisms.

CHAPTER 5

Impersonal Intimacy

Yan Geling's *Fusang* and Its English Translation

> Love is an ethical and social responsibility to open personal and public spaces in which otherness and difference can be articulated. Love requires a commitment to the advent and nurturing of difference.
>
> —Kelly Oliver, *Witnessing*

> "Asian American" connotes the violence, exclusion, dislocation, and disenfranchisement that has attended the codification of certain bodies as, variously, Oriental, yellow, sometimes brown, inscrutable, devious, always alien. It speaks to the active denial of personhood to the individuals inhabiting those bodies. At the same time, it insists on acknowledging the enormous capacity for life that has triumphed repeatedly over racism's attempts to dehumanize, over the United States' juridical attempts to regulate life and culture.
>
> —Kandice Chuh, *Imagine Otherwise*

M Y DISCUSSIONS of Kuo, Zhang, and Alameddine in previous chapters argue that these authors reconstruct histories of violent conflicts between the majority state and ethno-racial and religious minorities in a way that punctures the myth of an already achieved state of national harmony that prevails in both contemporary America and China. These authors engage, through their narratives, in the strenuous labor of reconceiving pluralist universalism in opposition to facile versions of it embodied in conciliatory multiculturalism. On the one hand, they suggest that building national solidarity, whether in civic or state-centric terms, frequently conflicts, sometimes violently, with assertions of historically shaped group differences within a nation. On the other, they argue that the resulting tensions are not to be confined or suppressed; they should instead be confronted by both dominant and marginal social groups through a process whereby they work together on revising the terms and conditions of national identity in an ethos of openness and generosity. Kuo's idea of dissenting nationalism, Zhang's model of competing collectivisms, and Alameddine's rethinking of Christian universalism share an investment in exploring conceptions of national identities that emphasize both coherence and inconclusiveness.

What these authors do not pay sufficient attention to, however, is the ways in which individual subjectivity mediates, and is mediated by, the ideals of national identity they envision. They are more concerned with reconstructing neglected histories from scattered fragments of collective memory than with imagining how these histories relate to the individual psyche. This chapter takes up the topic of how the individual, embodied subject can become a battleground for different nationalist discourses and a site of psychic labor through which these discourses can be reshaped. It does so through a discussion of *Fusang,* an unusual novel by Chinese immigrant author Yan Geling. Published first in Chinese in 1996 and translated into English in 2001 as *The Lost Daughter of Happiness,* the novel offers a provocative portrayal of the titular character Fusang, a Chinese prostitute in nineteenth-century San Francisco. To the uneasy surprise of many, Fusang is depicted not as a victim of racial and sexual violence but as an enigmatic figure who actively accommodates the violent penetrations of her body. Her accommodation of sexual violence entails a rejection of the self-possessed, autonomous liberal subject and thus figures as a tactic of survival *and* resistance that turns the character into an unlikely pioneer of a new regime of subjectivity and relationality.

Although the name of Yan Geling may mean very little to U.S.-based academics, most Asian Americanists included, she is often commended by scholars in China and Taiwan as one of the most important Chinese-language authors in the United States. Before she came to the United States as a student in 1989, Yan had published three novels in China, where she was born in the late 1950s. During and after her study at Columbia College in Chicago for an MFA in fiction writing, she published award-winning short stories, novellas, and novels in Chinese-language literary journals in the United States, Taiwan, and China.[1] In 1995, she won a *United Daily News* Novel Prize with

---

1. Yan is also known as the script writer for the 1992 film *Shaonu Xiaoyu,* based on her novella of the same title, and as a co-script writer (along with Joan Chen) for the 1998 *Tianyu,* directed by Chen.

Fusang, the story of a village girl in Canton who was abducted, brought to the United States on a cargo ship, and sold into a brothel in nineteenth-century San Francisco Chinatown.[2] Since then, Yan has continued to publish at a breathtaking pace, winning admiration from literary prize committees in both China and Taiwan and from established Chinese film directors, who have commissioned scripts from her or purchased the rights to her works.[3] Yan has also experimented with writing in English. Her first English-language novel, *The Banquet Bug,* came out in 2007 to positive reviews.

The most interesting aspect of the novel *Fusang,* which makes it quite rare among Chinese-language writings in the United States, is that it is a fully transnational narrative with a history of reception in both the United States and China. My reading of the novel therefore pays close attention to its translation and reception, both of which consist of a series of appraisive, interpretive acts. The English translation, *The Lost Daughter of Happiness,* excises or shortens many passages in the original, seeking to make the translation read, in the words of Cathy Silber, the translator, more like an "English-language novel."[4] I draw particular attention to the textual alterations that accompany the novel's entry into a different political and cultural context. In chapter 1, I point out a discrepancy between the English and Chinese versions of Jiang Rong's *Lang Tuteng.* In the case of Yan's *Fusang,* however, comparing the original and the translation is a much more crucial task. Passages that are excised from or abbreviated in the English translation, most of which contain descriptions (from the narrator's or other characters' perspectives) of Fusang's unruly sexuality, become a kind of constitutive absence that signals a certain cultural anxiety. These editorial changes, no doubt, have centrally shaped Anglo-American responses to the novel, but they are also critical moves in their own right that implicitly pass judgment on what the novel does right and what it does not. Not coincidentally, the deleted and shortened passages also play a crucial role, either by being highlighted or ignored, in Chinese critics' readings of the novel. I offer, in various sections of this chapter, an analysis of the interpretive, regulatory work that the translation

---

2. *United Daily News* literary prizes are among the most prestigious awards for Taiwan writers and Chinese-language writers around the world. Authors in China have also started to compete for the award.

3. Yan is the scriptwriter for Chen Kaige's film *Mei Lanfang,* an autobiographical film named after its subject, the most important icon of Chinese opera. Zhang Yimou acquired rights to one of her recent novels *Jinling shisan chai* [Thirteen women in Nanjing].

4. Cathy Silber, Telephone Interview, Nov. 27, 2004. Silber informed me during our telephone interview that she was sometimes at odds with the Hyperion editor as to what changes were necessary, although she agreed with him on some alterations that would make the translation read more like an "English-language" novel. The author was consulted on most of the revisions, though Silber added that she did not seek to exercise control over the process.

process performs and what it may say about the ways in which the novel challenges the conciliatory logic of U.S. liberal multiculturalism. My own understanding of the novel, which I get to shortly, also anchors itself on the missing and shortened passages.

Along with comparing the two different versions of the novel, I explore the divergences and confluences between the interpretations of the central character Fusang generated in the United States and China. Anglo-American critics, with access only to the sanitized, incomplete version of the novel via the translation, have largely construed Fusang as a frustratingly inscrutable character, even as they argue that she subverts the orientalist imagination of Asian women. In China, Fusang's accommodation of sexual and social violence and her ability to draw pleasure from it has caused misgivings in critics who read the character allegorically as a symbol of the Chinese nation that has been forced to contend with Western colonialism and political and cultural hegemony since the mid-nineteenth century. The characterization of Fusang is either criticized for its complicity with the orientalist feminization of Chinese culture or praised for accentuating the virtuous resilience that has enabled China to overcome its historical humiliations. The novel's reception in China, then, illuminates a postcolonial understanding of the Chinese nation that approaches racialized experiences of Chinese immigrants in the West as an extension of China–West relations. This understanding, though not unjustified, provides important ammunitions for the party-state's emphasis on national sovereignty and unity in all policy matters, including the policy of regional autonomy for ethnic minorities (as opposed to federalism), which was rationalized on the purported grounds that the different ethnicities in China forged unbreakable friendships during shared struggles against Euro-American (and Japanese) colonialisms during the first half of the twentieth century. The various competing interpretations of Fusang show us yet another way in which ideas of race and nation in contemporary America and China are interconnected. Even as Chinese immigration and Chinese immigrant writings reveal the limits of liberal acceptance of racial others in the United States, they broach the topic of U.S. racial dynamics in China, which often becomes entangled with discussions of U.S.–China relations and of such translated concepts as postcoloniality and orientalism.

Ultimately, I provide a new reading of *Fusang* that challenges nationalist discourses and nation-centered critical practices. These practices, I believe, suppress Fusang's inexplicable queerness, normalizing her into an autonomous ethnic subject or a coherent embodiment of national identity. In response, I analyze the character through the very lens of queerness. I argue that her accommodation of sexual violence encodes a set of queer practices that in effect challenge conventional (liberal as well as nationalist) configurations of individual subjectivity. The radical challenge embodied in Fusang suggests a psychic and corporeal basis for new forms of individual and collective identity and therefore the new models of national integration discussed in chapters 3 and 4. In dialogue with literary and theoretical traditions in both the United States and China, Yan's novel turns what could have been a narrative of sacrifice and pain into a productive inquiry into the possibility of transforming versions of multiculturalism that prioritize the coherence of the nation, a goal often contingent on the disciplining of the (raced) female body.

Opaque or Transparent?

A third of the novel *Fusang* consists of second-person narration of the titular character's experience. The rest is mostly third-person narration describing Fusang's interactions with johns and with the missionaries trying to rescue her. The novel is also sprinkled with first-person narration in which the embodied, explicitly female narrator compares her own life with Fusang's. There is certainly no linear narrative to be found in the novel, but the plot can be summarized as follows: Fusang is brought to California toward the end of the 1860s from a Canton village and sold into a brothel. She quickly attracts the attention of Chris, a white teenager; Da Yong, a Chinatown gangster; and Chinese laborers forced to live a bachelor's life because of the immigration restrictions on Chinese women. She becomes Da Yong's possession when she willingly allows him to take her away from the missionaries who are trying to save her. Meanwhile, Fusang develops a crush on Chris and initiates sexual relations with him several times. Their consummation does not happen, though, until a riot breaks out against the Chinese and Chris joins a group of rioters in gang-raping Fusang. Finally, she turns down Chris's marriage offer and weds herself to Da Young just before he is executed for killing a white merchant. She then returns to Chinatown and lives there until an old age.

Fusang is an imagined character based on and yet different from the descriptions of Chinatown prostitutes available in various historical documents.[5] Although the narrator claims that Fusang is an actual historical figure

5. Benson Tong, *Unsubmissive Women*. In this book-length study of Chinese prostitutes, Tong maps out the history of Chinese prostitutes in San Francisco and on the frontier in general. Before the passage of the Page Law in 1875, which prohibited the entry of women for the purpose of prostitution, the majority of the adult Chinese women in California declared

documented in some of the "one hundred and sixty histories of the Chinese in San Francisco that no one else has bothered to read,"[6] she implicitly undermines this claim by questioning the reliability of historical records, pointing out that they offer reductive or conflicting accounts of Chinatown prostitutes and the people surrounding them.[7] The novel further hints at the ambiguous status of its central character with the very name of Fusang, which coincides with the title of Stan Steiner's 1979 history of Chinese in America. Steiner explains that Fusang appeared in ancient Chinese chronicles as the name of a paradisiacal kingdom east of China discovered by a Buddhist priest Hui Shen in A.D. 499; modern scholars have quibbled over whether the discovery actually happened or whether the kingdom, if actually discovered, was an island off Japan or the Americas.[8] The debates around the meaning of the land of Fusang underscore the slippages between history and myth. "Fusang" has another, similarly mythical meaning in Chinese, namely, a giant tree in the East where the sun rises. By naming her main character Fusang, therefore, Yan draws attention to the ways in which her representation of a nineteenth-century Chinese prostitute blurs the boundary between history and fiction and questions the presumed stability of historical knowledge.

Most American and British reviewers of *The Lost Daughter of Happiness* highlight the narrator's disavowal of complete knowledge of Fusang's character. Some see this renunciation of narrative authority as an implicit challenge to the Western complacency about being able to know the non-West. British reviewer Julia Lovell, for example, contends that, by having its subject remain "at all times opaque," the novel subverts the "basic tenet of Orientalism—that the Orient *can* be read."[9] An American reviewer, Jeffrey C. Kinkley, also affirms the opacity of Fusang's characterization for allowing the novel's plot to break out of the predictable mold of "white men saving yellow women from yellow men."[10] Other reviewers interpret the lack of a

---

themselves as prostitutes in census forms (Tong, 30). Most of the prostitutes were imported and controlled by *Tongs,* secret societies in Chinatown (Tong, 10). Some of the women who came before 1853 operated as free entrepreneurs, the most notable example of which was Ah Toy, who arrived in San Francisco in late 1848 or early 1849 (Tong, 6). Also see Doris Muscatine, *Old San Francisco.* Muscatine also documents a "lone Chinese courtesan" who arrived in 1849. She was a "stunning twenty-two-year-old" with a dozen names, the most common of which were Ah Toy and Ah Choy (Muscatine, 205). Judy Yung's *Unbound Voices* focuses mainly on the first part of the twentieth century, but it provides a *California Illustrated Magazine* article that condemns prostitution in Chinatown and cites a few real examples.

6. Yan Geling, *The Lost Daughter of Happiness,* translated by Cathy Silber, 3.
7. Ibid., 274.
8. Stan Steiner, *Fusang,* 3–9.
9. Julia Lovell, "Chinatown Lady," 20; italics in the original.
10. Jeffrey C. Kinkley, review of *The Lost Daughter of Happiness,* 136 (2).

well-defined central character as a deliberate attempt to unsettle the reader's own sense of belonging. Rebecca Barnhouse, for example, speculates that the author consciously frustrates the readerly expectation for a sharply delineated protagonist in order to make the reader feel, along with Fusang, the pain of being "displaced in the physical and psychological landscapes" that one struggles to inhabit.[11] In general, the reviewers of *The Lost Daughter of Happiness* argue that the novel subverts its Orientalist trappings by refusing to make Fusang a transparent object. Their unanimous focus on Fusang's opacity, however, is not without problems.

While the Anglo-American readings just recapitulated do not reduce Fusang into a transparent racial stereotype, they are nevertheless reductive. In these interpretations, Fusang figures as little more than an empty signifier that warrants all manners of projections or subjective readings. This problem becomes more serious when we consider the less appealing implications of seeing Fusang as "opaque." Indeed, one critic complains that "Fusang never becomes a fully realized character" and suggests that only readers with a "strong interest in the subject" should pick up the novel.[12] We might say that Fusang's, and hence the novel's, purported opacity is yet another symptom of Western-centric approaches toward the non-West, which manifest, on the one hand, in subsuming the other as a known object and, on the other, in dismissing the other on grounds of inscrutable difference. By describing Fusang as "opaque," the reviewers are seeking, arguably, to rationalize their inability to decipher the character. If this is the case, Fusang is not the only Chinese American female literary figure to be denied the status of a meaningful character that merits close attention. Chinese American writer Gish Jen once wondered aloud, during a luncheon-discussion with her readers at the Public Square in Chicago, why some reviewers of her latest novel *The Love Wife* had characterized one of its central characters, Lan Lan, a nanny from China, as an opaque figure that the author does not allow the reader to sympathize with or understand.[13] Jen quipped that the reviewers had probably read "right past" the pages and pages of internal monologue attributed to Lan Lan.

For critics in China, in contrast, Fusang becomes an almost transparent signifier. Fusang's experiences as a Chinatown prostitute serve to allegorize

11. Rebecca Barnhouse, review of *The Lost Daughter of Happiness*, 97.

12. Cathleen A. Towey, review of *The Lost Daughter of Happiness*, 203.

13. As part of the Illinois Humanities Council, a nonprofit organization, the Public Square hosts readings, lectures, and public discussions of political issues. The occasion for Jen's reading and luncheon-discussion, held on October 27, 2004, was the publication of her *The Love Wife* in that year.

China's encounter with Western imperialism and the racialization of Chinese immigrants in the United States from the mid-nineteenth century onward. A critic goes as far as to proclaim that the value of the novel lies in its reflections on the various power dynamics outlined in "postcolonial theory" and reads the desire between Fusang and Chris as a parable of the mutual fascination between the "mature West" and the "ancient East."[14] Many endorse the character's indiscriminating hospitality, describing her as a Mother Earth figure, derived from archetypes in Chinese myth who absorb death and regenerate life.[15] For these critics, Fusan can be construed as a symbol of the survival instincts of Chinese immigrants or "traditional Chinese virtues" that allow China and Chinese around the world to overcome a long history of being overpowered by Westerners.[16] An almost equal number of critics, however, take Yan Geling to task for "internalizing" orientalist imaginings of China in her portrayal of Fusang.[17] Fusang, under this critical perspective, symbolizes a fantasy of cultural reconciliation that masks the tenacity of the racialist "prejudices" stemming from the persistently unequal relations between East and West.[18] Both the supporters and the detractors of the novel, however, converge on their use of an allegorical approach to it. They demonstrate that a certain postcolonial discourse—the notion that China has withstood successive waves of incursion by Western nations, which continue to exercise significant power over how China is perceived and positioned in the world—deeply influences how Chinese immigrant writings like *Fusang* are interpreted in China. Whether they warn of the continuing evil of Western neocolonialism or express confidence in China's ability to survive and rise above Western dominance, Chinese critics of *Fusang* seldom stop to question the Jamesonian critical framework they use (Jameson's theory of Third World writings is duly cited in some of the Chinese criticisms of *Fusang*) that interprets the character Fusang as a metaphor for the historical destiny of an undivided Chinese nation.

14. Li Xiaohua, "Fusang de renwu biaozheng he dongfangzhuyi wenhua duiying" [How characters in *Fusang* register orientalism], 211.

15. Cai Qing, Xu Xu, Zhang Hongwei, "Fusang zhong de shenhua yuanxing jiexi: zhuixun xin de minzu wenhua zhigen" [Mythical archetypes in *Fusang*: In search of new roots of national culture], 77.

16. Yang Hongyin, "Minzu yuyan yu fudian xushu" [National allegory and heteroglossic narration]; Lin Cuiwei. "Fusang zhong de Nu Xing Guan" [Femininity in *Fusang*].

17. Teng Wei, "Huaixiang zongguo de fangshi" [The remembering of China in Yan Geling's immigrant literature], 1.

18. Hu Shaoqing and Zhang Yueyuan, "Zhongguo-xifang de huayu laoyu, dui ershi shiji yilai jige "kuaguo jiaowang" wenben de kaochao" [The China–West dichotomy: Reading transnational narratives since the 1990s], 79.

Fusang's reception history, therefore, constitutes an important site for studying the ways in which such concepts as Orientalism, anti-Asian racism, and postcolonialism have circulated between contemporary America and China. The introduction of theories of orientalism and postcoloniality into China in the early 1990s, combined with the "Chinese economic success," has helped to consolidate Chinese nationalism, which justifies the heavy premium it places on the notion of unity, in a large measure, through invocations of China's continuing vulnerability in the international sphere.[19] The period since the 1990s has also seen a surge in state-centered expressions of Chinese nationalism, including renewed interest in traditional Chinese culture (in which state promotion plays a key role),[20] mass civil protests against foreign impingement upon Chinese sovereignty,[21] and, more recently, a heated online discussion of whether there is a constellation of cultural values that define Chineseness and how they might help or hinder China's rise in world economy and politics.[22] Heightened nationalist sentiments, naturally, inflect Chinese interpretations of Chinese immigrant writings in the United States, especially those written in Chinese, which often come to be read as allegories of China's responses to Western powers, the United States in particular, in the post–Cold War period. To extol *Fusang*'s "traditional Chinese

19. Arif Dirlik and Xudong Zhang, "Introduction"; Dai Jinhua, "Behind Global Spectacle and National Image Making"; Wang Hui, "Contemporary Chinese Thought and Modernity." Dirlik and Zhang point out that the appropriation of postcolonial critique in China "both indicates the heightened awareness of power relations in cultural production and manifests the kind of confidence derived from the Chinese economic success in the global market" (13, 14). Also see Dai, who notes that the surge of Chinese nationalism in the mid-1990s, often framed in anti-American terms, is closely related to "larger social critiques targeted at globalization, transnational capital, and the economic, cultural, and political imperialism of the West" (177). While Wang Hui takes notes of Chinese intellectuals' criticism of nationalist sentiments in the 1990s, he also acknowledges that "[in] Chinese postmodernism, postcolonial theory is often synonymous with a discourse on nationalism, which reinforces the China/West paradigm" (170).

20. In 1994, the Chinese government sponsored an international conference on Confucianism and designated Confucianism as an essential component of the nation's patriotic education curriculum. See Kang Liu, "Is There an Alternative to (Capitalist) Globalization?" 172.

21. Nationalistic protests in China in the late 1990s and early 2000s include, most notably, the demonstrations following NATO's bombing of the Chinese Embassy in Belgrade in 1999 and the public outrage over the collision between a U.S. Navy spy plane and a Chinese fighter in 2001.

22. This discussion was first organized by Sina.com, the third largest website in China, to commemorate the sixtieth anniversary of the founding of the PRC. It caught enormous public attention in May 2009, when an essay written by a college professor for the website received surprisingly enthusiastic responses from common readers and was republished in print media. As of now, the discussion has engaged a large number of well-known public intellectuals and bloggers, as well as common Chinese, many of whom have ventured ideas about the most "universal" characteristics among the (Han) Chinese.

virtues" reflects the nationalist desire to construct an indigenous culture as a counterweight to Western cultural hegemony. To repudiate the character as a symptom of internalized orientalism indicates anxiety over whether this hegemony can be dislodged.

Yan's novel, however, is not simply appropriated by different political and critical discourses; its translation into English, which in many ways conditioned its reception by English-speaking audiences, constituted a more forceful act of appropriation. The changes made in the translation, the removal and shortening of a large number of passages in the original, entail acts of interpretation that echo, even as it partially generated, Anglo-American reactions to the novel. These changes aim to make the novel safe for a liberal view of race, only to demonstrate the limits of liberal tolerance. To intervene in the existing readings of the translation, then, we need to recover what was taken away from the original Chinese version. This work of reconstruction allows us to see how the translation process, compounded by the politics of reading surrounding Chinese immigrant literature in the United States, severely obscures the novel's formal and political sophistication.

Suppressed Irony

Two important passages narrated from Chris's perspective are removed from the English translation, *The Lost Daughter of Happiness*. In the first passage, a sixty-year-old Chris remembers how he was surprised when, as a teenager, he first saw Fusang comply uncomplainingly with her johns. He believes that he is now finally able to understand Fusang's inexplicable ability to draw pleasure from forced sexual acts. He concludes that Fusang embodies a "primitive maternity," defined by "eternal suffering, boundless tolerance, and willing sacrifice:"[23] "Maternity is the highest level of femininity—she opens herself to be plundered and invaded. She does not reject. Her indiscrimination is the most elegant form of wantonness."[24] In the second passage, the narrator reveals the older Chris's reflections on Fusang's attempt to seduce him when she temporarily lived at the missionary house (from which she was soon to be taken by Da Yong). He concludes that Fusang is the "most authentic, most natural" woman because she lets everyone "plough" and "sow" her as "a plot of earth."[25]

These two passages undoubtedly prompt Chinese critics to interpret

23. Yan Geling, *Fusang*, 85.
24. Ibid., 85.
25. Ibid., 114.

Fusang as a Mother Earth figure, either criticizing her as a thoroughly orientalized fantasy or commending her as a symbol of Chinese resilience. The removal of these passages from the translation shows *not* that they would be unimportant from the perspective of English-speaking readers. Just the contrary. In fact, the translator explained their removal from the translation by saying that these passages are "too sentimental" and "overstated"—they are "telling, instead of showing" the reader what to make of the character Fusang.[26] In other words, these passages would give the moral of the novel away; their removal, on the other hand, would ideally leave the English-speaking critics guessing about Fusang's meaning. The critics of the English translation, consequently, became convinced of Fusang's opacity, despite all the other suggestive passages designed to "show" rather than "tell" about the character. The Anglo-American interpreters of the novel (including the translator) and the Chinese critics, therefore, are actually much more similar than different—they both base their readings on explicit rather than descriptive passages. They either claim a complete understanding of Fusang when another character offers a reading of her or give up on deciphering the character when the more explicit passages are absent. Both groups of critics, from different ideological vantage points, elide the formal complexity of the novel. Chris, in fact, can be read as an unreliable observer rather than a guide to Fusang's interiority. The novel's conscious exploration of the various contradictions in Chris's oedipal/orientalist longing for Fusang suggests that we do well to read irony into his paean to Fusang's "primitive maternity."

The narrator attributes Chris's infatuation with Fusang to a convergence of racial and sexual fantasies. When Chris first visits Fusang in her brothel as a twelve-year-old boy, he carries with him all the "fairy tales and adventure stories" he has consumed and the resultant view that the "Orient" is a realm of fascinating mysteries.[27] For Chris, Fusang brings to life a fairy tale, her "cavelike room" figuring as a "distant kingdom."[28] The narrator suggests that Chris approaches Fusang with a set of Orientalist assumptions, which fuel his infatuation with her. Chris perceives Fusang's accented, limited English phrases as primitive sounds that "predate human language," and in so doing, projects her as an infant, or an innocent savage, untouched by civilization.[29] Fusang's bound feet impress Chris as "fishtails" that signify both "stunted

---

26. I obtained this information through my telephone interview with Silber.

27. Yan, *Lost Daughter,* 15.

28. Ibid., 15.

29. Yan, *Fusang,* 10. The sentence that contains this phrase is missing from Silber's translation. See Yan, *The Lost Daughter of Happiness,* 13.

evolution" and cruel mutilation.[30] Thus, the younger Chris imagines Fusang as part of a primitive culture that insulates itself from modern civilization and metes out cruel treatment to its women. Chris's imagination is reminiscent of a range of orientalist discourses and images circulating in the nineteenth-century United States, such as the noble savage discourse (registered, for example, in Melville's *Typee*) and the sensual images of women in the harem (reappropriated for example in Poe's "Ligeia"). Yan's novel, therefore, reverberates with contemporary historical and literary scholarship by figuring nineteenth-century U.S. orientalism as a contradictory, unstable structure of knowledge that consists of a hodgepodge of images about different parts of what is known as the "Orient" or Asia.[31] Chris's various assumptions about Fusang constellate into a sexualized fantasy of rescue. In the days following his first visit to Fusang, Chris wanders around in daydreams. As the narrator puts it, addressing Fusang: "His infatuation with you has left him time for nothing else. In his dreams, he is much taller, brandishing a long sword. A knight of courage and passion. An Oriental princess imprisoned in a dark cell waits for him to rescue her."[32] The "mutilated points of [Fusang's] feet," again, figure prominently in the boy's fantasy.

The novel figures Chris's unconscious as a repository not only of Orientalist fantasies about white men saving women of color from men of color but also of oedipal stereotypes of alluring mature women. Chris taps quickly into these stereotypes as he comes into contact with a sensual "oriental" woman. In the eyes of the twelve-year-old Chris, Fusang's body is a "fruit heavy with juice," "ripe to the bursting point."[33] "Her pursed lips and lowered lashes lent her face all the gentleness of a mother."[34] Chris's desire for thrills turns into the kind of "adoration boys all over the world feel for ripe beautiful women."[35] While Chris regresses into childhood, Fusang is elevated to the status of a primal goddess, her thick long hair falling "like water, as black and impenetrable as sky began before time."[36] By juxtaposing Chris's

---

30. Yan, *Fusang*, 11. Here I depart from Silber's translation, which translates Yan's original as "a stage of evolution no one has imagined" (Yan, *Fusang*, 14). Yan's original literally translates as "a stage between evolution and regression" (Yan, *Lost Daughter*, 11), which I prefer to translate as "stunted evolution."

31. Malini Johar Schueller, *U.S. Orientalisms*. Schueller provides an analysis of the different constructions of the Orient in U.S. culture before 1890, including the orientalism induced by the U.S.–North African conflict of the late eighteenth century, Near Eastern orientalism, and Indic orientalism (ix).

32. Yan, *Lost Daughter*, 19.

33. Ibid., 16.

34. Ibid., 12.

35. Ibid., 16.

36. Ibid., 14.

oedipal infatuation with his heroic fantasy of coming to Fusang's rescue, the novel shows that, for Chris, Fusang is at once a hypersexualized mother who incites penetration and a chaste whore who awaits salvation. Chris's desire for Fusang, indeed, is a case that illustrates what Homi Bhabha terms "ambivalence" at the heart of colonial and racial desire.[37]

Chris's characterization not only gestures toward the intersections of heterosexuality and racialized desire in nineteenth-century America. It also shows that infatuation with the racial and sexual other is bound up with a more insidious emotional undercurrent. Chris's desire for Fusang is symbiotic with his fear of the otherness she embodies, a fear that is mostly displaced onto the Chinese men around her. As he goes through what seems to him Chinatown's shady establishments and becomes exposed to anti-Chinese protests starting to flare up in San Francisco, Chris is increasingly gripped by the conviction that the Chinese, especially the male laborers who account for most of the Chinatown population, are an "inferior race" that should be "wiped out."[38] At some points, Chris's desire to rescue Fusang seems to be motivated by or at least correlated with a different desire—the desire to distinguish himself from, as well as destroy, "those hideous Oriental buildings, all these grotesque feet and queues" and all these things that he "couldn't understand."[39] Fusang also becomes a victim of this racial hate in the rape scene, which I discuss in the following section.

The novel's orientalization of Fusang through Chris, therefore, might arguably be read as what Judith Butler calls, in her *Bodies That Matter*, a "critical mime,"[40] which refers to an act of citing or appropriating dominant discourse that aims to expose its foundational violence. Indeed, one can say that the novel mimics Chris's view of Fusang as a way of opening up a conceptual space beyond it. It suggests a critical vantage point from which one can see Chris's complicity with the inherently violent racial stereotypes of exotic, passive, submissive, and sexually available Asian women.[41] When the younger Chris believes that Fusang's passivity gives her freedom, because she

37. Bhabha, 69. He uses the concept of "ambivalence" to indicate the contradictions in the "polymorphous and perverse collusion between racism and sexism" and in the subjectivities of both the colonizer and the colonized (69). Extrapolating from Said's organization of "manifest" and "latent" orientalism into one congruent and intentional system of representation, Bhabha critiques the "closure and coherence attributed to the unconscious pole of colonial discourse" (72).

38. Ibid., 44.

39. Ibid., 198.

40. Judith Butler, *Bodies That Matter*, 47.

41. For a useful review of the Asian American feminist critique of these stereotypes, see Laura Hyun Yi Kang, *Compositional Subjects*, especially the chapter titled "Cinematic Projections."

is a "body not ruled over by the soul," he can be seen as positing an oriental and feminine other essentially opposed to his own repressed self, brought up on Calvinist teachings against physical desire and prohibited socially and legally to pursue his desire.[42] When the older Chris, cited in the beginning of this section, fantasizes about Fusang as a Mother Earth figure who rises above unspeakable violence through her uncomplaining passivity and her "elegant wantonness," he can be understood as enacting what Kristeva terms the ritual of "purifying the abject," which in the case of the novel figures as Fusang's othered, prohibited body.[43]

The Anglo-American and the Chinese interpretations of Fusang outlined in the previous section, which emphasize her opacity and transparent symbolic value (as a metaphor for the Chinese nation), respectively, elide the ways in which the novel undercuts Chris's perspective. The decision to remove these passages from the novel's English translation might have been motivated by the fear that the passages, described by the translator as too "sentimental" and "overstated," would repel the novel's potential critics and readers in the West, who are presumed to be largely white, middle-class, and liberal. They might very well attribute these two passages to the author and subsequently criticize her for perpetuating an essentialist, exoticist view of Asian femininity and femininity in general. Chinese and other Asian immigrant literature is expected to adhere to the tenets of liberal multiculturalism and stage a critique of *historical* configurations (as opposed to the continual presence) of orientalism. Parts of Yan's *Fusang*, however, might upset this liberal expectation and instead lead the average, supposedly careless American reader to believe that the novel is coopted by orientalism. The deletion of these two passages, then, provides a glimpse of how trade book publishing in the United States shapes Asian immigrant literature by exercising an overt form of censorship. The critics of *The Lost Daughter of Happiness*, one might say, exercise a more covert form of censorship by refusing to acknowledge parts of the novel that cannot be subsumed under a simple antiorientalist reading, literally dismissing them in describing Fusang as "opaque." While the English translation has been made safe and palatable for mass consumption in the United States, it loses much of the original's formal and thematic

42. Yan, *Fusang*, 86.
43. Julia Kristeva, *Powers of Horror*, 17. Kristeva defines the abject as what is fundamentally suppressed from the human psyche. The abject is "the jettisoned object, is radically excluded and draws me toward the place where meaning collapses" (2). The abject appears either as "a rite of defilement and pollution" or as "exclusion or taboo" in various religions; religions and art both comprise various means of "purifying the abject" (17). In *Bodies That Matter*, Judith Butler defines the abject more generally as a social and psychic zone of uninhatability that "constitutes the defining limit of the subject's domain" (3).

sophistication. The Chinese critics unquestioningly equate Chris's perspective on Fusang with the novel's largely to support their allegorical readings of the character as an emblem of the Chinese at home and abroad. As they use the novel to construct coherent narratives of the historical trajectory of China's relation to the West, especially the United States, the Chinese critics fail to consider the possibility that the novel could at once imitate and subvert orientalist stereotypes in creating the figure of Fusang. The critics on both sides of the Pacific, therefore, converge in reducing Fusang to an unambiguous character and subordinating her to nation-centered interpretative frameworks. Fusang is turned either into a proper ethnic subject attesting to racial progress in contemporary American culture or into the quintessential modern Chinese subject struggling under Western domination.

Signifying Excision

I argued that the existing criticisms of Yan's *Fusang* and its English translation show how different audiences, from different cultural and political standpoints, appropriate Chinese immigrant literature in the United States. Equally important, these critical appropriations are anticipated and mirrored within the novel itself, which dramatizes how various characters compete to possess Fusang in both epistemological and sexual terms. While the Chinese laborers and gangsters in the novel try to confine Fusang to the social and domestic structures of Chinatown, Chris, in both his younger and older versions, projects onto her, as I demonstrate in my previous section, an incoherent panoply of cultural stereotypes. One can see strong echoes between the male characters' competing interpretations of Fusang and those of the novel's critics. The allegorical readings generated in the Chinese context naturalize Fusang's Chineseness, as does the heterosexual economy of Chinatown presented in the novel. Just as Chris turns Fusang into a desirable oriental by distinguishing her from the "hideous" surroundings of San Francisco Chinatown, the Anglo-American critics of the novel, along with its translator and publisher, are engaged in restaging Fusang as a proper racial subject who does not yield willingly to the sexual depravations of Chinatown's male denizens and visitors.

Despite the competing efforts to comprehend and possess her, Fusang consistently fascinates, baffles, and disorients the novel's male characters with her boundlessly open sexuality. Her at-home-ness with forced sexual transactions sets her apart from common tropes of fallen women, such as veteran prostitutes hardened against the world and prostitutes with a heart of gold, who embody moral virtues under a worldly guise. She does not, apparently, see her role in terms of sexual slavery. Surprised at Chris's age at their first encounter, Fusang nevertheless decides not to "cut a single corner with him," instead smiling at him "as if he were a man every bit [her] match."[44] She also willingly accommodates Da Yong when she comes under his control. When Chris tries to kill Da Yong while the latter is asleep, Fusang quietly deters him by continuing to wash Da Yong's hair as she was ordered.

Many of Fusang's Chinese clients construe her effortless accommodation of their sexual needs as an expression of submissive affection and consequently propose to buy her out of prostitution and marry her.[45] Da Yong quickly overwhelms his rivals and takes possession of Fusang, petting her the same way he treasures his "dog," "parrot," and "jewelry case."[46] In a scene that literalizes Eve Sedgwick's argument about male homosociality being triangulated through the female body, a brawl breaks out between Da Yong's gang and a group of white passengers on a ship over the latter's insulting remarks about Fusang and her music.[47] Throughout the novel, the male Chinese characters vie with each other and with the dominant race for control over Fusang, all the while under the illusion of her willing submission. Though the novel fully acknowledges the historical, legal, and psychic structures that resulted in the gendered racialization of early Chinese migrants in San Francisco, it does not romanticize this racialized group. Just as it implicitly subverts Chris's orientalist desire for Fusang through critical mimicry, the novel suggests the cost of Da Yong's desperate defense of his own and the other Chinese men's endangered masculinity by showing how it is predicated on the possession of Fusang's body.

Each of the "readers" within the text seeks to stabilize Fusang's implications for particular ethnic or national identities by domesticating her capacious, indiscriminate sexuality. Likewise, as we can see in the competing critical discourses around the novel, turning an enigmatic female figure in Chinese immigrant fiction into a modern ethnic or national subject is contingent upon shearing her sexuality of its inexplicable excess. The interpretive battles both within and around Yan's novel demonstrate the ways in which Asian American women's sexuality and subjectivity become, to quote

44. Yan, *Lost Daughter*, 15.

45. The slippage between prostitutes and domestic women, as presented in the novel, is peculiar to early Chinese immigrant history. Chinatowns in the U.S. had a predominantly male population until after World War II, when the 1945 War Brides Act started to increase the number of Chinese women immigrating to the United States. See Tong, 159.

46. Yan, *Lost Daughter*, 156.

47. Ibid., 164.

Leslie Bow, a "register of international and domestic struggle," defined in conflicting terms by competing nationalist discourses.[48]

At one point, the novel seems to acquiesce with reductive readings of Fusang by toying with the possibility of her domestication through racially inflected heterosexual desire. Upon meeting Chris after a long absence, although Fusang draws a blank when trying to remember who Chris is, as would be the case with any of her other johns, she is eventually moved by Chris's persistence at being accepted sexually. The narrator goes on to project a parallel between Fusang's feelings for Chris and her own affection for her husband. Just as the narrator feels both infatuated with and distanced from her husband because of their perceived "differences," Fusang develops a heightened sensitivity to Chris by becoming aware of how she is different from him: "You are aware of your strange feet, your cold faux jade bracelet. You're aware of the heartbeat of every embroidered blossom on your peach silk blouse."[49] For a brief moment, Fusang seems to have been interpellated into the racialized economy of heteronormative desire that Chris inhabits and to have become a recognizable object of that desire. The younger Chris's erotic gaze puts her through a process of subjectification, turning her into a desiring subject as well as a desired object.

However, the novel soon thwarts its own movement toward a standard interracial romance. The various legal and social restrictions prohibiting Fusang's desire for Chris do not lead her to take her own life in the fashion of a betrayed Madame Butterfly. The novel gradually suggests that Fusang's all-accepting sexuality, characterized as a form of pristine femininity by the older Chris, can be construed as a process of dismantling the normative desire that threatens to claim her. It is not a stretch to say that the novel not only critically mimics and therefore self-consciously critiques the various acts of appropriation to which Fusang is subjected but also illustrates how these forces can potentially be resisted and neutralized.

When Chris, as a young man in his twenties, proposes to marry her and then move with her to Montana toward the end of the novel, Fusang quietly leaves to prepare and stage a wedding with Da Yong, who is soon to be executed. Fusang's apparent submission to the institution of marriage signifies just the opposite. Her marriage with the dead Da Yong, as the last part of the novel suggests, becomes an implicit statement of her refusal to marry in real life. It is indeed a final, definitive rejection of marriage. This ending decidedly distinguishes the novel *Fusang* from Ruthanne Lum McCunn's

48. Leslie Bow, *Betrayal and Other Acts of Subversion*, 10.
49. Yan, *Lost Daughter*, 43.

Thousand Pieces of Gold, a novel based on the life of Lalu Nathoy, a nine-teenth-century Chinese prostitute working in a mining town in Idaho.[50] While McCunn's novel largely revolves around Lalu's love for and marriage with Charlie Bemis, a saloon owner, *Fusang* does not offer the satisfaction of a conventional interracial romance between a white man and an Asian woman.

Although Fusang's rejection of marriage triggers profound confusion in the young Chris and, as he gets older, eventually compels him to think of the Chinatown prostitute as a form of primitive materiality that cannot be socially integrated, it is actually prefigured in a number of long passages that appeared earlier in the novel. In one scene, Chris follows Fusang back from a teahouse to her brothel. Dying to find out whether Fusang is in danger, Chris climbs up a small tree beneath Fusang's window. When he flings himself forward and lands on Fusang's window ledge, however, Chris is greeted by a shocking scene:

> Her body was taking in a man. It was sleek with a faint film of sweat. She wasn't resisting as he had expected, but accommodating herself completely to the man. The way the beach accommodates the tide.
>
> . . .
>
> He thought there should be struggle, some sign of suffering. But what he saw instead was harmony. No matter that the man wore a queue, or that his sallow back was covered with grotesque tattoos—the harmony was beautiful.[51]

Fusang's embrace of this experience, for one thing, undercuts Chris's fantasy of rescue and the underlying gendered pattern of racialization (Asian women are seen as hypersexual while Asian men are seen as either asexual or sexually perverted). The sight of Fusang drawing pleasure from her intercourse with a random Chinese man, unsurprisingly, baffles Chris, who has been conditioned to associate the masculinity of Chinatown laborers with grotesqueness.

But Yan's staging of intraracial "harmony" in this scene is not a cultural nationalist proclamation of a natural erotic bond between Asian men and Asian women.[52] Instead, it amounts to a description of a nonnormative sex-

---

50. Ruthanne Lum McCunn, *Thousand Pieces of Gold.*
51. Yan, *Lost Daughter,* 62.
52. A recent example of this version of cultural nationalism is Darrel Hamamoto's film, *Yellowcaust: A Patriot Act* (2003), in which the University of California Davis professor includes clips from a self-made pornographic film that stars Asian actors. His expressive purpose was to

ual practice that can potentially challenge the reification of sexual, racial, and national differences. Fusang conveys her desire both for the Chinese man and for Chris (whom she sees) through bodily movements that are seductive, almost phallic:

> Her body was [the harmony]'s basis; she controlled the advance and retreat.
> . . .
> And [the pleasure] did not reside solely in her, the movement of her body spread it to the man, and her gaze sent it toward Chris.
>
> Chris realized that now he was crying for a different reason. With the onslaught of the mysterious pleasure, his body unfolded and quickened in ways he'd never known. The movements of their bodies drew him into their rhythm.[53]

Fusang's desire in this passage is not only active but expansive, contagious, and implicitly nonmonogamous as well. At this moment, probably against his own will, Chris's murderous jealousy toward the Chinese john, his wish to "rescue the beautiful slave girl on her dying breath," morphs into the pleasure of an imaginary sexual union.[54] Although the sexual pleasure Fusang experiences and helps generate in Chris remains ambiguous, indefinable, and "mysterious," it is clearly differentiated from what Chris sees as passive submission characteristic of primordial femininity.

How do we, then, understand Fusang's apparently unintelligible sexuality? I submit that we consider Leo Bersani's theory of impersonal intimacy, which builds on a series of writings since his 1988 article "Is the Rectum a Grave," as a possible interpretive framework.[55] In his 2002 article "Sociability and Cruising," Bersani questions the disparaging definition in Freudian psychoanalysis of a male homosexual as one who "cruises the world . . . in search of objects that will give him back to himself as a loved and cared for subject,"

"re-eroticize Asian America" and to bring Asian men and women together sexually. See *Masters of the Pillow* (2003), James Hou's documentary film about the making of the pornographic film.

53. Ibid., 62, 63.

54. Ibid., 61.

55. Leo Bersani, "Is the Rectum a Grave?"; *Homos;* "Sociability and Cruising." In "Is the Rectum a Grave?" Bersani points out that while sex is often practiced to create "a hyperbolic sense of self, it also potentially implies "a loss of all consciousness of self" (218); he posits the enhancement of the latter aspect of sex as the aim of radical sexual politics. He builds on this argument in *Homos,* where he considers the possible manners in which male homosexuality provides a "privileged vehicle" for self-shattering sex (10). "Sociability and Cruising" continues the line of thinking presented in *Homos,* explaining in more detail the psychic resources and labor required for constructing new forms of intimacy dissociated from the fortification of the self.

recasting this longing as a radial form of sexuality. By loving others as the self, Bersani argues, the gay cruiser recognizes that "difference can be loved as the non-threatening supplement of sameness," thus providing an alternative to the normative, heterosexual approach to sexual difference.[56] Cruising, therefore, constitutes a form of training in "impersonal intimacy," namely, sexual relations that do *not* result in psychic individuation through the simultaneous eroticization and repudiation of the gendered other.[57] Embracing impersonal intimacy, for Bersani, helps build a psychic foundation for relating to the other in general, on both sexual and nonsexual levels, as supplementary to the self. That is to say, both heterosexuals and homosexuals can practice impersonal intimacy, to different extents and at different costs, and, in so doing, disrupt normative heterosexual desire organized around reified sexual difference.

Sexual difference, it needs to be emphasized, claims a unique position in Bersani's theory of impersonal intimacy. Although he allows in his essay that sexual difference should not be "prejudicially sanctified in our psychoanalytically oriented culture as the ground of all difference," he adds that it perhaps "does have a unique epistemological function in human growth as an early and crucial model for structuring difference."[58] In contrast to Bersani's proposition, the representation of Fusang's sexuality in this important passage unsettles the normative operation of both sexual and racial differences without attributing to one mode of differentiation more psychic and social importance than it does the other. In *Racial Castration,* David Eng argues that psychoanalytical theories and queer discourses can be useful for Asian American and critical ethnic studies if we open them "upon a social terrain marked not by singular difference but by multiple differences.[59] Indeed, the passage where Fusang derives pleasure from forced intercourse shows both the usefulness and the limitations of psychoanalytically informed queer theories for analyzing how Chinese immigrant literature interrogates the construction of social differences.

Although Fusang's desire is not exactly homosexual and she of course does not cruise the world, she, like the gay man posited in Bersani's article, shows the same ability to approach the threatening other as the "non-threatening supplement" of herself. One can, therefore, simultaneously claim a kind

56. Ibid.

57. Leo Bersani, "Sociability and Cruising," 17.

58. Ibid., 17. This view of sexual difference is a slight change from the one expressed in a slightly earlier article "Against Monogamy." In that essay, Bersani explicitly parallels sexual difference with "national, racial, religious, ethnic" differences (4).

59. Eng, *Racial Castration,* 2.

of queerness for Fusang and reinscribe queerness as disruptions of not only sexual but also racial and ethnic differences and as a process of becoming rather than a stable component of one's identity. As demonstrated in her interactions with Chris, Fusang manages racial and sexual trauma, registered on her body in the form of violent penetration, by being hospitable to and drawing pleasure from it. She goes through a ritual of coquetry with any random client, as she does with Chris: she would pour some tea, turn to smile at the customer, adjust her shirt, and then wait a moment.[60] In one of the passages deleted from the English translation, the narrator describes, from Fusang's perspective, one of her sexual experiences, in which she reaches the acute pleasure lying at the far end of "a vast plain of pain" by treading over "resistance and unwillingness, shame and anger."[61] By showing how Fusang turns the pain of sexual servitude into a source of pleasure, this passage might very well disturb middle-class American readers. This concern might have motivated the removal of this passage from the English translation. The omission obscures the ways in which the novel appropriates conventional forms of female sexual service, like prostitution, in order to stage new modes of relating to the racial and sexual other. Inserted back into the translation, the passage suggests that the peculiar form of sexual hospitality that Fusang exhibits not only reconciles her with the violent world around her but actively intervenes in it as well. Fusang's vastly expansive desire temporarily dissolves Chris's hatred of the Chinese johns. The visual pleasure he feels signifies either a cross-racial identification (with the Chinese john) or a cross-gender and cross-racial identification (with Fusang), both of which are precluded from the racial and sexual economy of the nineteenth-century San Francisco presented in the novel and, to a different extent, from today's America.

As Bersani argues, impersonal intimacy entails both self-extension and self-subtraction. By practicing sexual acts like cruising, one can learn to refrain from the wish to be individuated from all otherness and embrace one's numerous inaccurate replications in the world, thus extending oneself into the world in a nonaggressive way. Just as Bersani's notion of impersonal intimacy, an expansive connectedness, is predicated upon the work of self-subtraction, Fusang's all-accepting sexuality is based on the stripping away of her sense of an enclosed, autonomous self. Right after the scene just discussed, Fusang gets up and "splash[es] herself with water to wash off [menstruation] blood."[62] Watching her from outside the window, Chris is "shocked" at

---

60. Yan, *Lost Daughter*, 11–13.
61. Yan, *Fusang*, 88.
62. Yan, *Lost Daughter*, 64.

Fusang's "nonchalance" toward blood.[63] Fusang seems indifferent to, or intent upon dismantling, the difference between inside and outside, private and public. As blood trickles down her leg, Fusang fails to cohere into a subject with easily recognizable boundaries. She has become a kind of uncountable body inextricable from the world. As the narrator puts it, Fusang's body "doesn't count now."[64] This image emblematizes Fusang's resistance toward being counted, or categorized as a normative female subject that upholds a specific set of nationalist discourses. The novel's representation of Fusang's open-ended sexuality suggests that acts of survival can be continuous with the process of forging new kinds of subjectivity that do not strive toward autonomy or coherence.

The novel stages the most extreme implications of Fusang's sexuality in the gang-rape scene. The race riot that occasions the rape of Fusang bears some resemblance to historical accounts of race riots against the Chinese that happened in the 1870s in Los Angeles, Chico, and other parts of the American West.[65] As the English translation shortens the extensive description of the rape in the original (which underscores, again, that the translator of *Fusang* and the publisher of the translation construed parts of the novel to be unacceptable to mainstream American readers), I have to quote mainly from the Chinese original in my following analysis. Speaking in second person, the narrator equates Fusang's experience of being raped and her daily interactions with her johns, "You can't tell the difference between selling your body and gang-rape."[66] If an important difference between rape and prostitution is the supposition of female consent, this difference is all but nonexistent in the case of Fusang as presented in the novel. The novel's equation of rape and prostitution mirrors inversely the analogy Andrea Dworkin draws between prostitution and gang rape in her essay "Prostitution and Male Supremacy."[67] Both the novel and Dworkin's essay point out that women do not consent to prostitution, just as they do not consent to rape, because they are not legally or socially defined as sovereign subjects in full possession of their bodies. However, while Dworkin calls for changes in social structures that will enable women to attain to subjecthood, Yan gestures toward a critique of the very

63. Ibid.
64. Ibid.
65. Sucheng Chan, *Asian Americans*, 48–49.
66. Yan, *Fusang*, 183.
67. Andrea Dworkin, "Prostitution and Male Supremacy." Dworkin criticizes the tendency among academic feminists to discuss prostitution in abstract, theoretical terms. She explains how prostitution facilitates unmitigated violence against women by making the following statement, "The only analogy I can think of concerning prostitution is that it is more like gang rape than it is like anything else" (3).

notion of subjectivity, characterized by autonomy and individuation, as a source of social violence. We cannot expect to universalize access to subjectivity, that is to say, without changing its premises.

From the translator and publisher's perspective, perhaps, Fusang, with all her provocative complexity, would not be able to strike a chord in the novel's mainstream reader who is likely to have been socialized into liberal notions of the sovereign subject. It is perhaps why the rest of the paragraph that begins with the sentence just quoted is completely deleted. I therefore translate it as follows:

> One can even say that you never felt you were selling your body at all, because you accept the men. There is equality in your interactions with the men: You find pleasure even as you are physically violated, and you take away from the men what you give them. Instinctively, you have transformed the traffic in your body into exchanges between and among bodies. Your body is so hospitable that you never realized that you had had to exchange it for money. Encounters between and among bodies allow different lives to converse with and learn from each other.
>
> This makes me suspect again that you, Fusang, are from a very old time.[68]

The last sentence of this passage seems to suggest that the narrator is aligned with the older Chris, who sees Fusang as a symbol of primitive, pristine femininity. But if this passage indeed posits an originary femininity, it does not signify, as the older Chris believes, a boundless ability to countenance suffering and regenerate life. It does not justify rape by implying that it satisfies women's masochistic sexual fantasies or, in other words, their proclivities for suffering, nor does it stop at critiquing rape as traffic in the female body. Instead, it proposes a possible antidote to rape impulses by teasing out the radical implications of the survival tactic Fusang uses in this scene. As Fusang imagines the process of the rape as "exchanges between and among bodies," she becomes a conduit of a subversive, self-subtracting sexual practice. This passage suggests, therefore, that, by embracing differently configured bodies without feeling threatened, in other words, by practicing a form of impersonal, indiscriminate intimacy, we could start, as Fusang does in this passage, to dissolve conventional notions of subjectivity grounded in entrenched social difference. The dissolution, in turn, would make impossible the resentment of the other that feeds such misogynist (and racist, in this particular case) practices as rape.

68. Yan, *Fusang,* 183.

The novel's representation of Fusang, as I pointed out earlier, is in conversation with various historical studies of the experience of Chinese prostitutes in nineteenth-century America. It rewrites conventional historical narratives that cast these women as either victims or agents seeking control of their own lives and, in so doing, resonates with and contributes to contemporary critical inquiries into subjectivity and relationality. Bersani's ideas of impersonal intimacy and self-divestiture are by no means the only critical resource useful for our understanding of the radical implications of Yan's novel. Contemporary feminist theories have also questioned the idea of autonomous, individuated identity by reimagining the female body.[69] Some feminists, borrowing from different intellectual and scientific traditions, focus particularly on theorizing the interconnectivity between different bodies as a sexual corollary of intersubjective conceptions of identity. Christine Battersby, for example, builds her conception of the female body over and against the equation of embodiment with an experience of containment posited in Lakoff and Johnson's theories of metaphor (which believes that the experience of containment gives rise to mental patterns—or schemata—that constrain metaphorically how we conceptualize other relations). Battersby argues for a fluid understanding of the body by citing embodied experiences peculiar to women (menstruation, pregnancy, and childbirth), modern topological theory (which sees form or structure as a temporary stability in patterns of flow) and new scientific paradigms of form, and historical formulations of the body (as seen in Nietzsche and Bergson, among others) that broke from a rigidly masculine view of the body as coherent and well-contained. As Battersby points out, she is not alone in making this argument; many others, including Irigaray, Harraway, Emily Martin, and Kelly Oliver, to name only the most obvious suspects, have reenvisioned the (female) self/body in terms of "patterns of potentiality and flow."[70] The queer and feminist theories cited in this chapter are directly

69. Autonomy has always been a key idea in feminist philosophy, not always connected to the issue of the body. See Marilyn Friedman, "Feminism in Ethics: Conceptions of Autonomy." Friedman points out that "[t]he standard current feminist account of autonomy may be called a social or relational account," variants of which have been offered by many feminist philosophers, including "Evelyn Fox Keller, Jennifer Nedelsky, Seyla Benhahib, Lorraine Code, Morwenna Griffiths, Alison [sic] Weir and Susan Brison" (217).

70. Christine Battersby, "Her Body/Her Boundaries," 355. For two more examples of this theoretical negotiation, see Allison Weir, Sacrificial Logics; Jane Caputi, "'Take Back What Doesn't Belong to Me': Sexual Violence, Resistance, and the 'Transmission of Affect.'" Weir uses Kristeva to distinguish between dominating and nondominating identity, arguing that the "separateness or identity of the self" does not have to presume the suppression of nonidentity; in fact, "[i]deally, the identity of the self is based on the acceptance of the nonidentity of others, and of the nonidentity within oneself" (13). Caputi discusses sexual violence toward women as a transmission of affect, the "dumping" of negative emotions from the masculine subject to the

relevant to efforts in U.S. ethnic studies, including Asian American studies, to reconfigure identities organized around race, ethnicity, and nation. Kandice Chuh's argument against referential understandings of the term "Asian American," for example, grounds itself in the larger argument against taking the universal "citizen-subject" and the proper, rights-bearing "subject of the law" on face value.[71] Such a poststructural project requires not only intervention in conventional narratives but also investment in reimagining and reorganizing embodied practices. As Yan suggests through *Fusang*, a necessary ingredient of the ongoing theoretical efforts to break the false dichotomy between reified national identities and reified minority identities is to intervene in the corporeal and psychic dimensions of the process of identity formation.

The idea of an embodied subject seeking disembodiment by circulating itself among other bodies might seem unattainable. But the novel suggests that it could be concretized in the future and that a condition of possibility for attaining this new kind of subjectivity resides in reflections on the violence inherent in normative sexual desire. The narrator relates that Fusang feels her strength drained away and experiences a taste of "humiliation" when Chris joins the rapists and yet tries to set himself apart from them by being tender toward her.[72] The "little bit of tenderness" that Chris tries to give her generates in Fusang a traumatized reaction—she feels humiliated and tries to break away from Chris.[73] Fusang's humiliation suggests a perception of the profound contradictions within the racialized economy of heterosexual desire. Chris's sexual longing for Fusang, expressed through violent penetration in the rape scene, becomes literally intertwined with an outburst of racial hate. His attempt to instill some "tenderness" into this sexual act does not offset its violence; instead it overlays the violence of subjectification upon that of physical domination. Fusang tries to manage the traumatic effects of this redoubled violence by treating Chris like everyone else, biting off one of his buttons as a reminder of her "peculiar contact" with him.[74] It can be argued that Fusang's resistance toward heteronormative, monogamous desire, manifest later in her refusal to marry Chris and in her decision to wed herself to

---

feminine other. Healing from such abuse, for Caputi, entails self-cleansing through reconnecting with the positive, elemental forces in the world. This process repudiates sexual violence as a form of, but "as force of connection, linking us energetically to each other, to the elements, and to a divinity that is experienced not as a transcendent White father god . . . but on earth, . . . and in other sexual bodies" (12). One's embodied connections to the environment thus facilitate the reconstitution of a female self in the wake of masculine violence.

71. Kandice Chuh, *Imagine Otherwise*, 22–23.

72. Yan, *Fusang* 185; *Lost Daughter* 225.

73. Yan, *Fusang* 231; *Lost Daughter* 189.

74. Yan, *Fusang*, 184; *Lost Daughter* 224.

Da Yong right before his execution, derives from her intuitive understanding of the contradictory and traumatic nature of this desire. Her social position as a racialized, sexualized object and her refusal to be coopted by socially instituted desire enable her to personify a new mode of subjectivity and relationality. Although Fusang's rejection of normative subjectivity does not immediately produce an ideal alternative within or outside the text, she at least suggests a condition of possibility for approaching this ideal.

A Chinese Peasant Woman

We should certainly not read *Fusang* only through the scrim of literary and cultural theories produced in the United States. The author, in fact, has made it clear that the novel, to her mind, engages with multiple cultural contexts. In an interview she gave in 2003, Yan Geling indicates that she has become aware of the critical resistance to and appropriations of the novel. She takes pain to distinguish the figure Fusang from the more well-known prostitute figures in Chinese and Western literary canons, including, in particular, Dumas's Camille, who is remembered for her "helplessness and sacrifices."[75] Fusang, by contrast, embodies a new form of feminism. As the author puts it, "Fusang is a feminist with strength that surpasses men's. She embodies a modern ethos—she values freedom, refuses to bind herself to one man, and is completely open to physical pleasure."[76] Fusang is a figure who "transcends reality" in a politically meaningful way, the author adds, implicitly refuting the Anglo-American critics' comment that the character comes across as pointlessly opaque.[77] In the same interview, Yan also indicates that she is apprised of some Chinese critics' complaint that the novel made them "feel uneasy," speculating that this may be a reaction to her dispiriting description of the male Chinese immigrants.[78] In her own defense, she describes the characterization of Fusang as a deliberate critique of a kind of reactionary mindset that fuels some of the "senseless resentment" that the Chinese sometimes display against Westerners.[79] The character is meant to frustrate the nationalist sentiments of many Chinese and provide a corrective to their oscillation between "excessive pride" and "excessive shame" in perceiving themselves vis-à-vis the West.

75. Ya fei, "Zai haiwai xiezuo: zuojia yan geling fangtanlu, zuojia Yan Geling fangtan lu" [Writing from overseas: An interview of Yan Geling].
76. Ibid.
77. Ibid.
78. Ibid.
79. Ibid.

Though Fusang should not be read as an embodiment of a unified, triumphant Chinese nation, she speaks to an important strain in contemporary Chinese literature. Another point the author makes in the interview is that, while the character is surreal, she is solidly grounded in the author's understanding of what a "sturdy Chinese peasant woman" might look and think like. Fusang's peasant origin (she is literally born a peasant girl in Canton in the novel) suggests the novel's possible affinity with the concept of *minjian* proposed by Chinese critic Chen Sihe, who, not coincidentally, has written some of the most widely cited critical essays on Yan. Chen defines the concept of *minjian,* which translates literally as the "sphere of the people," as the cultural customs, sentiments, and aesthetic preferences of the lower strata of people in rural and ethnic areas, over which state power has weakened or incomplete control. The most important characteristic of *minjian* is its relative freedom from dominant ideologies and mores, although it can generate its own, sometimes extremely oppressive, power structures. *Minjian* figures in contemporary Chinese literature as "invisible structures" that slyly throw into question its more politically conformist elements.[80] Chen's idea of *minjian* resonates with some of the subversive tactics that have been identified in American literature, including critical reappropriation, signifying, and, as I invoked earlier, critical mimicry. The passages deleted from the English translation of *Fusang* can be aptly described as manifestations of *minjian* in the novel, as they present unconventional modes of pleasure and resistance that belie the novel's superficial resemblance with an allegory of China's struggles against the West. Disrupting the master narratives of official, postcolonial Chinese nationalism, the novel *Fusang* runs in the same vein as *Xinling Shi,* where the idea of *minjian* also registers. Chen explicitly associates Yan's portrayal of Fusang with his conception of *minjian* in his comments on Yan's 2006 novel *Dijiuge guafu* [The ninth widow], which portrays a Fusang-like character in a rural part of Henan, a province in central China. The peasant woman Wang Putao weathers the series of political movements during the second half of the twentieth century in the same way that Fusang weathers her various sexual encounters, that is, with indiscriminating openness and tenacious simple-mindedness. For Chen, Wang Putao represents an extension of the indomitable, undisciplined life force already present in Fusang.[81]

80. For Chen, representations of *minjian* became self-conscious with the rise of the "roots-seeking" writers in the 1980s. The politics and aesthetics of *minjian* reached a new level in the 1990s, when many writers turned to *minjian* for new forms of idealism that do not derive from state ideologies. See Chen, *Zhongguo xiandangdai wenxueshi jiaochen* [History of modern and contemporary Chinese literature], 12–14.

81. Chen Sihe, *Ziji de shujia* [My own bookshelf].

Drawing from and addressing cultural coordinates in both the United States and China, *Fusang* is an appropriate work with which to end my discussion of the two multiculturalisms. In the novel, moments of violence become a plea for narrative and intellectual labor aiming to uncover new grounds for radical, noncomplicitous responses to power. The character Fusang, a product of this labor, bodies forth a self-subtracting, nonaggressive mode of subjectivity shaped in the active accommodation of a web of otherness. Simultaneously one and many, Fusang can be read as a study of the subjective conditions for the construction of functional but maximally heterogeneous collective identities, whether ethno-racial or national. The novel, therefore, helps imagine and broker a radical kind of pluralist universalism, an ideal shared, albeit imperfectly, by Kuo, Zhang, and Alameddine alike.

CONCLUSION

A S A GLOBAL PROJECT, multiculturalism's search for workable formulas for balancing national coherence and ethnic justice is always already characterized by cross-national comparisons and borrowing. Even as they propose expansive models of multiculturalism, the authors studied in this book help bridge, consciously or unconsciously, the imagined chasm between two multiculturalist projects. In other words, they translate between two national contexts against the grains of existing modes of translation. Herein lies the crux of this study. The double critique that it performs does not simply intervene in two different cultural and political processes simultaneously; it also revises the comparative discourses that have emerged between them. The existing comparative discourses, as I pointed out throughout this study, are mostly marked by a conservative impulse toward self-justification. This impulse is visible whether the other country (as opposed to one's own) is criticized for minority rights violations or exalted as a commendable example of cultural tolerance. When U.S. liberal multiculturalism is affirmed and embraced in China as an instructive precedent, as we saw in the chapter on Kuo, it usually works slyly to legitimize the privileging of the national over the ethnic in China's own ethnic policy. The literary readings offered here counter the banal universalism—

"excusing one bad deed by pointing to another," that is, in colloquial terms—entailed in such self-defensive modes of comparison.

The double critique framework determines the specific interpretative tactics employed in each of the literary chapters, which examine how the literary narratives at hand interact with political, cultural, and theoretical discourses emanating from a particular national context *and* the ways in which they mediate between two different national contexts. It also shapes the structure of the entire study, destabilizing the boundaries between diasporic Chinese American literature and U.S.–Chinese comparative literature. If authors inhabiting the liminal space between the United States and China can be resituated in both national contexts, then those working more squarely within one national context can be paired together and read as commentaries on what happens in between the two nations.

Over the past decade, Chinese investments in Western multiculturalisms, especially the U.S. variety, have been on the rise. New U.S.–China comparisons have emerged in discussions of possible antidotes to the more recent upheavals in Tibet and Xinjiang. In an immediately catchy turn of phrase, sociologist Ma Rong has put forth an argument for the "depoliticization of ethnic minority issues" in China. Ma faults the regional autonomy model and its Soviet antecedent for institutionizing, or politicizing, group differences and destabilizing national identity. For an alternative, he turns to the kind of pluralism that he personally experienced as a doctoral student at Brown University in the 1980s. Echoing the U.S. Ethnicity School of the 1980s, Ma portrays American multiculturalism as a de-essentializing, "culturalist" approach to conceptualizing ethnic difference that can be instructive for China's battle against ethnic conflicts.[1] Ma's call for depoliticization recalls the Habermasian subordination of ethno-cultural communities to an inclusive national community. One may regard it as a Chinese variation upon, indeed a belated translation of, Western liberal criticisms of official multiculturalism and state-sanctioned ethnic identities. Ma's concern with the Chinese state's manufacturing and consolidation of minority identities does not lack parallels in new U.S. studies of the Chinese ethnic policy. Benedict Anderson's Foreword for Thomas Mullaney's *Coming to Terms with the Nation* claims explicitly that the more populous minorities in China—Tibetans and the Uyghurs, for example—develop their ethnic self-awareness and antagonism against the Han as a reply to the state's "incessant 'Who are you?'"[2]

1. Ma Rong, "Lijie minzu guanxi de xinsilu" [New Approaches to Understanding Ethnic Relations], 126–27.

2. Benedict Anderson, Foreword to *Coming to Terms with the Nation*, xx.

While Ma Rong invokes the American model as a liberal alternative to China's official multiculturalism, critic Wang Hui warns against adopting the narrow culturalism of the liberal "politics of recognition," which obscures the nonlocalizable material processes at work in the shaping of ethnic relations in China.[3] In an implicit response to the rhetoric of depoliticization, Wang offers an analysis of the history of Tibet–Han conflicts, suggesting that it cannot but be a political issue. What truly "depoliticizes" the Tibet issue is the reduction of ethnic differences to purely cultural and religious divisions, as we can see in Western condemnations of religious suppression in Tibet, a conceptual error that has long acquired the name of "orientalism." Instead, the social upheavals and religious revival in Tibet have to be situated in the development of a market economy in China over the last few decades, which have created new social inequities that deprive many poor and rural Tibetans of opportunities to compete effectively within this economy. This, for Wang, has reversed the many policies, implemented before the 1990s, geared toward integrating Tibet economically with the rest of the nation. Only by recognizing the material underpinnings of ethnic differences in China, can the Chinese version of the "politics of respect" have a real possibility for living up to its purpose of facilitating the advance of the socialist revolution in both Han and non-Han areas and creating a shared (though not necessarily narrowly nationalist) identity among the inhabitants of these different areas. Wang's argument against the "depoliticization" of ethnic relations resonates strongly with my argument against conciliatory multiculturalism. The reframing of "the politics of respect" is a critique of tepid culturalist conceptions of ethnic justice that has assumed a kind of global traction, traveling from the United States to China, to say the very least, and setting severe limits for the multicultural projects in both places, among other parts of the world. This recent intellectual discussion of the "depoliticization" of ethnic policy helps illustrate, yet again, the need for a transnational, comparative framework for any new studies of the configurations and politics of multiculturalism.

Comparative critique, however, is by necessity a collective, collaborative project. Let me conclude my envoi, then, with the hope that this book will pass through the minds of others and give rise to ideas that eventually return to me, unrecognizable yet familiar.

---

3. Wang Hui, "Dongfang zhuyi, minzuquyu zhengzhi he zuiyan zhengzhi" [Orientalism, ethnic regional autonomy, and the politics of respect].

ENGLISH BIBLIOGRAPHY

"About NUMA." NUMA website, http://www.numa.net/ (accessed November 2007).

"About *Windhorse:* The Story behind the Story." *Windhorse* website. http://www.windhorsemovie.com/aboutWindhorse/storyBehindTheStory.php (accessed May 18, 2008).

Alameddine, Rabih. *Koolaids: The Art of War.* New York: Picador USA, 1998.

Alcock, Susan et al., eds. *Empires: Perspectives from Archaeology and History.* Cambridge, MA; New York: Cambridge University Press, 2001.

Allen, Michael. Review of *America at the Crossroads,* by Francis Fukuyama. *Democratiya* (Summer 2006): 44–55.

Alsultany, Evelyn. "Selling American Diversity and Muslim American Identity through Nonprofit Advertising Post-9/11." *American Quarterly,* special issue: *Religion and Politics in Contemporary United States,* ed. R. Marie Griffith and Melani McAlister, *American Quarterly* 59, no. 3 (2007): 593–622.

Anaya, S. James. *Indigenous People in International Law.* New York: Oxford University Press, 2004.

Anderson, Benedict. Foreword. *Coming to Terms with the Nation: Ethnic Classification in Modern China,* by Thomas Shawn Mullaney, xv–xx. Berkeley: University of California Press, 2010.

———. "Nationalism, Identity, and the World-in-Motion: On the Logics of Seriality," in *Cosmopolitics: Thinking and Feeling beyond the Nation,* ed. Pheng Cheah and Bruce Robbins, 117–33. Minneapolis: University of Minneapolis Press, 1998.

Anidjar, Gil. *Semites: Race, Religion, and Literature.* Stanford, CA: Stanford University Press, 2008.

———. *The Jew, the Arab: A History of the Enemy.* Stanford, CA: Stanford University Press, 2003.

Annaud, Jean-Jacques, John H. Williams, and Iain Smith. *Seven Years in Tibet,* directed by Jean-Jacques Annaud, 1997. Culver City, CA: Columbia TriStar Home Video, 2003. Blu-ray and VHS.

Asad, Talal. *On Suicide Bombing.* New York: Columbia University Press, 2007.

———. *Formations of the Secular: Christianity, Islam, Modernity.* Stanford, CA: Stanford University Press, 2003.

"Asia Society Awards Osborn Elliott Journalism Prize to Evan Osnos for Examining the Global Effects of China's Growth." Asia Society website, April, 1, 2007, http://www.asiasociety.org/media/press-releases/asia-society-awards-osborn-elliott-journalism-prize-to-evan-osnos-for-examining (accessed October 4, 2007).

Atwill, David G. *The Chinese Sultanate: Islam, Ethnicity, and the Panthay Rebellion in Southwest China, 1856–1873.* Stanford, CA: Stanford University Press, 2005.

Azuma, Eiichiro. *Between Two Empires: Race, History, and Transnationalism in Japanese America.* Oxford: Oxford University Press, 2005.

Badiou, Alain. *Saint Paul: The Foundation of Universalism,* trans. Ray Brassier. Stanford, CA: Stanford University Press, 2003.

Baldwin, Kate. *Beyond the Color Line and the Iron Curtain: Reading Encounters between Black and Red, 1922–1963.* Durham, NC: Duke University Press, 2002.

Barfield, Thomas J. "The Shadow Empires: Imperial State Formation along the Chinese-Nomad Frontier," in *Empires: Perspectives from Archaeology and History,* ed. Susan Alcock et al., 11–41. Cambridge: Cambridge University Press, 2001.

Barnhouse, Rebecca, review of *The Lost Daughter of Happiness,* by Yan Geling. *English Journal* 91, no. 5 (May 2002): 97–99.

Barry, Brian. *Culture and Equality: An Egalitarian Critique of Multiculturalism.* Cambridge, MA: Harvard University Press, 2001.

Battersby, Christine. "Her Body/Her Boundaries," in *Feminist Theory and the Body: A Reader,* ed. Janet Price and Margrit Shildrick, 341–58. New York: Routledge: 1999.

Bedeski, Robert. "Western China: Human Security and National Security," in *China's West Region Development,* ed. Ding Lu and William A. W. Neilson, 41–52, Singapore: World Scientific Publishing, 2004.

Benn Michaels, Walter. *Trouble with Diversity: How We Learn to Love Identity and Ignore Inequality.* New York: Metropolitan Books, 2006.

Bercovitch, Sacvan. *Rites of Assent: Transformation in the Symbolic Construction of America.* New York: Routledge, 1993.

Bersani, Leo. "Sociability and Cruising." *Umbr(a): A Journal of the Unconscious* (2002): 9–24.

———. "Against Monogamy." *Oxford Literary Review* 20 (1999): 3–21.

———. *Homos.* Cambridge, MA: Harvard University Press, 1995.

———. "Is the Rectum a Grave?" in *AIDS: Cultural Analysis/Cultural Activism,* ed. Donald Crimp, 197–222. Cambridge, MA: MIT Press, 1988.

Berthrong, John H. *All under Heaven: Transforming Paradigms in Confucian-Christian Dialogue.* Albany: State University of New York Press, 1994.

Bhabha, Homi. *Location of Culture.* New York, London: Routledge, 1994.

Black, Lydia T. "Bear in Human Imagination and in Ritual." *Ursus* 10 (1998): 343–47.

Blau, Joel. *Dynamics of Social Welfare History in the United States.* Oxford: Oxford University Press, 2004.

Bloemraad, Irene. *Becoming a Citizen: Incorporating Immigrants and Refugees in the United States and Canada.* Berkeley: University of California Press, 2006.

Boelhowever, William Q. *Through a Glass Darkly: Ethnic Semiosis in American Literature.* Venice: Edizioni Helvetia, 1984.

Bovingdon, Gardner. *Autonomy in Xinjiang: Han Nationalist Imperatives and Uyghur Discontent.* Washington, DC: East-West Center Washington, 2004.

Bow, Leslie. *Betrayal and Other Acts of Subversion.* Princeton: Princeton University Press, 2001.

Breslin, Paul. *Nobody's Nation: Reading Derek Walcott.* Chicago: University of Chicago Press, 2001.

Bromley, Julian and Viktor Kozlov. "The Theory of Ethnos and Ethnic Processes in Soviet Social Sciences." *Comparative Studies in Society and History* 31, no. 3 (1989): 425–38.

Brook, Timothy and Andre Schmid, eds. *Nation/Work: Asian Elites and National Identities.* Ann Arbor: University of Michigan Press, 2000.

Brown, Joseph Epes. *The Spiritual Legacy of the American Indian.* Wallingford, PA: Pendle Hill Publications, 1964.

Butler, Judith. *Bodies That Matter: On the Discursive Limits of "Sex."* New York: Routledge, 1993.

Bulag, Uradyn Erden. "The Yearning for 'Friendship': Revisiting 'the Political' in Minority Revolutionary History in China." *Journal of Asian Studies* 65 (2006): 3–32.

———. *The Mongols at China's Edge: History and the Politics of National Unity.* Lanham, MD: Rowman & Littlefield Publishers, 2002.

Callahan, William A. "Remembering the Future—Utopia, Empire, and Harmony in 21st-Century International Theory." *European Journal of International Relations* 10.4 (2004): 569–601.

Cao, Zuoya. *Out of the Crucible: Literary Works about the Rusticated Youth.* Lanham, MD: Lexington Books, 2003.

Caputi, Jane. "'Take Back What Doesn't Belong to Me': Sexual Violence, Resistance, and the 'Transmission of Affect.'" *Women's Studies International Forum* 26.1 (2003): 1–14.

Casanova, Jose. "Religion, the New Millennium, and Globalization." *Sociology of Religion* 62.4 (2001): 415–41.

Chan, Sucheng. *Asian Americans: An Interpretive History.* Boston: Twayne Publishers, 1991.

Chang, Leslie. *Factory Girls: From Village to City in a Changing China.* New York: Spiegel and Grau, 2008.

Cheah, Pheng. "Given Culture: Rethinking Cosmopolitical Freedom in Transnationalism," in *Cosmopolitics: Thinking and Feeling beyond the Nation,* ed. Bruce Robbins and Pheng Cheah, 290–328. Minneapolis: University of Minnesota Press, 1998.

Chen, Yong. *Chinese San Francisco, 1850–1943: A Trans-Pacific Community.* Stanford, CA: Stanford University Press, 2000.

Cheung, King-kok. "The Woman Warrior versus the Chinaman Pacific: Must a Chinese American Critic Choose between Feminism and Heroism?" in *Maxine Hong Kingston's The Woman Warrior: A Casebook,* ed. Sau-ling Wong, 113–34. New York: Oxford University Press, 1999.

Chiang, Mark. *The Cultural Capital of Asian American Studies: Autonomy and Representation in the University.* New York: New York University Press, 2009.

Chicago Cultural Studies Group. "Critical Multiculturalism," in *Multiculturalism: A Critical Reader,* ed. David Theo Goldberg, 114–139. Oxford: Blackwell.

Chin, Frank. "The Most Popular Book in China," in *Maxine Hong Kingston's The Woman Warrior: A Casebook,* ed. Sau-ling Wong, 23–28. New York: Oxford University Press, 1999.

Chin, Frank et al. *The Big Aiiieeeee: An Anthology of Chinese American and Japanese American Literature.* New York: Meridian, 1991.

———. *Aiiieeeee!: An Anthology of Asian-American Writers.* Washington, DC: Howard University Press, 1974.

Choy, Catherine Ceniza. *Empire of Care: Nursing and Migration in Filipino American History.* Durham, NC: Duke University Press, 2003.

Chu, Patricia P. "Asian American Narratives of Return: Nisei Representations of Prewar and Wartime Japan," in *Ethnic Life Writing and Histories: Genres, Performance, and Culture,* ed. Rocio G. Davis et al., 204–21. Berlin: Lit, 2007.

Chua, Beng Huat. "The Cost of Membership in Ascribed Community," in *Multiculturalism in Asia,* ed. William Kymlicka and Baogang He, 170–95. New York: Oxford University Press, 2005.

Chuh, Kandice. *Imagine Otherwise, on Asian American Critique.* Durham, NC: Duke University Press, 2003.

Coetzee, J. M. *The Lives of Animals.* Princeton: Princeton University Press, 1999.

Connolly, William. *Why I Am Not a Secularist.* Minneapolis: University of Minnesota Press, 1999.

Compamanes, Oscar V. "Filipinos in the United States and Their Literature of Exiles," in *Read-*

ing the Literatures of Asian America, ed. Shirley Geok-Lin Lim and Amy Ling, 49–78. Philadelphia: Temple University Press, 1992.

Cornwell, Grant H. and Eve Walsh Stoddard. *Global Multiculturalism: Comparative Perspectives on Ethnicity, Race, and Nation.* Lanham, MD: Rowman & Littlefield Publishers, 2001.

Crossley, Pamela Kyle. "Thinking about Ethnicity in Early Modern China." *Late Imperial China* 11, no. 1 (June 1990): 1–35.

———. "The Qianlong Retrospect on the Chinese-Martial (*hanjun*) Banners." *Late Imperial China* 10, no. 1 (June 1989): 63–107.

Crossley, Pamela Kyle, Helen F. Siu, and Donald S. Sutton. *Empire at the Margins: Culture, Ethnicity, and Frontier in Early Modern China.* Berkeley: University of California Press, 2005.

Cussler, Clive. *Black Wind: A Dirk Pitt Novel.* New York: Penguin, 2004.

———. *Flood Tide: a Novel.* New York: Simon & Schuster, 1997.

———. *Dragon: A Novel.* New York: Simon & Schuster, 1990.

Cussler, Clive and Dirk Cussler. *Treasure of Khan.* New York: Putnam and Sons, 2006.

Dai, Jinhua. "Behind Global Spectacle and National Image Making," trans. Jonathan Scott Noble. *Positions: East Asian Cultures Critique* 9, no. 1 (2001): 161–86.

Darder, Antonia and Rodolfo D. Torres. *After Race: Racism after Multiculturalism.* New York: New York University Press, 2004.

Davies, Gloria. *Worrying about China: The Language of Chinese Critical Inquiry.* Cambridge, MA: Harvard University Press, 2007.

Dearborn, Mary V. *Pocahontas's Daughters: Gender and Ethnicity in American Culture.* New York: Oxford University Press, 1986.

De Fina, Barbara. *Kundun,* directed by Martin Scorsese. Burbank, CA: Touchstone Home Video: Distributed by Buena Vista Home Entertainment, 1998. Blu-ray and DVD.

De Man, Paul. "Anthropomorphism and Trope in the Lyric," in *The Rhetoric of Romanticism,* 239–62. New York: Columbia University Press, 1984.

———. "Reading (Proust)." *Allegories of Reading: Figural Language in Rousseau, Nietzsche, Rilke and Proust.* 57–78. New Haven, CT: Yale University Press, 1979.

Dikötter, Frank. "Racial Discourse in China: Continuities and Permutations," in *The Construction of Racial Identities in China and Japan: Historical and Contemporary Perspectives,* ed. Frank Dikötter, 12–33. London: C. Hurst, 1997.

———. The *Discourse of Race in China.* Stanford, CA: Stanford University Press, 1992.

Dillon, Michael. *Xinjiang—China's Muslim Far Northwest.* London: Routledge Curzon, 2004.

Dirlik, Arif. "Globalization, Indigenism, and the Politics of Place." *Ariel* 34:1 (2003): 15–29.

Dirlik, Arif and Xudong Zhang. "Introduction: Postmodernism and China." *Boundary 2* special issue: Postmodernism and China, edited by Dirlik and Zhang, 24:3 (1997): 1–18.

Dittmer, Lowell and Samuel S. Kim. "In Search of a Theory of National Identity," in *China's Quest for National Identity,* ed. Dittmer and Kim, 1–31. Ithaca, NY: Cornell University Press, 1993.

Dreyer, June T. *China's Forty Millions: Minority Nationalities and National Integration in the People's Republic of China.* Cambridge, MA: Harvard University Press, 1976.

Dudziac, Mary. *Cold War Civil Rights: Race and the Image of American Democracy.* Princeton, NJ: Princeton University Press, 2000.

Dworkin, Andrea. "Prostitution and Male Supremacy." *Michigan Journal of Gender and Law* (1993): 1–12.

Elliott, Emory. "Diversity in the United States and Abroad: What Does It Mean When American Studies Is Transnational?" *American Quarterly* 59, no. 1 (2007): 1–22.

Elliott, Mark. *The Manchu Way: Banners and Ethnic Identity in Late Imperial China.* Stanford, CA: Stanford University Press, 2001.

Eng, David. *Racial Castration: Managing Masculinity in Asian America.* Durham, NC: Duke University Press, 2001.

Feng, Lan. "The Female Individual and the Empire: A Historicist Approach to Mulan and Kingston's *Woman Warrior.*" *Comparative Literature* 55, no. 3 (Summer 2003): 229–45.

Feng, Peter. "Decentering the Middle Kingdom: ABC and the PRC," in *Identities in Motion: Asian American Film and Video,* 103–27. Durham, NC: Duke University Press, 2002.

Fish, Stanley. "Boutique Multiculturalism, or Why Liberals Are Incapable of Thinking about Hate Speech." *Critical Inquiry* 23, no. 2 (Winter 1997): 378–95.

Fishkin, Shelley Fisher. "Crossroads of Cultures: The Transnational Turn in American Studies." *American Quarterly* 57, no. 1 (2005): 17–57.

French, Howard W. "Letter from China: China Could Use Some Honest Talk about Race." *New York Times,* July 31, 2009.

Friedman, Marilyn. "Feminism in Ethics: Conceptions of Autonomy," in *Cambridge Companion to Feminism in Philosophy,* ed. Miranda Fricker and Jennifer Hornsby, 205–24. Cambridge: Cambridge University Press, 2000.

Fukuyama, Francis. *America at the Crossroads: Democracy, Power, and the Neoconservative Legacy.* New Haven, CT: Yale University Press, 2006.

Gana, Nouri. "Introduction: Race, Islam, and the Task of Muslim and Arab American Writing." *PMLA* 123, no. 5 (2008): 1573–80.

Genesan, N. "Liberal and Structural Ethnic Political Accommodation in Malaysia," in *Multiculturalism in Asia,* ed. William Kymlicka and Baogang He, 136–51. New York: Oxford University Press, 2005.

Gertz, Bill. *The China Threat: How the People's Republic Targets America.* Washington, DC: Regnery Publishing, 2000.

Gilmour, David. *Lebanon: The Fractured Country.* Oxford, UK: M. Robertson, 1983.

Gitlin, Todd. *The Twilight of Common Dreams: Why America Is Wracked by Culture Wars.* New York: Holt Paperbacks, 1995.

Gladney, Dru C. "Islam in China: Accommodation or Separatism?" *China Quarterly* 174 (2003): 451–67.

———. *Muslim Chinese: Ethnic Nationalism in the People's Republic.* Cambridge, MA: Council on East Asian Studies, Harvard University: distributed by Harvard University Press, 1991.

Glazer, Nathan. "The Emergence of an American Ethnic Pattern," in *Affirmative Discrimination: Ethnic Inequality and Public Policy,* 3–32. New York: Basic Books, 1975.

Goldberg, David Theo. *The Racial State.* Malden, MA: Blackwell Publishers, 2002.

———, ed. *Multiculturalism: A Critical Reader.* Boston: Blackwell Publishers, 1994.

Goldstein, Melvyn C. "Tibet and China in the Twentieth Century," in *Governing China's Multiethnic Frontiers,* ed. Morris Rossabi, 186–229. Seattle: University of Washington Press, 2004.

Gopinath, Gayatri. *Impossible Desires: Queer Diasporas and South Asian Public Cultures.* Durham, NC: Duke University Press, 2005.

Griffith, R. Marie and Melani McAlister. "Introduction: Is the Public Square Still Naked?" in *American Quarterly,* special issue on *Religion and Politics in the Contemporary United States,* ed. R. Marie Griffith and Melani McAlister, 59, no. 3 (2007): 527–63.

Gutierrez-Jones, Carl. "Color Blindness and Acting Out," in *The Futures of American Studies,* ed. Donald Pease and Robyn Wiegman, 248–265. Durham, NC: Duke University Press, 2002.

Gutman, Amy, ed. *Multiculturalism: Examining the Politics of Politics of Recognition.* Princeton, NJ: Princeton University Press, 1994.

Habermas, Jürgen. "Struggles for Recognition in the Democratic Constitutional State," trans. Shierry Weber Nicholsen, in *Multiculturalism: Examining the Politics of Politics of Recognition,* ed. Amy Gutman. 107–48. Princeton, NJ: Princeton University Press, 1994.

Hardt, Michael and Antonio Negri. *Empire.* Cambridge, MA: Harvard University Press, 2001.

Harrell, Stevan. *Way of Being Ethnic in Southwest China.* Seattle: University of Washington Press, 2001.

Hassan, Salah D. "Unstated: Narrating War in Lebanon." *PMLA* 123, no. 5 (2008): 1621–29.

Hayot, Eric. "The Asian Turns." *PMLA* 124, no. 3 (2009): 906–17.

———, Haun Saussy, and Steven G. Yao. *Sinographies: Writing China.* Minneapolis: University of Minnesota Press, 2008.

He, Baogang. "Multiculturalism with Chinese Characteristics," in *Multiculturalism in Asia,* ed. Will Kymlicka and Baogang He, 56–79. New York: Oxford University Press, 2005.

Hero, Rodney E. and Robert R. Preuhs. "Multiculturalism and Welfare Policies in the USA: A State-Level Analysis," in *Multiculturlaism and the Welfare State: Recognition and Redistribution in Contemporary Democracies,* ed. Keith Banting and Will Kymlicka, 122–29. Oxford: Oxford University Press, 2006.

Hirsch, Francine. *Empire of Nations, Ethnographic Knowledge and the Making of the Soviet Union.* Ithaca, NY: Cornell University Press, 2005.

Hollinger, David. *Postethnic America: Beyond Multiculturalism.* 1995. Reprinted with revisions. New York: Basic Books, 2000.

Hou, James. *Masters of the Pillow,* directed by James Hou, 2003. DVD.

Hsu, Madeline. *Dreaming of Gold, Dreaming of Home: Transnationalism and Migration between the United States and South China, 1882–1943.* Stanford, CA: Stanford University Press, 2000.

Hu, Jintao. "Speech at Yale University," April 22, 2006, trans. anonymously. Chinese-English Bilingualist, April 28, 2006, http://www.bilinguist.com/data/hy04/messages/135813.html (accessed November 8, 2010).

Huang, Guiyou, ed. *Greenwood Encyclopedia of Asian American Literature.* Westport, CT: Greenwood Press, 2009.

Hughes, C. R. "Nationalism and Multilateralism in Chinese Foreign Policy: Implications for Southeast Asia." *Pacific Review* 18, no. 1 (March 2005): 39–66.

Israeli, Raphael. *Islam in China: Religion, Ethnicity, Culture, and Politics.* Lanham, MD: Lexington Books, 2002.

Issac, Allan Punzalan. *American Tropics: Articulating Filipino America.* Minneapolis: University of Minnesota Press, 2006.

Jen, Gish. *The Love Wife.* New York: Alfred A. Knopf, distributed by Random House, 2004.

Jenkins, Jerry and Tim LaHaye. *Left Behind: A Novel of the Earth's Last Days.* Wheaton, IL: Tyndale House, 1995.

Jervis, Robert, review of *America at the Crossroads,* by Francis Fukuyama. *Millennium: Journal of International Studies:* 201–5.

Jiang, Rong. *The Wolf Totem,* trans. Howard Goldblatt. New York: Penguin Press, 2008.

Jiang, Zenpei, ed. *Zhongguo liuxuesheng wenxue daxi* [An anthology of literature by Chinese students overseas]. Shanghai: Wenyi chubanshe, 2000.

Johnson, Chalmers. *Sorrows of Empire: Militarism, Secrecy, and the End of the Republic.* New York: Metropolitan Books, 2004.

Jun, Helen. "Black Orientalism: Nineteenth-Century Narratives of Race and U.S. Citizenship." *American Quarterly* 58, no. 4 (2006): 1047–66.

Kang, Laura Hyun Yi. *Compositional Subjects: Enfiguring Asian/American Women.* Durham, NC: Duke University Press, 2002.

Kaplan, Amy. "'Left Alone with America': The Absence of Empire in the Study of American Culture," in *Cultures of United States Imperialism,* ed. Donald Pease and Amy Kaplan, 3–21. Durham, NC: Duke University Press, 1993.

Karl, Rebecca. *Staging the World: Chinese Nationalism at the Turn of the Twentieth-Century.* Durham, NC: Duke University Press, 2002.

Kaup, Katherine. *Creating the Zhuang: Ethnic Politics in China.* Boulder, CO: L. Rienner, 2000.

Khalaf, Samir. "The Background and Causes of Lebanese/Syrian Immigration to the United States before World War I," in *Crossing the Waters: Arabic-Speaking Immigrants to the United States before 1940,* ed. Eric J. Hooglund, 17–36. Washington, DC: Smithsonian Institution Press, 1987.

Kim, Claire Jean. *Bitter Roots: The Politics of Black-Korean Conflict in New York City*. New Haven, CT: Yale University Press, 2000.

Kingston, Maxine Hong. *The Woman Warrior*. New York: Vintage Books, 1976.

Kinkley, Jeffrey C., review of *The Lost Daughter of Happiness*, by Yan Geling. *World Literature Today* 76, no. 2 (2002): 136.

Klare, Michael. *Blood and Oil: The Dangers and Consequences of America's Growing Petroleum Dependency*. New York: Metropolitan Books, 2004.

Kövecses, Zoltán. *Metaphor in Culture: Universality and Variation*. Cambridge: Cambridge University Press, 2005.

Kremb, Jürgen. "A Wolf in Sheep's Clothing: Beijing's Unwanted Best Seller." *Spiegel Online International*, October 20, 1998, http://www.spiegel.de/international/0,1518,407184,00.html (accessed October 30, 2010).

Kristeva, Julia. *Powers of Horror: An Essay on Abjection*, trans. Leon S. Roudiez. New York: Columbia University Press, 1982.

Kristof, Nicholas. "Calling China." *New York Times*, May 18, 2008, http://kristof.blogs.nytimes.com/2008/03/30/calling-china/ (accessed October 30, 2010)

Kuo, Alex. *White Jade and Other Stories*. Oregon: Wordcraft of Oregon, LLC, 2008.

———. *Panda Diaries*. Indianapolis: University of Indianapolis Press, 2006.

———. "10,000 Dildoes." *Amerasia Journal* 29, no. 2 (2003): 254–264.

———. *Lipstick and Other Stories*. Hong Kong: Asia 2000 Ltd., 2001.

———. *Chinese Opera*. Hong Kong: Asia 2000 Ltd., 2000.

———. *This Fierce Geography: Poems*. Boise, Idaho: Limberlost Press, 1999.

———. *Chinese Opera*. Hong Kong: Asia 2000, 1998.

———. *Changing the River*. Berkeley: I. Reed Books, 1986.

———. *New Letters from Hiroshima and Other Poems*. Greenfield, NY: Greenfield Review Press, 1974.

———. *The Window Tree*. Peterborough, NH: Windy Row Press, 1971.

Kurlantzick, Joshua. "Beijing's Safari: China's Move into Africa and Its Implications for Aid, Development, and Governance." *Policy Outlook* (November 2006): 1–7.

Kymlicka, Will. *Politics in the Vernacular*. Oxford: Oxford University Press, 2007.

———. *Multicultural Odysseys: Navigating the New International Politics of Diversity*. Oxford: Oxford University Press, 2001.

———. *Can Liberal Pluralism Be Exported: Western Political Theory and Ethnic Relations in Eastern Europe*. Oxford: Oxford University Press, 2001.

———. *Multicultural Citizenship: A Liberal Theory of Minority Rights*. Oxford: Clarendon Press; New York: Oxford University Press, 1996.

Lee, James Kyung-Jin. *Urban Triage: Race and the Fictions of Multiculturalism*. Minneapolis: University of Minnesota Press, 2004.

Lee, Robert G. "*The Woman Warrior* as an Intervention in Asian American Historiography," in *Approaches to Teaching Kingston's The Woman Warrior*, ed. Shirley Geok-lin Lim, 52–63. New York: The Modern Language Association of America, 1991.

Lee, Steven S. "Cold War Multiculturalism: The Clash of American and Soviet Models of Difference." PhD diss., Stanford University, 2008.

———. "Borat, Multiculturalism, Mnogonatsional'nost'." *Slavic Review* 67, no. 1 (2008): 19–34.

Leenhouts, Mark. "Culture against Politics: Roots-Seeking Literature," in *Columbia Companion to Modern East Asian Literature*, ed. Joshua Mostow, 543–50. New York: Columbia University Press, 2003.

Levy, Jacob T. "Contextualism, Constitutionalism, and modus Vivendi," in *Multiculturalism and Political Theory*, ed. Anthony Simon Laden and David Owen, 173–97. New York: Cambridge University Press, 2007.

Li, David Leiwei. "The Production of Chinese American Tradition: Displacing American Orientalist Discourse," in *Reading the Literatures of Asian America*, ed. Shirley Geok-lin Lim and Amy Ling, 319–31. Philadelphia: Temple University Press, 1992.

Lieven, Anatol. *America Right or Wrong: An Anatomy of American Nationalism*. New York: Oxford University Press, 2004.

Lin, Yutang. *Between Tears and Laughter*. New York: Kessinger Publishing, 2005. First published 1943 by John Day.

Lipman, Jonathan. *Familiar Strangers: A History of Muslims in Northwest China*. Seattle: University of Washington Press, 1997.

Litzinger, Ralph. *Other Chinas: The Yao and the Politics of National Belonging*. Durham, NC: Duke University Press, 2000.

Liu, Kang. "Is There an Alternative to (Capitalist) Globalization? The Debate about Modernity in China," in *The Cultures of Globalization,* ed. Fredric Jameson and Masao Miyoshi. Durham, NC: Duke University Press, 1998.

———. "Is There an Alternative to (Capitalist) Globalization? The Debate about Modernity in China." *Boundary 2* 23, no. 3 (1996): 193–218.

Liu, Lydia. "A Folk Song Immortal: Official Popular Culture in Twentieth-Century China," in *Writing and Materiality in China,* ed. Judity T. Zitlin and Lydia Liu. 553–609. Cambridge, MA: Harvard University Press, 2003.

Lockman, Zachary. *Contending Visions of the Middle East: The History and Politics of Orientalism*. Cambridge: Cambridge University Press, 2004.

London, Jack. "The Yellow Peril," in *Revolution and Other Essays,* 269–89. New York: Macmillan, 1910.

Lovell, Julia. "Chinatown Lady." *Times Literary Supplement* 10 (August 2001): 20.

Lowe, Lisa. "Immigration, Citizenship, and Racialization," in *Immigrant Acts: On Asian American Cultural Politics,* 1–36. Durham, NC: Duke University Press, 1996.

Lu, Ding and William V. W. Neilson, eds. *China's West Region Development: Domestic Strategies and Global Implications*. World Scientific Publishing, 2004.

Lye, Colleen. "The Sino-Japanese Conflict of Asian American Literature." *Genre* 39 (2006): 43–63.

———. *America's Asia: Racial Form and American Literature, 1893–1945*. Princeton, NJ; Oxford: Princeton University Press, 2005.

Mackerras, Colin. *China's Ethnic Minorities and Globalization*. London: Routledge Curzon, 2003.

———. *China's Minorities: Integration and Modernization in the Twentieth Century*. Hong Kong: Oxford University Press, 1994.

Mackerras, Colin and Michael Clarke. *China, Xinjiang and Central Asia: History, Transition and Crossborder Interaction into the 21st Century*. London: Routledge, 2009.

Malik, Kenan. *The Meaning of Race: Race, History and Culture in Western Society*. New York: New York University Press, 1996.

Martin, Terry. *The Affirmative Action Empire: Nation and Nationalism in the Soviet Union, 1923–1939*. Ithaca, NY: Cornell University Press, 2001.

Mason, Andrew. "Political Community, Liberal-Nationalism, and the Ethics of Assimilation." *Ethics* 109 (January 1999): 261–86.

Mazumdar, Sucheta. "Asian American Studies and Asian Studies: Rethinking Roots," in *Asian Americans: Comparative and Global Perspectives,* ed. Shirley Hune, Hyung-chan Kim, Stephen S. Fugita, and Amy Ling, 29–44. Pullmann: Washington State University Press, 1991.

McCunn, Ruthanne Lum. *Thousand Pieces of Gold: A Biographical Novel*. Boston: Beacon Press, 1988. First published in 1981 by Beacon.

Mesic, Milan. *Perspectives of Multiculturalism—Western and Transitional Countries*. Zagreb: Faculty of Philosophy: Croatian Commission for UNESCO, 2004.

Mignolo, Walter. *Local Histories/Global Designs: Coloniality, Subaltern Knowledges, and Border Thinking*. Princeton, NJ: Princeton University Press, 2000.

Mirsky, Jonathan. "A Decade in the Grasslands," review of *The Wolf Totem,* by Jiang Rong. *Literary Review* (online edition), http://www.literaryreview.co.uk/mirsky_03_08.html (accessed October 24, 2008).

Mishra, Pankaj. "Call of the Wild." *New York Times,* May 4, 2008. http://www.nytimes. com/2008/05/04/books/review/Mishra-t.html (accessed May 5, 2008).

Mullaney, Shawn Thomas. *Coming to Terms with the Nation: Ethnic Classification in Modern China.* Berkeley: University of California Press, 2010.

———. "Coming to Terms with the Nation: Ethnic Classification and Scientific Statecraft in Modern China, 1928–1954," PhD diss., Columbia University, 2006.

Muscatine, Doris. *Old San Francisco: The Biography of a City from Early Days to the Earthquake.* New York: Putnam, 1975

Nash, Roberts and Harriett Hawkins. *Classics and Trash: Traditions and Taboos in High Literature and Popular Modern Genres.* New York: Harvester Wheatsheaf, 1990.

Nash, Walter. *Language in Popular Fiction.* London: Routledge, 1990.

Nepal, Sanjay K. "Involving Indigenous Peoples in Protected Area Management: Comparative Perspectives from Nepal, Thailand, and China." *Environmental Management* 30, no. 6 (December 2002): 748–63.

Ngai, Mae. *Impossible Subjects: Illegal Aliens and the Making of Modern America.* Princeton, NJ: Princeton University Press, 2004.

Omi, Michael and Howard Winant. *Racial Formation in the United States: From the 1960s to the 1980s.* New York: Routledge and Kegan Paul, 1986.

Osnos, Evan. "China's Great Grab." *Chicago Tribune,* December 16, 18, 19, 2006, http://www.chicagotribune.com/news/local/chi-china-special,0,2208838.htmlpage.

Palumbo-Liu, David. *Asian/American: Historical Crossings of a Racial Frontier.* Stanford, CA: Stanford University Press, 1999.

Parekh, Bhikhu. *Rethinking Multiculturalism: Cultural Diversity and Political Theory.* Basingstoke, UK: Palgrave Macmillan, 2006.

Parikh, Crystal. *An Ethics of Betrayal: the Politics of Otherness in Emergent U.S. Literatures and Culture.* New York: Fordham University Press, 2009.

Pease, Donald. "Exceptionalism," in *Keywords for American Studies,* ed. Bruce Brugett and Glenn Hendler, 108–12. New York: New York University Press, 2007.

———. "The Global Homeland State: Bush's Biopolitical Settlement." *Boundary 2* 30, no. 3 (2003), 1–18.

Pease, Donald and Amy Kaplan, ed. *Cultures of United States Imperialism.* Durham, NC: Duke University Press, 1993.

Pease, Donald and Robyn Wiegman, eds. *Futures of American Studies.* Durham, NC: Duke University Press, 2002.

Phillips, Anne. *Multiculturalism without Culture.* Princeton, NJ: Princeton University Press, 2007.

Pholsena, Vatthana. "A Liberal Model of Minority Rights for an Illiberal Multiethnic State? The Case of the Lao PDR," in *Multiculturalisms in Asia,* ed. Will Kymlicka and Baogang He, 80–19. Oxford: Oxford University Press, 2005.

Pomeroy, William J. *American Neo-Colonialism: Its Emergence in the Philippines and Asia.* New York: International Publishers, 1970.

"President Orders Strategic Petroleum Reserve Filled." The White House website, November 2001, http://georgewbushwhitehouse.archives.gov/news/releases/2001/11/20011113.html (accessed October 12, 2008).

Radway, Janice. *A Feeling for Books: The Book-of-the-Month Club, Literary Taste, and Middle-Class Desire.* Chapel Hill: University of North Carolina Press, 1997.

Ramazani, Jahan. *The Hybrid Muse: Postcolonial Poetry in English.* Chicago: University of Chicago Press, 2001.

Raz, Joseph. "Multiculturalism." *Ratio Juris* 11, no. 3 (1998): 193–205.

Robbins, Bruce. "The Worlding of the American Novel." Computer print. Department of English, Columbia University, 2009.

Rockwell, David. *Give Voice to Bear: North American Indian Myths, Rituals, and Images of the Bear.* Niwot, CO: Roberts Rinehart, 1991.

Roberts, Thomas J. *An Aesthetics of Junk Fiction.* Athens: University of Georgia Press, 1990.

Sailata, Steven. *Arab American Literary Fictions, Cultures, and Politics.* New York: Palgrave Macmillan, 2007.

———. *Anti-Arab Racism in the USA: Where It Comes from and What It Means for Politics Today.* London: Pluto, 2006.

Schell, Orville. "Expert Roundtable." *The New York Times* August 29, 2007. http://china.blogs.nytimes.com/2007/08/29/answers-from-orville-schell/.

Schultz, Kevin. "'Favoritism Cannot Be Tolerated': Challenging Protestanism in American's Public Schools and Promoting the Neutral State," in *American Quarterly,* special issue, *Religion and Politics in Contemporary United States,* ed. R. Marie Griffith and Melani McAlister, 59, no. 3 (2007): 565–91.

Shakir, Evelyn. "Arab American Literature," in *New Immigrant Literatures in the United States: A Sourcebook to Our Multicultural Literary Heritage,* ed. Alpana Sharma Knippling, 3–18. Westport, CT: Greenwood Press, 1996.

Schein, Louisa. *Minority Rules: The Miao and the Feminine in China's Cultural Politics.* Durham, NC: Duke University Press, 2000.

———. "The Consumption of Color and the Politics of White Skin in Post-Mao China," in *The Gender/Sexuality Reader: Culture, History, Political Economy,* ed. Roger N. Lancaster and Micaela di Leonardo, 473–86. New York: Routledge, 1997.

Schlesinger, Arthur. *The Disuniting of America.* New York: Norton, 1992.

Schueller, Malini Johar. *U.S. Orientalisms: Race, Nation, and Gender in Literature, 1790–1890.* Ann Arbor: University of Michigan Press, 1998.

Shakya, Tsering. *The Dragon in the Land of Snows: A History of Modern Tibet since 1947.* New York: Columbia University Press, 1999.

Shih, Chih-yu. *Negotiating Ethnicity in China: Citizenship as a Response to the State.* London: Routledge, 2002.

Shih, Shu-mei. *Visuality and Identity: Sinophone Articulations across the Pacific.* Berkeley: University of California Press, 2007.

Shoha, Ella and Robert Stam, eds. *Multiculturalism, Postcoloniality, and Transnational Media.* New Brunswick, NJ: Rutgers University Press, 2003.

Shirmer, Jennifer. "Appropriating the Indigenous, Creating Complicity: The Guatemalan Military and the Sanctioned Maya," in *The Politics of Ethnicity: Indigenous Peoples in Latin American States,* ed. David Maybury-Lewis, 51–77. Cambridge, MA: Distributed by Harvard University Press, 2002.

Singh, Amritjit and Peter Schmidt, eds. *Postcolonial Theory and the United States.* Jackson: University Press of Mississippi, 2000.

Singh, Nikhil Pal. *Black Is a Country: Race and Unfinished Struggles for Democracy.* Cambridge, MA: Harvard University Press, 2004.

———. "Culture/Wars: Recoding Empire in an Age of Democracy." *American Quarterly* 50, no. 3 (1998): 471–522.

Slezkine, Yuri. "The USSR as a Communal Apartment, or How a Socialist State Promoted Ethnic Particularism." *Slavic Review* 53, no. 2 (Summer 1994): 414–52.

Sofield, Trevor and F. M. S. Li. "Processes in Formulating an Ecotourism Policy for Nature Reserves in Yunnan Province, China," in *Ecotourism Policy and Planning,* ed. David A. Fennell and Ross K. Dowling, 141–168. Cambridge, MA: CABI Publishing, 2003.

Sollors, Werner. *Beyond Ethnicity: Consent and Descent in American Culture.* New York: Oxford University Press, 1986.

———, ed. *The Invention of Ethnicity.* New York: Oxford University Press, 1989.

Sonntag, Selma. "Self-Government in the Darjeeling Hills of India," in *Emancipating Cultural Pluralism,* ed. Cris E. Toffolo, 181–94. Albany: State University of New York Press, 2003.

Steiner, Stan. *Fusang: The Chinese Who Built America.* New York: Harper & Row, 1979.

Stevens, Stan. *Conservation through Cultural Survival: Indigenous Peoples Are Protected Areas.* Washington, DC: Island Press, 1997.

Stilz, Anna. *Liberal Loyalty: Freedom, Obligation, and the State.* Princeton, NJ: Princeton University Press, 2009.

Suettinger, Robert L. "The Rise and Descent of 'Peaceful Rise.'" *China Leadership Monitor,* no. 12 (Fall 2004): 1–10.

———. *Beyond Tiananmen: The Politics of U.S.-China Relations.* Washington, DC: Brookings Institution Press, 2003.

Suleiman, Michael W. "Early Arab-Americans: The Search for Identity," in *Crossing the Waters: Arabic-Speaking Immigrants to the United States Before 1940,* ed. Eric J. Hooglund, 37–55. Washington, DC: Smithsonian Institution, 1987.

Sullivan, Michael. "The 1988–89 Anti-African Protests: Racial Nationalism or National Racism?" *China Quarterly* 138 (June 1994): 438–57.

Suny, Ronald Grigor. *The Revenge of the Past: Nationalism, Revolution, and the Collapse of the Soviet Union.* Stanford, CA: Stanford University Press, 1993.

Tamir, Yael. *Liberal Nationalism.* Princeton, NJ: Princeton University Press, 1995.

Takaki, Ronald. "Reflections on Racial Patterns in America: An Historical Perspective," in *Debating Diversity: Clashing Perspectives on Race and Ethnicity in America,* ed. Ronald Takaki, 23–36. New York; Oxford: Oxford University Press, 2002. First published in *Ethnicity and Public Policy* 1 (1982): 1–23.

Tapper, Richard. "Animality, Humanity, Morality, Society," in *What Is an Animal?* ed. T. Ingold, 47–62. London: Unwin Hyman, 1988.

Taylor, Charles. *A Secular Age.* Cambridge, MA: Belknap Press of Harvard University Press, 2007.

———. "The Politics of Recognition," in *Multiculturalism: Examining the Politics of Politics of Recognition,* ed. Amy Gutman, 25–74. Princeton, NJ: Princeton University Press, 1994.

Taylor, Diana. *Disappearing Acts: Spectacles of Gender and Nationalism in Argentina's "Dirty War."* Durham, NC: Duke University Press, 1997.

Terrill, Ross. *The New Chinese Empire; and What It Means for the United States.* New York: Basic Books, 2003.

Thompson, H. *Theories of Ethnicity: A Critical Appraisal.* New York: Greenwood Press, 1989.

Tisdell, Clem and Zhu Xiang. "Reconciling Economic Development, Nature Conservation and Local Communities: Strategies for Biodiversity Conservation in Xishuangbanna, China." *The Environmentalist* 16, no. 3 (September 1996): 203–11.

Tong, Benson. *Unsubmissive Women: Chinese Prostitutes in Nineteenth-Century San Francisco.* Norman: University of Oklahoma Press, 1994.

Tong, Zhang, ed. *An Anthology of Chinese American Literature.* Nankai, China: Nankai University Press, 2004.

Towey, Cathleen A., review of *The Lost Daughter of Happiness,* by Yan Geling. *Library Journal* 126, no. 3 (15 Feb. 2001): 203.

Townsend, James. "Chinese Nationalism," in *Chinese Nationalism,* ed. Jonathan Unger, 1–30. Armonk, NY: M. E. Sharpe, 1996.

Tremblay, Rodrigue. *The New American Empire.* West Conshohocken, PA: Infinity Publishing, 2004.

U.S. Department of State. *2008 Human Rights Report: China (includes Tibet, Hong Kong, and Macau).* U.S. Department of State website, http://www.state.gov/g/drl/rls/hrrpt/2008/eap/119037.htm (accessed August 5, 2009).

Venturino, Steven J. "Signifying on China: African-American Literary Theory and Tibetan Discourse," in *Sinographies: Writing China,* ed. Eric Hayot, Haun Saussy, and Steven G. Yao, 271–99. Minneapolis: University of Minnesota Press, 2008.

Vizenor, Gerald. *Griever: An American Monkey King in China: A Novel.* New York: Illinois State University, 1987.

Wagner, Paul. *Windhorse*, directed by Paul Wagner. New York: New York Video, 2005. DVD.

Wald, Alan. "Theorizing Cultural Difference: A Critique of the 'Ethnicity School.'" *MELUS* 1 no. 2 (Summer 1987): 21–33.

Waltzer, Michael. "Multiculturalism and Individualism." *Dissent* (Spring 1992): 185–91.

Wang, Hui. "Contemporary Chinese Thought and Modernity," in *China's New Order: Society, Politics, and Economy in Transition,* trans. Theodore Huters and Rebecca Karl, 141–86. Cambridge, MA: Harvard University Press, 2003.

Weir, Allison. *Sacrificial Logics: Feminist Theory and the Critique of Identity.* New York: Routledge, 1996.

Whaley, Lindsay. "The Growing Shadow of the Oroqen Language and Culture." *Cultural Survival Quarterly* 25, no. 2 (Summer 2001): 13–15.

Winant, Howard. *Racial Conditions: Politics, Theory, and Comparisons.* Minneapolis: University of Minnesota Press 1994.

Wines, Michael. "A Strong Man Is China's Rock in Ethnic Strife." *New York Times,* July 10, 2009.

Wong, Sau-ling. "The Stakes of Textual Border-Crossing: Hualing Nieh's Mulberry and Peach in Sinocentric, Asian American, and Feminist Critical Practices," in *Orientations: Mapping Studies in the Asian Diaspora,* ed. Kandice Chuh and Karen Shimakawa, 130–52. Durham, NC: Duke University Press, 2001.

———. "Autobiography as Guided Chinatown Tour? Maxine Hong Kingston's *The Woman Warrior* and the Chinese American Autobiographical Controversy," in *The Woman Warrior: A Casebook,* ed. Sau-Ling Wong, 29–53. New York: Oxford University Press, 1999.

———. "Denationalization Reconsidered: Asian American Cultural Criticism at a Theoretical Crossroads." *Amerasia Journal* 21, no. 1–2 (1995): 1–27.

———. "Kingston's Handling of Traditional Chinese Sources," in *Approaches to Teaching Kingston's* The Woman Warrior, ed. Shirley Geok-lin Lim, 26–36. New York: Modern Language Association of America, 1991.

Weston, Timothy. "A Defense of Jiang Rong's Wolf Totem." *China Beat,* July 25, 2008, http://thechinabeat.blogspot.com/2008/07/defense-of-jiang-rongs-wolf-totem.html (accessed November 24, 2008).

Wolfe, Cary. *Animal Rites: American Culture, the Discourse of Species, and Posthumanist Theory.* Chicago: The University of Chicago Press, 2003.

Xu, Jian. "Radical Ethnicity and Apocryphal History: Reading the Sublime Object of Humanism in Zhang Chengzhi's Late Fictions." *Positions* 10, no. 3 (2002): 525–46.

Xu, Jianchu et al. "Integrating Sacred Knowledge for Conservation: Cultures and Landscapes in Southwest China." *Ecology and Society* 10, no. 2 (2005): Art. 7. http://www.ecologyandsociety.org/vol10/iss2/art7/.

Yan, Geling. *The Lost Daughter of Happiness,* trans. Cathy Silber. New York: Hyperion, 2001.

Yin, Xiao-huang. *Chinese American Literature since the 1850s.* Urbana: University of Illinois Press, 2000.

Young, Iris. *Justice and the Politics of Identity.* Princeton, NJ: Princeton University Press, 1990.

Yung, Judy. *Unbound Voices: A Documentary History of Chinese Women in San Francisco.* Berkeley: University of California Press, 1999.

Zhang, Ya-Jie. "A Chinese Woman's Response to Maxine Hong Kingston's *The Woman Warrior,*" in *Maxine Hong Kingston's* The Woman Warrior: A Casebook, ed. Sau-ling Wong, 17–22. New York: Oxford University Press, 1999.

Zhao, Suisheng. "Chinese Foreign Policy in Hu's Second Term: Coping with Political Transition Abroad." *Foreign Policy Research Institute E-Notes,* May 10, 2008, http://www.fpri.org/enotes/20080510.zhao.chineseforeignpolicyhu.html (accessed December 12, 2008).

———. *A Nation-State by Construction: Dynamics of Modern Chinese Nationalism.* Stanford, CA: Stanford University Press, 2004.

Žižek, Slavoj. "Multiculturalism, or, the Cultural Logic of Multinational Capitalism." *New Left Review* I/225 (September–October 1997): 28–51.

CHINESE BIBLIOGRAPHY

Cai, Qing, Xu Xu, and Zhang Hongwei, "Fusang zhong de shenhua yuanxing jiexi: zhuixun xin de minzu wenhua zhigen" [Mythical archetypes in *Fusang*: In search of new roots of national culture]. *Qiqi ha'er shifan gaodeng zhuanke xuexiao xuebao,* no. 5 (2007): 76–78,

Cao, Glen. *Beijingren zai Niuyue* [A Beijinger in New York]. Beijing: Zhongguo wenlian chuban gongci, 1991.

Chang, Shiyan. "Minzu hexie yu ronghe: shixian minzu yu zhenzhi yiti de guanjian" [Ethnic harmony and amalgmation: The key to the unity and political integration of the nation]. *Zhenzhi wenming yanjiu,* no. 2 (2007): 69–71.

Chen, Joan and Alice Chan. *Tianyu* [Heavenly bath], directed by Joan Chen. New York: Unapix Entertainment, 1998. DVD.

Chen, Sihe. "Ziji de shujia, Yan Geling de *dijiuge guafu*" [My own bookshelf: Yan Geling's *Ninth Widow*]. *Minzuo xinshuang,* no. 5 (2008), 102–4.

———. *Zhongguo xiandangdai wenxueshi jiaochen* [A history of modern and contemporary Chinese literature]. Shanghai: Fudan daxue chubanshe, 1999.

Cussler, Clive, with Dirk Cussler. *Kehan de baozang* [Khan's treasure], trans. Yao, Hong et al. Changsha: Hunan renmin chubanshe, 2008.

Gao, Guoli. "Guowai qianfada diqu duiyu woguo xibu dakaifa de jidian qishi" [Lessons from underdeveloped areas in other countries]. *Jingji yanjiu cankao,* no. 34 (2000): 32–36.

Gao, Jianguo. "Shilun meiguo minzu duoyanxing he wenhua duoyuan zhuyi" [Comments on ethnic diversity and multiculturalism in the U.S.]. *Shijie lishi,* no. 4 (1994): 2–10.

Gao, Ruiquan et al. "Renwen jingshen xunsilu zhier" [Reflections on the humanistic spirit: Part II], *Dushu,* no. 4 (1995): 73–81.

Gu, Jun and Yuan Li. "Meiguo wenhua ji ziran yichan baohu de lishi yu jingyan" [History of the protection of cultural and natural heritage]. *Xibei minzu yanjiu,* no. 3 (2005): 167–76.

Guan, Kai. "Duoyuan wenhua zhuyi yu minzu quyu zizhi—minzu zhengce guoji jianyan fenxi" [Multiculturalism and ethnic regional autonomy—An analysis of ethnic policies in the world]. *Xibei minzu yanjiu,* no. 2 (2004): 40–92.

Han, Sanping. *Mei Lanfang* [Mei Lanfang: The legend of Peking Opera], directed by Chen Kaige. Guangzhou: Guangdong yinxiang chubanshe, 2009. DVD.

He, Chansheng, Niu Shuwen, and Cheng Shenkui, "Meiguo xibu fazhan dui zhongguo xibu dakaifa de qishi" [Lessons from development of the U. S. West to China's West Development Program]. *Ziyuan kexue* 27, no. 6 (2005): 188–93.

He, Shaoyin. "Quanqiuhua yu haiwai minzu wenhua duoyuan fazhan de qishi" [Globalization and lessons from multiculturalisms in foreign countries], in *Jingji quanqiuhua yu minzu wenhua duoyuan fazhan* [Economic globalization and the pluralist development of ethnic cultures], ed. Yunnan minzu xueyuan, 57–70. Beijing: Shehui kexue wenxian chubanshe, 2003.

He, Tongbin. "Wenming yu yexing de jitai hejie—guanyu 'lang tuteng' de wenhua zhenghou" [A perverse reconciliation of civilization and wilderness: On cultural symptoms in *Lang Tuteng*]. *Wenyi zhenming*, no. 5 (2006): 88–92.

He, Yuping. "'Mulanci' chuangzuo shidai yu zuozhe zhi tanjiu" [A study of the composition and authorship of the "Ballad of Mulan"]. *Luoyang daxue xuebao* 19, no. 1 (March 2004): 20–21.

Hu, Shaoqing and Zhang Yueyuan. "Zhongguo-xifang de huayu laoyu, dui ershi shiji yilai jige 'kuaguo jiaowang' wenben de kaochao" [The China-West dichotomy: Reading transnational narratives since the 1990s]. *Wenyi lilun yu piping*, no. 1 (2004): 75–85.

Information Office of the State Council of the PRC. *2008 nian meiguo renquan baogao* [2008 report on human rights in the United States]. Xinhua News Agency, http://news.xinhuanet.com/world/2009-02/27/content_10908695.htm (accessed August 5, 2009).

Jiang, Rong. *Lang Tuteng.* Wuhan: Changjiang wenyi chubanshe, 2004.

Kubin, Wolfgang. "89 nian qianhou, zhongguo zuojia ziji beipan le wenxue" [Chinese authors betrayed literature since 1989]. *Deutsche Welle* (Chinese online edition), July 3, 2009, http://www.dw-world.com/dw/article/0,,4453664,00.html (accessed November 24, 2008).

Li, Jianjun. "Zhenzu haishi wandou" [Pearls or peas]. *Hunan shifan xueyuan yuanbao*, no. 6 (2006), 66–74.

Li, Xiaohua. "Fusang de renwu biaozheng he dongfangzhuyi wenhua duiying" [How characters in *Fusang* register orientalism]. *Qiusuo*, no. 12 (2004): 210–11.

Lin, Cuiwei. "Fusang zhong de nuxingguan" [Femininity in *Fusang*]. *Huawen Shixue*, no. 62 (2004): 65–68.

Liu, Daxian. "Zhongguo Shaoshu Zuyi de Rentong yu Zhuti Wenti" [Identification and subjectivity among China's minorities]. *Wenyi lilun yanjiu* 5 (2009): 1–9.

Liu, Fusheng. "Linglei de zongjiao xiezuo: Zhang Chengzhi zongjiao xiezuo de yiyi" [Religion in literature: Meaning of Zhang Chengzhi's writings]. *Zhongguo bijiao wenxue*, no. 3 (2006): 57–65.

"'Liuxuesheng wenxue' zuotan jiyao" [Minutes from the Shanghai roundtable on "Overseas Student Literature"]. *Xiaoshuo jie*, no. 1 (1989): 180–93.

Ma, Lirong. "Jin bainian huizu zuojia gailun" [Hui writers: A hundred year précis]. *Minzu wenxue yanjiu*, no. 4 (2004): 95–101.

Ma, Rong. "Lijie minzu guanxi de xinsilu—shaoshu zuqun wenti de quzhengzhihua" [New approaches to understanding ethnic relations: Depoliticizing of ethnic issues]. *Beijing daxue xuebao* 41, no. 6 (2004): 122–33.

"Ninyue chenbianshe 'liuxuesheng wenxue' zuotan jiyao" [Minutes from New York Morningside Society's roundtable on "Overseas Student Literature"]. *Xiaoshuo jie*, no. 1 (1988): 148–56.

Pan, Ying. "Xibei wushenqu qian xieyi lianshou daji 'sangu shili'" [Five northwest provinces signed agreement to clamp down on "Three Forces"]. *Xinhua news* (web portal for the official Xinhua News Agency), November 21, 2009. http://news.xinhuanet.com/politics/2009-11/21/content_12517592.htm (accessed May 12, 2010).

Qi, Meiqin. "Guanyu shinianlai 'hanhua' yiji xiangguan wenti yanjiu de kaochao" [A review of research on "Sinicization" and related issues]. *Xiyu yanjiu*, no. 2 (2006): 103–13.

Qian, Hao. "Meiguo minzu lilun kaoshi" [On American ethnic theories]. *Shijie minzu,* no. 2 (2003): 10–16.

Qin, Feng. "Cong wulumuqi 7–5 shijian kan xifang meiti shuangchong biaozhun" [The July 5 Urumqi incident reveals double standards in Western media]. *Beijing ribao,* July 12, 2009.

Rao, Pengzi. "Haiwai huawen wenxue zai zhonguo xuejie xingqi de jiqi yiyi" [The development of studies in world literature in Chinese and its implications]. *Huaxia wenhua luntan,* no. 0 (2008): 3–9.

Shao, Fen. "Meiguo xibu kaifa lifa jiyi jingyan jiaoxun" [Development of the West in the United States and Its Lessons]. *Faxuejia,* no. 5 (2002): 119–24.

Shi, Yu. *Daofeng xia de mangdian* [The blind spot beneath the scalpel]. Special issue on new novels. *Xiaoshuo yuebao* 4 (2006): 76–135.

Shu, Jinyu. "Jiemi *Lang Tuteng* banquan shuchu shenhua" [Decoding the successful handling of publishing rights for *Lang Tuteng*]. *Zhonghua dushu bao,* September 2, 2009.

State Council Information Office. *Zhongguo de minzu zhengce yu ge minzu gongtong fanrong fazhan baipishu* [China's ethnic policy and the common prosperity and development of all ethnic groups]. Official website of the State Ethnic Affairs Commission. http://www.seac. gov.cn/gjmw/zt/2009-09-27/1254039198754918.htm (accessed August 20, 2009).

State Ethnic Affairs Commission of PRC. *Zhongguo Minzu Nianjian* (2009) [Chinese ethnicities yearbook 2009]. Beijing: Zhongguo minzu nianjian chubanshe, 2009.

Teng, Wei. "Huai Xiang Zhongguo de Fangshi" [The remembering of China in Yan Geling's immigrant literature]. *Huawen wenxue* 62 (2004): 1–10.

Wang, Hui. "Dongfang zhuyi, minzuquyu zhengzhi he zuiyan zhengzhi—guanyu Xizang wenti de yidian sikao" [Orientalism, ethnic regional autonomy, and the politics of respect— Thoughts on the Tibet question]. *Tianya,* no. 4 (2008): 173–91.

Wang, Xi. "Duoyuan wenhua de qiyuan, shijian yu juxianxin" [Origins, practices, and limits of multiculturalism]. *Meiguo yuanjiu,* no. 2 (2000): 44–80.

Wang, Zhongjun et al. *Guasha* [The guasha treatment], directed by Zheng Xiaolong. Beijing: Beijing dianshi yishu zhongxin yinxiang chubanshe, 2001. DVD.

Wu, Xuan et al. "Renwen jingshen xunsilu zhisi" [Reflections on the humanistic spirit: Part IV]. *Dushu,* Issue 6 (1995): 66–74.

Xiaoping, Wang. *Guasha* [The guasha treatment]. Beijing: Xiandai chubanshe, 2001.

Xu, Jilin et al. "Renwen jingshen xunsilu zhisan" [Reflections on the humanistic spirit: Part III]. *Dushu,* no. 5 (1995): 46–55.

Xu, Xinjian. "Dangdai zhongguo de minzu shenfen biaoshu" [Articulations of national identity in contemporary China]. *Minzu wenxue yanjiu,* no. 4 (2006): 107–11.

Xu, Yingguo. *Meiguo wenxue xuandu* [An anthology of Chinese American literature]. Tianjing: Nankai daxue chubanshe, 2008.

Ya, fei. "Zai haiwai xiezuo: zuojia yan geling fangtanlu, zuojia Yan Geling fangtan lu" [Writing from overseas: An interview of Yan Geling]. May 27, 2003, douban.com. http://www.douban.com/group/topic/3157380/ (accessed July 5, 2009).

Yan, Geling. *Jinling shisan chai* [Thirteen women in Nanjing]. Beijing: Zhongguo gongren chubanshe, 2007.

———. *Dijiuge guafu* [The ninth widow]. Bejing: Zuojia chubanshe, 2006.

———. *Fusang.* Vol. 3 of *The Collected Works of Yan Geling.* 7 vols. Beijing: Dangdai Shijie Chubanshe, 2003. First published in 1996 by Lianjing chubanshe (Taibei).

Yang, Hongyin. "Minzu yuyan yu fudian xushu" [National allegory and heteroglossic narration]. *Huawen wenxue,* no. 5 (2003): 62–65.

Yang, Jiguo, "Dangdai huizu wenxue de chuangzuo tezheng" [Characteristics of contemporary Hui literature]. *Huizu yanjiu,* no. 1 (1996), 67–74.

Yin, Wenjia and Yu Li. "Xifang duoyuan zhuyi ji dui zhongguo de jiejian yiyi—zai hexie wenhuaguan de shiyu zhong" [Western multiculturalism and its instruction for China's construction of a discourse of cultural harmony]. *Xueshu luntan,* no. 1 (2008): 165–67.

Zha, Jianying, *Congling xia de binghe* [The ice river in the jungle]. Chang Chun: Shidai Wenyi Press, 1995.

Zhang, Chengzhi. "Sanfen meiyou yinzai shushang de xuanyan" [Three prefaces that did not come to print], in *Qingjie de jingshen* [The clean spirit], 154–64. Beijing: Zhongxin chubanshe, 2008.

———. "Zhenzheng de ren shi X" [X embodies true humanity], in *Qingjie de Jingshen* [The clean spirit], 85–93. Beijing: China Citic Press, 2008.

———. "Gou de Diaoxiang" [A statue of a dog], in *Zhang Chengzhi sanwen* [Zhang Chengzhi essays], 23–33. Beijing: Renmin wenxue chubanshe, 2005.

———. "Toushi de Sushuo" [A story of stone throwing], in *Zhang Chengzhi sanwen* [Zhang Chengzhi essays], 258–66. Beijing: Renmin wenxue chubanshe, 2005.

———."Wuyuan de Sixiang" [Helpless thought], in *Zhang Chengzhi sanwen* [Zhang Chengzhi essays], 34–49. Beijing: Renmin wenxue chubanshe, 2005.

———. *Xinling Shi* [History of the soul]. Changsha, Hunan: Hunan wenyi chubanshe, 1999. First published in 1991 by Huscheng chubanshe.

Zhang, Hong. "Zhuti rentong, geming yishi yu renmin meixue—lun zhang chengzhi zai xin shiqi de wenxue shijian" [Identification, revolutionary consciousness, and people's aesthetics: Zheng Chengzhi's literary writings since the Reform Era]. *Wenyi lilun yu piping,* no. 6 (2005): 78–84.

Zhang, Rulun et al. "Renwen jingshen xunsilu zhiwu" [Reflections on the spirit humanistic: Part V]. *Dushu,* no. 7 (1995): 49–56.

———. "Renwen jingshen xunsilu zhiyi" [Reflections on the humanistic spirit: Part I]. *Dushu,* no. 3 (1995): 3–13.

Zhong, Hubin. *Shaonu Xiaoyu* [Young Xiaoyu], directed by Zhang Aijia. Taibei: Taisheng duomeiti gufenyouxian gongsi, 1995. DVD.

Zhong, Jialian and Ye Xinyuan. "'Yanshan Huji' dang zhishui?" [What does the "Yan Mountain Barbarian Calvary" refer to?]. *Dushu* no. 4 (1997): 146–48.

Zhu, Lianbi. "Duoyuan wenhua zhuyi yu minzu-guojiao de jiangou, jianping wei'er jinlika de shaoshu de quanli" [Multiculturalism and the construction of nation-states: Will Kymlicka's *Politics in the Vernacular*]. *Shijie minzu* no. 1 (2008): 10–19.

INDEX

Printed in Great Britain
by Amazon